Property and Power in
English Gothic
Literature

EDITED BY RUTH BIENSTOCK ANOLIK

*Demons of the Body and Mind: Essays on
Disability in Gothic Literature* (McFarland, 2010)

*Horrifying Sex: Essays on Sexual Difference in
Gothic Literature* (McFarland, 2007)

EDITED BY RUTH BIENSTOCK ANOLIK
AND DOUGLAS L. HOWARD

*The Gothic Other: Racial and Social Constructions
in the Literary Imagination* (McFarland, 2004)

Property and Power in English Gothic Literature

Ruth Bienstock Anolik

McFarland & Company, Inc., Publishers
Jefferson, North Carolina

LIBRARY OF CONGRESS CATALOGUING-IN-PUBLICATION DATA

Anolik, Ruth Bienstock, 1952–
    Property and power in English Gothic literature / Ruth Bienstock Anolik.
        p.   cm.
    Includes bibliographical references and index.

    ISBN 978-0-7864-9850-5 (softcover : acid free paper) ∞
    ISBN 978-1-4766-2264-4 (ebook)

    1. English fiction—18th century—History and criticism. 2. Horror tales, English—History and criticism. 3. Gothic revival (Literature)—Great Britain—History—18th century. 4. Power (Social sciences) in literature. 5. Property in literature. I. Title.

PR868.T3A56 2016
823'.0872909—dc23   2015035357

BRITISH LIBRARY CATALOGUING DATA ARE AVAILABLE

© 2016 Ruth Bienstock Anolik. All rights reserved

No part of this book may be reproduced or transmitted in any form or by any means, electronic or mechanical, including photocopying or recording, or by any information storage and retrieval system, without permission in writing from the publisher.

Front cover artwork: *Le Chateau*, Frieda Lefeber, artist; photograph by Robert Anolik

Printed in the United States of America

McFarland & Company, Inc., Publishers
    Box 611, Jefferson, North Carolina 28640
        www.mcfarlandpub.com

To my dear friend, Vincent Hausmann.

With gratitude for our time together,
laughing and talking about texts and ideas,
as we careen around the streets of Philadelphia.

Acknowledgments

With eternal thanks to those who were present at the creation, those many eons ago: Carol Bernstein, Sandra Berwind, Peter Briggs, Susan Dean, and Katrin Burlin.

With ongoing thanks for the love and support I receive from my Anolik family, Bob, Jon, Rachel and Sarah.

For my Bienstock family, Josh and Linda, and Clara. In memory of Herbert Bienstock and June Klein Bienstock, the foundation of my accomplishment.

And to Warren and Cecily, and Dorene—for being like family.

To Kate Henry, for her constant inspiration and challenge.

In memory of Steve Asher, who never doubted the outcome.

Table of Contents

Acknowledgments vi

Introduction. Possessions: Property and Propriety in the English Gothic Mode 1

Part I. Castle and Moat: Property Possession in the English Gothic

1. Slippery Properties: *The Castle of Otranto* and *The Old English Baron* 13
2. A Century of Loss: Historical Contexts for Property Anxieties 19
3. Fantasies of Return: Property Restoration Imagined 28
4. Nineteenth-Century Expansions 35

Part II. Ghosts: Possession of Person in the English Gothic

5. Self-(Dis)Possession in *The Woman in White* 47
6. Dispossessions of the Mind and the Body: A Gothic Tropology 56
7. The Double and the Ghost: Refusals of Self-(Dis)Possession 67
8. Resurrection Fantasies: Defying Death's Dispossessions 76
9. Slavery and Marriage: Gothic Reflections of Political Rhetoric 81
10. Missing Mothers and Suppressed Sisters: The Dangers of Primogeniture 103

Part III. Fragmented Stories; Appropriated Voices: Possession of the Narrative in the English Gothic

11. Gothic Conventions; Narrative Dispossessions 123

12. Contexts of Contested Narratives: Can the Text Be Possessed? 132

13. The Theology of Narrative Dispossession in Maturin's
   Melmoth the Wanderer 137

14. Dispossessed and Dispossessing: The Wandering Jew's
   Possession of Voice and Narrative 150

Part IV. Beyond the End: Dispossessing Closure

15. "It is only the theory I want": Repossessing Fiction
   in Sarah Waters's *Affinity* 169

16. The Political Fantastic 191

*Conclusion. Toward a Transatlantic Investigation:
   Possession and Dispossession in American Gothic Literature* 197

Chapter Notes 203

Bibliography 223

Index 231

Introduction

Possessions: Property and Propriety in the English Gothic Mode

> Possession: actual holding or occupancy, as distinct from ownership [OED]

Immediately after the Fall, after the first moment of dispossession that informs Western thought through the millennia, Eve appropriates Adam's role as namer of creatures and assigns her two sons their names. These names, like most biblical nomenclature, have a literal meaning: Cain signifies "possession" (*kinyan*) and Abel "vanity" (*hevel*). Thus, as the medieval biblical commentator Nachamanides observes, the names of the first men born of humans form a simple sentence that haunts the Western imagination: "possession is vanity."

This early implicit statement later emerges from the unconscious of Western culture to organize and to inform the tradition of English Gothic literature, distinguished by its preoccupation with issues of possession and with the paradoxical immateriality of the objects of possession, as captured by K. Gray in *The Cambridge Law Journal*: "The ultimate fact about property is that it does not really exist; it is mere illusion" (252). The unfolding of Eve's fateful sentence lends continued weight and enduring power to the Gothic imagination, haunted by the postlapsarian awareness that human attempts to possess (to fix property within the material world of law and economics) always fail because property is illusion.

Indeed, the typical moment of the English Gothic text is the moment after the fall from the idyllic past in which possession had been securely fixed. The ostensible project of the Gothic is to return to the idyllic moment of secure and undisrupted possession. However, the actual effect of the Gothic narrative is to undermine the certainties of secure possession, the kind of certainty that is popularly expressed as "possession is nine-tenths of the law." The English Gothic moves to untangle the distinction between the concepts of "ownership" and of "possession," to disrupt the relationship between the two, and to explore the many forms that "possession" may take. In the English Gothic text the security of legal ownership is persistently destabilized in the repeated replay of the moment in which the legal owner is dispossessed and possession is effected through extra-legal means. Thus the tradition moves toward a subversive interrogation of the laws and statutes upon which rest not only the rights of possession but also all systems of social and political organization.

The ideologies of possession are central to modern civilization. Thinking no doubt of Jean-Jacques Rousseau and John Locke among others, Jeremy Bentham remarks on "the prodigious importance attached by so many to the term *property*: as if the value of it were intrinsic, and nothing else had any value: as if man were made for property, not property for man" (quoted by Kenneth Burke, *Permanence and Change* 209–210). Certainly it is the fixation of society upon property and the unavailability of property to women that leads Mary Wollstonecraft (drawing upon Gothic imagery) to inveigh against "the demon of property [that] has ever been at hand to encroach on the sacred rights of men, and to fence round with awful pomp laws that war with justice" (*A Vindication of the Rights of Men* 7).

The English Gothic is taken up by the issue of possession and is preoccupied with the legal and seemingly literal questions of ownership: the questions of who actually owns the *property* (the frequently contested castle[1]), who owns the *self*, including the body and mind, who owns the *narrative* and the *text*. These obsessively repeated questions generally receive ambiguous and ambivalent answers that work to desynonymize ownership and possession rather than stabilize the terms. The ease with which property is lost and found, the inevitable thwarting of the male plot to dominate and possess the woman, the inability of the narrator and the text to convey meaning and of the reader to apprehend signification: these Gothic tendencies all indicate an unstable and anxious notion of possession.

The linguistic and conceptual project of the Gothic—to disentangle the meanings of ownership and of possession and to interrogate the categories of possession—reflects the complex of tangled and opposing meanings and possibilities associated with the word *possession*.[2] Real estate, human beings and texts may be legally possessed, commodified as private property through various systems, including property rights, marriage, slavery and copyright. Concurrently, bodies may also be possessed sexually. Conversely, edifices, bodies, and texts may be imaginatively possessed by haunting ghosts. Sane, self-possessed and enlightened minds may rationally possess knowledge and perception, yet minds may also be supernaturally possessed by ghosts and by the related dispossessions of madness and hallucinations (induced by fever, drugs or other forces). Significantly, a related form of mental possession, "obsession"—which in contemporary terms means the state of being overwhelmed by a preoccupation—indicates the cultural movement toward the psychological from the supernatural: an earlier definition of "obsession" referred to the state of being possessed by an evil spirit.[3] The English Gothic text is obsessed with all these forms and means of possession; indeed this obsession unifies and informs the Gothic canon.

The preoccupation of the English Gothic with possession and with dispossession is apparent in the complex of conventional motifs by which the mode is often defined; it is this central concern that unites and unifies the seemingly unrelated complex of motifs. Each of the many apparently unvarying conventions reveals anxieties about possession and dispossession of property, self and narrative. Questions of property possession take form in the conventional image of the decaying haunted castle that is typically the center of a property dispute. Radiating from this central anxious image of unstable property are related motifs that reflect questions concerning problems of inheritance and identity, the unreliable indicator of property ownership in the aristocratic model. The complex of motifs that arise in response to anxieties of property possession (that is, real estate) will be the topic of Part I of this book, Castle and Moat: Property Possession in the English Gothic. Questions of personal possession, ownership of the body and of the mind—touching on both social/economic and philosophical/psychological notions of personal possession and self-possession—also surface in a vast complex of conventional Gothic tropes, including imprisonment and rape (sexual possession), madness, the double, and supernatural possession. The entire complex of tropes that express anxieties of personal possession and self-possession is explored in the discussion of Part II, Ghosts: Possession of Person in the English Gothic. Questions of ownership of voice, narrative, and text (questions that recognize the plot of the narrative is as insecurely held as is the plot of land) also surface in a set of conventional Gothic motifs. The conventional tropes of multiple narrators, the appropriated voice, the fragmented narrative, and the recovered manuscript contribute to the Gothic representation of text as contested and indeterminate, insecurely possessed by both reader and writer. These questions and the motifs that express them are the topic of Part III, Fragmented Stories; Appropriated Voices: Possession of the Narrative in the English Gothic. Part IV, Beyond the End: Dispossessing Closure, comprises two chapters. Chapter 15—"'It is only the theory I want': Repossessing Fiction in Sarah Waters's *Affinity*"—focuses on the neo-Victorian novel published in 1999. This text, poised at the cusp of the twenty-first century, illustrates the continuation of the paradigm of possession in the English Gothic, while simultaneously disputing and dispossessing the defining and confining power of scholarly paradigms, including mine. The final chapter, "The Political Fantastic," interrogates the political stance of the English Gothic tradition, dedicated as it is to political situations, wavering as it does between support and subversion of the *status quo*.

Gothic narratives thus tend to deploy anxious tropes of possession and dispossession in order to refute certainties of possession. These motifs work to subvert the certainties of ownership and the ideologies that support them by asserting that property, the self and the narrative are ultimately and inherently unpossessible. The situation of the haunted property that is typically lost and randomly restored subverts the stability of the legal and economic systems that attempt to secure property ownership. The tropes of personal dispossession—madness, the double and the ghost—work to discredit the Enlightenment valorization of the power of the rational mind to effect epistemological possession and self-possession and subvert the legal systems that allow for the ownership of the bodies and persons of others. Enlightenment certainties regarding epistemological apprehension are also refused by the resistance of the indeterminate Gothic narrative to possession by any one reader or narrator. The tropes of vocal and narrative possession—for example, the indeterminate and the multi-vocal narrative, the appropriated voice—also dispute the claim of commercial possession of texts. Thus the Gothic repeatedly and insistently counters certainties of possession with images and moments of dispossession.[4]

The utility and aptness of an examination of these images and moments comes into clearer focus against the backdrop of the social and cultural changes in the structures of possession that Michel Foucault and others see occurring in Western Europe during the eighteenth century,[5] the period that also saw the rise of the Gothic novel. The eighteenth century was a time of enormous upheaval and consolidation as the structures of the modern world came into being. The increase in trade and commercialism—and the resultant rise of what Neil McKendrick, John Brewer and J.H. Plumb identify as the "consumer society" with its focus on purchase rather than inheritance as a means of achieving possession—resulted in the creation of new commodities that were subject to possession, such as slaves and texts: the development of capitalist England's first major overseas empire led to the rise of the slave trade; the development of the new systems of copyright led to new notions of ownership of the text. The changes of the Industrial Revolution resulted in the diminished position of women in the economic systems and the consequent diminishment of female power. The changes brought about by the Agricultural Revolution resulted in an expansion of the process of the enclosure of the common lands. Changes in the economy led to the rise of the middle class, a new class distinguished from the aristocracy and from the lower classes in its methods of acquiring and transmitting property and in its attitudes toward marriage and the family.[6]

The changes in the means and methods of economic possession were also reflected in the development of Enlightenment ideology that promoted the powers of the independent rational mind to possess the world and itself. As Michel Foucault asserts, the Enlightenment advanced the notion that the human was the proper focal point of the rational mind, with particular interest paid to the model of the human norm derived from binary opposition to the non-normative. As Foucault asserts in *The Order of Things* (1973) the concept of "man" as an object of study was developed in the eighteenth century through the construction of linguistic and epistemological barriers of new discourses in order to place man at the center of intellectual scrutiny, thereby as the cynosure of social control.

The influence of the paradigm that Foucault[7] developed in the course of his work to account for the ways that the modern forms of thinking and social control came into being during the eighteenth century derives in large measure from its usefulness in explaining and contextualizing the radical changes of that century, as well as in accounting for the development of various institutions and structures that rose to disseminate the new form of social power that was generated by these transformations. Through the course of Foucault's investigations, a model of social control develops: Foucault asserts that heightened control in the eighteenth century was effected through the development of new conceptual categories regarding normative human behavior, new definitions of human activity that required the attention of social control with the attendant construction of the physical structures needed to contain these newly defined threats to social order. This paradigm is clear in *Madness and Civilization* (1988), in which Foucault argues that the newly defined non-normative category of human madness was also cast as a social danger, requiring a new mode of social response: containment and confinement within the walls of the madhouse. Similarly in *Discipline and Punish* (1979) Foucault asserts that the new category of criminals, burglars and thieves, called into being by the increase in consumer commodities—that is by new, more mobile forms of property in need of greater protection—also posed a new social danger and thus needed to be contained within the walls of the penitentiary. Foucault traces a similar process of containment in his other works.

Although the boundaries of containment that he sees constructed in other areas of social life are conceptual and are not accompanied by physical walls, they are no less confining since, as Foucault demonstrates in *Discipline and Punish*, power in its modern forms is amplified because it is located within the mind of the subject. Since modern power is internalized within the mind, it exerts confining powers even when physical containing walls are absent. Thus, for example, the new power over sexuality that Foucault discovers in *The History of Sexuality* (1990) as the internalized deployment of sexuality replaces the external social force of the deployment of alliance and is effected through conceptual barriers like the incest taboo which is no less breachable for being intangible. And, for another example, the newly developed concept of the author that Foucault identifies as arising in the late eighteenth century in "What is an Author?" is a concept that paves the way for greater legal control through the system of copyrights: in fact, the status of text "as property is historically secondary to the penal code controlling its appropriation" (124).

The paradigm that Foucault thus develops for understanding the social and intellectual movement of the eighteenth century is an essential backdrop for an understanding of the simultaneous counter-movement of the English Gothic preoccupied by issues of possession and dispossession, and images of social and institutional breakdown. The Foucauldian master narrative imagines the grand movement of the eighteenth century as the construction of physical and epistemological barriers of containment that work to demarcate areas for the application of power and social control or, to use the language of this study, the movement of the eighteenth century is to carve up physical and conceptual territory so that it may be more readily possessed.[8] In Foucault's terms, the boundaries are constructed for the purpose of exercising power; in my terms boundaries are constructed for the purpose of creating commodities that may then be possessed to effect power and control. The work of eighteenth-century European culture, then, is to render possessible that which was previously unpossessible. To provide a concrete example, the enclosure movement (that peaked in the eighteenth century, as will be demonstrated in the next chapter) redefined waste land as a commodity to be owned by encircling it with a fence.

The Gothic masterplot is thus a reversal of this ongoing and all-encompassing cultural process. For if the history of Western culture is the history of the commodification of property, person and text through the construction of categories of containment (a commodification that facilitates the enactment of possession and power) then the history of the Gothic is the interrogation and refusal of this movement. The Gothic mode shares Foucault's distrust of the modern tendency toward containment and the Gothic canon is informed by this distrust. The Gothic narrative is replete with images of walls being broken, boundaries of identity being breached and codes of behavior (most emphatically including sexual codes) being transgressed. The Gothic text constantly works to destabilize the categorical certainties of thought, the epistemes that Foucault locates as the founding principles of the culture. For example, as will be asserted in Part II, the Gothic insistently questions the consolidating integrity of "man," positing instead a fragmented, decentered and unstable figure and thus refusing the unifying concept of "man" as the focus of scrutiny and control; similarly Gothic conventions work to fragment and decenter the monolithic figure of the author, as discussed in Part III. The masterplot of the Gothic narrative is then a reversal of the paradigm that Foucault delineates.

The Gothic metanarrative that tells the story of the refusal of all the boundaries of containment, physical and conceptual, arises at the end of the eighteenth century during the time that Foucault associates with the consolidation of the categories of containment, the time of "epistemic disruption" which Foucault, in *The Order of Things*, marks as the beginning of the modern age at the end of the eighteenth century and the beginning of the nineteenth. Thus, if the masterplot of Western culture from the eighteenth century on is as Foucault imagines, the creation of boundaries, physical and intellectual, to reify and commodify property, physical and intellectual—to declare that everything is containable, controllable and possessible—then the masterplot of the Gothic tradition is the transgression of these boundaries, to resist their implications. The Gothic announces, echoing Eve, that first transgressor, "possession is vanity."

The Gothic tendency to resist the dissemination of power and control that Foucault detects in the eighteenth century points to a lacuna in Foucault's paradigm. In Foucault's model, power is absolute and unstoppable because it penetrates invisibly into every arena of social life. In this, Foucault fails to recognize the premise that underlies Marxist criticism and that informs the argument of this study: close reading reveals the resistance of literature and art to the forces of power.⁹ Indeed, the subversive potential that all literature contains is fulfilled with a vengeance by the Gothic, the form that has been recognized for centuries as the poetics of revolution. The eighteenth century was a time that saw a number of revolutionary transformations. Although walls of containment were being constructed, they were also being broken down, as for example the revolutionary destruction of the walls of the Bastille. The Gothic mode is a response to and a reflection of these revolutionary transformations.

A sustained critical focus on the English Gothic preoccupation with possession can be of scholarly use in sustaining the critical gaze and keeping generic chaos at bay to allow space for critical analysis. Occasionally when one reads the critical literature of the Gothic, it seems that no text exists outside of this mode; without some definition, the term Gothic remains so broad as to be useless. Indeed, the Gothic refusal of categories of containment extends to a refusal of generic containment; the transgressive power of the Gothic is demonstrated in the infiltration of Gothic tropes into almost every genre of literature. Thus the critic who pretends to fully possess the Gothic ends up looking as foolish as George Eliot's Casaubon with his "Key to All Mythologies."¹⁰ The Gothic resists comprehension and containment, the hermeneutic possession imposed by definition and interpretation, and thus the project that attempts to fix and contain this mode is ultimately subject to dispossession. What I shall assert instead is that Gothic texts share an interest in the problem of possession and that this shared preoccupation justifies the creation of a generic category more than does the list of creaky motifs that are usually invoked to define the Gothic.¹¹

Indeed, a close look at that ancient list reveals its inadequacies in defining the mode. Every critic seems to recognize the Gothic when it appears, bearing the conventional accouterments of haunted decaying castles, villainous heroes, innocent heroines in distress, secretively dysfunctional families and decaying manuscripts. Yet John Ruskin quite correctly dismisses the project of defining the Gothic through example. Writing of Gothic architecture, he states:

> We all have some notion, most of us a very determined one, of the meaning of the term Gothic; but I know that many persons have this idea in their minds without being able to define it: that is to say, understanding generally that Westminster Abbey is Gothic, and St. Peter's is not, they have, nevertheless, no clear notion of what it is that they recognize in the one or miss in the other ["The Nature of the Gothic" 158].

Thus, as Ruskin suggests, a listing of conventional Gothic motifs does not adequately prepare for an understanding of the mode. For one thing, the set of motifs is fluid; while some ur-texts like Horace Walpole's *Castle of Otranto* (1764) might contain every motif, other texts that inhabit the Gothic canon contain few or none of these motifs. Mary Shelley's *Frankenstein* (1818) for example has no haunted castle and no ghosts for that matter but it *feels* like a Gothic text. Frederick Garber's model of the Gothic as "a meeting of modes" (156) seems to work as a way to encompass the Gothic without reducing it to a single meaning. To Garber's model I add that the Gothic is a meeting of modes that all share an interest in the questions of possession.

The preoccupation of the English Gothic with questions of possession accounts paradoxically for both the cohesiveness and the variety of the mode. For while each text exhibits an interest in questions of possession, and while this interest is what centers the mode, each textual response is informed by a particular set of legal, social and cultural contexts. Thus, the picture of the English Gothic that emerges is not that of a series of texts presenting the same conventional motifs in an unremitting flow but instead a series of texts that presents a theme with infinite variations and transformations. As the terms of possession change in time, the terms of the Gothic text change as well. What does not change, as we shall see, is the Gothic tendency to respond with anxious skepticism to the ideologies. The skeptical stance toward conditions of possession and containment and the tendency to transgress the boundaries of containment also works to center the mode. This transgressiveness results in a genre that resists critical, readerly and canonical possession and that as a result is attractive to writers who write from the margins.

Indeed, a challenge unmet by this study is whether such a preoccupation informs the non-English Gothic tradition, with a different set of contexts and anxieties of possession. That is, as national contexts of possession change, do Gothic conventions evolve to reflect this? Certainly, as the centuries unfold in Britain, the English Gothic remains a vivid and visible presence; it is very likely that the continuing preoccupation with the always-pressing questions of possession accounts for its continuing popularity and power in addition to giving it weight and meaning as a literary tradition. As interesting are the conventions of the early Gothic as they rise in response to the new terms of possession that arise in eighteenth-century England, even more interesting are the transformations and mutations as the mode evolves to accommodate the new anxieties of possession in the centuries that follow, and in our already-haunted twenty-first century.

Part I

Castle and Moat

*Property Possession
in the English Gothic*

1

Slippery Properties
The Castle of Otranto *and* The Old English Baron

Although the Gothic mode insistently resists the confinement of definition, one central image often serves to link a text to the Gothic tradition: the haunted—and contested—building. This iconic trope highlights the Gothic struggle between the rule of law (real estate as property) and realism (house as locus of the domestic), and the misrule of fantasy (the building as habitation of the supernatural ghost). The image of the haunted house, or its close relative, the haunted castle, dominates two texts that greatly influence, if not generate, the Gothic mode in English literature: Walpole's *The Castle of Otranto* (1764)[1] and Clara Reeve's *The Old English Baron* (1777).[2] Each narrative poses the question that haunts the Gothic masterplot: who will be authorized to own, bequeath and inherit the property? It is this central question, obsessively repeated throughout the Gothic canon, which reveals the Gothic preoccupation with the real economic concerns of property ownership and transmission.

The right to possess property is a cornerstone of Western economic ideology, a concept that supports and generates the structures of European society and culture. This was certainly the case in the eighteenth century. The eighteenth-century legal writer William Blackstone articulates the sentiments of his age in declaring that "there is nothing which so generally strikes the imagination, and engages the affection of mankind, as the right of property" (II.2).[3] Other eighteenth-century writers[4] were inclined to share this view. A common thread that unites legal discourse regarding property is an insistence that the primary function of the legal code is to uphold the right to possess property. In "A Discourse on the Origin of Inequality" (1755) Rousseau observes (not uncritically): "The first man who, having enclosed a piece of ground, bethought himself of saying 'This is mine,' and found people simple enough to believe him, was the real founder of civil society" (192). As Rousseau suggests, property rights, though essential, are also inherently unstable, unable to stand without the support of a powerful legal structure.

❧

Until the eighteenth century, the property protected by laws and the state was generally defined as real estate. Martin Kayman notes, "When Blackstone represented the Common Law as the anonymous epic tale of how the English had established and defended their rights to liberty and property, the property in question was understood paradigmatically as physical property" (376). With the advent of mercantilism and commerce, other more portable forms of property came into being and it became even more important that laws exist to define and protect the terms of possession.

In this transformation of the terms of property possession, James Thompson discovers an explanation for the literary interest in economic concerns in the eighteenth century. "Economic discourse and novelistic discourse are both forms of ideological expression.... Both perform the main cultural work of the eighteenth century: reconceptualizing property relations, or, in other words, representing capitalist property, the relation between the individual subject and the object he owns" (30). Alan Ryan considers the literary imagination as supplement to the legal imagination: "the English legal inclination to enquire what gave a man good title to possession and no more than that, seems to have diverted a certain psychological or metaphysical interest into other channels" (7). In fact, the English literary imagination steps in to fill the void left by the limits of the legal imagination.

Conventions of the Gothic: Reflections on the Instability of Property

Gothic literature, preoccupied as it is with the terms and problems of property rights, is particularly suited to fill this void. Indeed, the tense Gothic text consistently resonates with the cultural and political awareness that "fleeting possessions [can] only be captured and secured by the institutions of property" (Avner Offer xiii), institutions that are themselves fallible. The subversive Gothic text consistently represents the conflict between the (conservative) desire for legal protection of property, and liberal desire for freedom from the codes and rules of the law. In reflecting this conflict, the Gothic presents an unstable picture of property rights. Indeed the Gothic is marked by a complex of conventions that tend to resist the certainties of legal possession and to discredit the stability of property as an entity that can be owned or transmitted. Given the centrality of property possession in western society, this is a radical stance indeed.

The Gothic tendency to interrogate the stability of property ownership evidences in the various motifs that appear, if not originate, in *Otranto* and *Baron*. The conventional Gothic property—dark, massive, labyrinthine and mysterious—works to construe property as legally and epistemologically unpossessible, resisting legal and rational attempts at control.

Resistance of Gothic Property to Epistemological Possession

Within the caverns of the massive Castle of Otranto,[5] with its numerous apartments, chambers, galleries and staircases, its lord, Manfred, encounters the resistance of his property to his epistemological possession when he pursues Isabella, who is fleeing his advances. Isabella flees to the subterranean passage that leads from the "vaults of the castle" (15) to the church of Saint Nicholas and there the labyrinths of the castle refute Manfred's control. Pursuing Isabella and confident that she is within his reach, Manfred is taken aback to discover in an underground vault, where he expected to find Isabella, a young peasant whom he thought imprisoned elsewhere (18). Although he owns the castle, Manfred discovers that he cannot mentally map its intricate spaces, nor rationally control what happens within; the very size of his property renders it resistant to his apprehension. The conventional representation of the Gothic property—dark, mysterious, labyrinthine, evoking the old irrational powers of Church and State—thus rebuts Enlightenment confidence in the apprehending powers of the human mind.

Resistance of Gothic Property to Legal Possession

The tendency of Gothic properties to being haunted also stands in opposition to Enlightenment notions of possession—legal as well as epistemological. The susceptibility to ghostly haunting is a dominant feature of Gothic property that works to undermine the power of legal modes of possession.[6] Indeed, the Gothic posits a ludic, supernatural world in which the principles of legal ownership, founded on rationality, law and power, de-materialize in the irrational presence of ghostly possession.[7] Indeed, the true owner of the haunted castle is the possessing ghost.[8] In *The Old English Baron*, the material, legal owner of Castle Lovel, Lord Fitz-Owen, discovers the supernatural constrictions upon his ownership as he must build a new apartment on the west side of his castle because the ghostly possession of the east side prevents him from occupying and fully possessing it. The east side is actually possessed by the ghosts of the rightful owners, the displaced and murdered Lord and Lady Lovel (33–34), who appear to their son, Edmund, in a dream. When Wenlock and Markham, the enemies of Edmund, attempt to sleep in a haunted room, the ghost of the displaced Lord Lovel appears in full armor and ejects them from the usurped space: "He stood with one hand extended, pointing to the outward door; they took the hint, and crawled away as fast as fear would let them" (78). As in most Gothic narratives, these ghosts represent the original, rightful, dispossessed owner from whom the property was usurped in the distant past. In destabilizing the legal rights of the current owner, the haunting ghost disrupts the certainty of legal ownership, undermining the system of law and rule that is based on rational order and revealing the lawless underpinnings of legal possession.

Paradoxically, it is the ghost that also represents order and legality, operating as the agent of normalization, effecting the restoration of the usurped property in *Baron*, and in *Otranto* where the first step toward restoration of the property is the manifestation of the giant ghostly helmet in the opening scene. The restoration of order is typically accompanied by the disappearance of the ghost, once its task of restoration has been accomplished. After his closing declaration of order and law—"Behold in Theodore, the true heir Alfonso"—the ghost of Alfonso departs, presumably forever, ascending "solemnly towards heaven, where the cloud parting asunder, the form of saint Nicholas ... receiving Alfonso's shade, they were soon wrapt from mortal eyes in a blaze of glory" (Walpole 108).

The shifting pattern of property possession—the ebb and flow of usurpation and restoration—is yet another Gothic motif that reveals anxiety about the possibilities of owning property, and skepticism regarding the legal systems that seek to support property possession and transmission. By the opening of *Otranto*, the castle, as well as the entire province of Otranto, seems to be securely held by Manfred, who has inherited the dynasty from his grandfather. The action of the novel moves inexorably through a variety of sensational plot devices—ghostly manifestations, threatened maidens, quasi-incest—toward the final revelation of the murder that resulted in the theft of the property, and to the discovery and restoration of the rightful heir. Manfred, the seemingly aristocratic owner, is revealed to be the grandson of Ricardo, the chamberlain who poisoned his master, Alfonso, the rightful aristocratic owner, in order to steal Alfonso's property (109). The seeming peasant, Theodore, is revealed as the grandson of Alfonso, the last rightful owner, whose likeness, as represented by the church statue, he bears; the novel ends with the restoration of the property to Theodore.

The Old English Baron—which Reeve acknowledges as "the literary offspring of *The Castle of Otranto*" (3)—also traces the complicated restoration of usurped property and identity. In *Baron*, even the legal purchase of a property does not ensure full possession. Although the eponymous Lord Fitz-Owen has legally bought Castle Lovel from Walter, Lord Lovel, and has further reinforced his claim to the castle by marrying the sister of Sir Walter (10), he is ultimately dispossessed: first by the ghosts who haunt the east wing and later in the novel's denouement by the revelation that Sir Walter had murdered Sir Arthur, the rightful owner, and stolen the property (and identity) from his son Edmund, who was an infant when his parents died and who has been raised as a peasant.

In the recurrence of the pattern of usurpation and restoration of property, then, the Gothic reveals skepticism toward the possibility of owning and securing property through law, and toward the reliability of personal identity, the underpinning of property ownership and transmission in the eighteenth-century aristocratic model. As in *Otranto* and *Baron*, the typical Gothic property is slippery, easily lost by the seemingly aristocratic owner and casually restored to an owner who occupies a seemingly marginal position within the economic framework. The seeming aristocratic owner is revealed to be a usurper[9]; the seemingly marginalized peasant revealed to be an heir.

The Limits of Gothic Imagination; Imperatives of Law and Society

In the eighteenth century, though, even the Gothic imagination has its insurmountable barriers. The usurped properties in *Otranto* and *Baron* are returned to *seeming* peasants: Theodore of *Otranto* supports himself by "the labour of my hands" (*Otranto* 82); Edmund of *Baron* is believed to be the "son of a cottager" (17). However, each is in fact a hidden member of the aristocracy; each is a descendant of the original aristocratic rightful owner. Each quasi-peasant reveals the signs of the aristocrat. The secretly noble Theodore contains a "mixture of grace and humility," contrasted to the "temper" of the usurping Manfred (18); Manfred's daughter recognizes that "the youth [is] the exact resemblance of Alfonso's [his ancestor's] picture in the gallery" (52). Edmund too, in his guise of peasant, demonstrates "uncommon merit, and gentleness of manners [that] distinguishes him from those of his own class" (17), and a friend of his dead aristocratic father notes "a strong resemblance he bears to a certain dear friend I once had, and his manner resembles him as much as his person; his qualities deserve that he should be placed in a higher rank" (19). Yet it is of course neither accomplishment nor manner that elevates Theodore and Edmund from the peasantry to the aristocracy—such visions of social mobility, based on merit rather than birth, are absent even from the radical Gothic imagination—it is the revelation and stabilization of their true, aristocratic identity that ultimately ensures their secure possession of the property. In eighteenth-century England even the subversive Gothic has its limits and cannot imagine the restoration of the land to an actual peasant.

The shifting narrative pattern of usurpation and restoration in the Gothic works, finally, to problematize the very existence of property, to reveal the economic fact, or secret, that the very idea of owning property is a legal fiction. Thus exposed, the legal fiction of land-holding is displaced from the seemingly rational realm of law and removed to the less steady realm of haunted fiction. And so, in the Gothic narrative, transmission of property is effected not through the smooth legal and rational means of aristocratic inheritance, but through disruptive usurpation and equally disruptive restoration, often supported by supernatural agents, in the realm of fantasy and fiction.[10]

2

A Century of Loss

Historical Contexts for Property Anxieties

The Enclosure Movement

A consideration of the social, political and historical realities of eighteenth-century England, the century that engenders *Otranto* and *Baron* and thus their many literary heirs, reveals occasion for skepticism and anxiety regarding the security of property possession. Although historians disagree on the exact chronology of the English enclosure movement, there is agreement that much common land was enclosed prior to and during the eighteenth century.[1] "Much of England was still open in 1700; but most of it was enclosed by 1840" (Neeson 5). "For a very long time commoners had lived with the possibility and the reality of enclosure but in the middle of the eighteenth century enclosers began to use private Acts of Parliament to enclose whole parishes" (187). This time frame indicates the synchronization of enclosure and the origins of the Gothic mode.[2] The Gothic mode and resistance to enclosure also coincide. Neeson, arguing that "commoners were more active in their own defence than historians ... have allowed" (262), asserts that there was a pattern of resistance to enclosure on the part of the commoners, what Neeson calls "wars of attrition waged skillfully over a decade or longer" (262).

One indication of Walpole's involvement with Parliamentary appeals of the process is recorded in his letters; George Montagu, his close friend, writes to Walpole (3 February 1761—three years before the publication of *Otranto*):

> I have been solicited by two ladies in my neighborhood to desire any friends I have in Parliament to attend in their behalf if they find their cause just. It is

with regard to an enclosure of Sulgrave which they oppose by a petition in the house. They are ladies of the manor, and apprehend they shall be injured ... if the weather will permit when the petition is heard, I shall be obliged to you [9. 336–337].

An examination of the pattern of property movement in the Gothic reveals a literary analogue to the political reaction.[3] The enclosure movement, with its amplified notions of privately owned land, is countered by the representation of property ownership in the Gothic mode that tends to resist and refuse the possibility of holding private property. The movement of property in the Gothic, shifting from the aristocrat landowner to the apparent peasant, is a reversal of the actual movement of property through the process of enclosure whereby common land previously available to the peasantry was secured by wealthy landowners. Thus the (mis)rule of the enclosure movement is reflected, reversed and interrogated in the misrule of the Gothic. In actuality, land is usurped from the peasant by the landed aristocracy; in the imaginative response, land is seized from the aristocrat and restored to the peasant. It is particularly appropriate that property in the Gothic is represented by the grand house that is, as Raymond Williams notes, the emblem of class power, exploitation, and struggle.[4]

Boundaries and Barriers

One particular aspect of the enclosure movement is particularly resonant within the context of the Gothic preoccupation with walls and boundaries. The enclosure movement was itself preoccupied by the construction of boundaries:

> Regional expression of this enclosure movement varies considerably ... the quickset hedge of much of the midlands contrasts vividly with the heavy stone walls of the Pennine counties and the combination of enclosure and drainage schemes so typical of the fenland parts of Lincolnshire, Norfolk, Cambridgeshire, and Somerset [Turner 16].

In a letter dated June 14, 1763, George Montagu describes to Walpole the impact that such barriers will have on Walpole's journey to him: "The next day you have about twenty miles here, and my servant shall meet you, show you the best way, and open the hundred portals of our enclosures" (10.82).[5]

The physical barriers of enclosure were used in the eighteenth century as means to effect control (in this case economic control), a tendency that

Foucault identifies with the early modern era. Foucault sees the construction of walls as one technique by which early modern society effected discipline through the "distribution of bodies in space." Recalling the walls that confined "vagabonds and paupers," students of secondary schools upon whom "the monastic model was gradually imposed," "the military barracks," surrounded by high walls, and factories that were "explicitly compared with the monastery, the fortress, a walled town," Foucault remarks that "discipline sometimes requires *enclosure* [Foucault's italics] the specification of a place heterogeneous to all others and closed in upon itself" (*Discipline and Punish* 141–142). In the Foucauldian paradigm, the physical barriers constructed to divide and to contain private property become, like the walls of the madhouse and the penitentiary, emblems for the epistemological and legal barriers of containment constructed in early modern society as means to consolidate social control.

Seen through a Foucauldian prism, the preoccupation of the Gothic with walls, barriers and enclosures evidences a refusal of the disciplinary tendency of modern society and a re-enactment of the actual destruction of fence posts, hedges and rails—the barriers of enclosure—that was subversively accomplished by the opponents of that movement. For while the Gothic narrative is dominated by the presence of enclosing walls and barriers, sources of discipline and control, these barriers tend, sometimes magically, to open and break down. The social control of the aristocracy that the walls emblematize and effect is countered by the supernatural power of fiction, deployed in the cause of those disempowered by the structures of society, generally peasants and women.

Variations of this trope abound in the Gothic text: Isabella, fleeing in the bowels of the castle from Manfred's unwelcome advances, discovers with the aid of a helpful "ray of moonshine streaming through a cranny of the ruin above" the trap door to freedom for which she conveniently holds the key (Walpole 27). When Edmund, Reeve's quasi-peasant, returns to his ancestral home to reclaim his usurped property, "a sudden gust of wind arose, and the outward gates flew open.... The moment Edmund entered the hall, every door in the house flew open" (130).[6] The conventional closure of the Gothic narrative, the destruction of the enclosing walls of the aristocratic castle and the destruction of aristocratic barriers, as in *Otranto* and *Baron*, is a variation of this trope. In each instance, the physical barriers erected by the aristocracy, barriers that emblematize actual social and economic control, are destroyed by the supernatural powers deployed by Gothic fiction, placed at the service of the enclosed, disciplined, dispossessed and powerless.

A Century of Revolutions

The enclosure movement is not the only example of property slippage in the eighteenth century. There is also a larger political context for Gothic representations of lost, stolen and destroyed property. For more than a century preceding the publication of Walpole's *Otranto* in 1764, the course of English history was marked by a pattern of political revolution, a cycle of usurpation and restoration. Three British revolutions[7] prefigured the anxious reversals of the Gothic mode: the Puritan Revolution in 1640 (followed by the Restoration in which usurped power and property were returned to the King and to the House in 1660), the Glorious Revolution in 1688, and the American Revolution in 1776, in which land was stolen from the King by usurping revolutionaries.[8] There were also, of course, the repercussions of the French Revolution of 1789, an association that is asserted by many critics, including de Sade, who declares in writing of the Gothic of Ann Radcliffe and Matthew Lewis that "twas the inevitable result of the revolutionary shocks which all of Europe has suffered" (109). Indeed, Lewis was "an eyewitness to the French Revolution, just as later he heard hair-raising stories from its victims" (Markman Ellis 96), stories that would suggest the mob scene in *The Monk* (1796). It is from this perspective that Miles reads the Gothic castle as an evocation of the Bastille and its destruction as an echo of the French Revolution: "The Bastille was typically figured as an instrument of gothic live burial" (70).

The echoes of revolution (French and American) in the Gothic mode also indicate a source for yet another conventional Gothic trope: the dysfunctional family. Within this reading, the relationship between the tyrannic father (originating with and exemplified by Manfred) and the terrorized although somewhat rebellious family is an emblem for the disrupted relation between monarch and people. Lynn Hunt notes that "most Europeans in the eighteenth century thought of their rulers as fathers and of their nations as families writ large" (xiv). "Authority in the state was explicitly modeled on authority in the family" (3). Thus, disruptions of the relationship between monarch and people may readily be emblematized as family disruption: "collective, unconscious images of the family order ... underlie revolutionary politics" (xiii) where deposition and murder of the king was analogous to murder of the father. The representation of Manfred as the tyrannic head of the patriarchy who appropriates the lands and the Castle of Otranto and who is opposed by his family and deposed by an apparent member of the peasantry, then, may be read as an allegory for and endorsement of revolution that ends, in Walpole's fantasy, in restoration, stability and harmony.

Walpole's sympathy for revolutionary politics surfaced during the time of the American Revolution when he stated to his friend Horace Mann in 1775, "I am what I always was, a zealot for liberty in every part of the globe and consequently, I most heartily wish success to the American.... If England prevails, English and American liberty is at an end!" (qtd. in Mowl 244). Writing to Henry Seymour Conway, his "favourite cousin" (Mowl 18), on 5 June 1779, Walpole declares, "I rejoice that there is still a great continent of Englishmen who will remain free and independent, and who laugh at the impotent majorities of a prostitute Parliament" (39.327). It is telling that in a political satire in support of American independence Walpole redeploys the image of the giant that he originates in *Otranto* (where the usurped owner returns as giant statue). In "An Account of the Giants Lately Discovered" (1766) the giant is also the emblem for the dispossessed.[9]

Yet, as a member of the upper classes, Walpole also revealed in his letters a sympathetic view towards monarchs and the monarchy, both of England and France. Thus, his portrait of Manfred is ultimately ambiguous. After Manfred has dismissed his newly dead son as "a sickly puny child" (22), cruelly banished his daughter from his presence (21), proposed to divorce his wife and rape his dead son's bride, the narrator tells us "Manfred was not one of those savage tyrants who wanton in cruelty unprovoked. The circumstances of his fortune had given an asperity to his temper, which was naturally humane; and his virtues were always ready to operate, when his passion did not obscure his reason" (30).

One way to account for this improbable statement is to remember that the first edition was published pseudonymously as the work of "Onuphrio Muralto," supposedly translated from "the Original Italian" by "William Marshal, Gent." Since Walpole constructs an imaginary narrator to tell his story, it is tempting to see in the comments on Manfred an attempt by Walpole to discount the acuity of his fictional narrator. However, the general narrative tone of *Otranto* belies this possibility. Nowhere else does the presumed narrator appear as a distinct speaking voice; the otherwise transparent, uni-level narrative invites unskeptical reading, a reading that conflates the narrative voice with Walpole's voice, collapsing the narrative gaps necessary for irony. Rather than betoken comic narrative irony, Walpole's comments reveal the tension of a member of the upper classes who cannot resist empathizing with the tyrannous monarch he condemns. Yet this empathy remains tense and ambivalent throughout the text. Manfred, despite his naturally good temper, is warped by his dynastic obsessions and is appropriately punished by the end of the narrative. Manfred's fate, too, reveals Walpole's ambivalent stance toward his tyrant. Manfred repents, willingly signs "his abdication of the principality" (110), and withdraws to a convent. The denouement of *Otranto* (and of *Baron*, where order is also harmoniously restored) unfolds, then, as a thinly veiled enactment of revolution *cum* restoration; the tyrant is peacefully, even lawfully, opposed by the peasant. The result of the radical revolution is the conservative restoration of original order. *Otranto*, then, like the "Account of Giants," unfolds as an apology for revolution, softening its radicalism and in fact erasing the boundaries between radical revolution and conservative restoration.

In addition to the upheavals of the enclosure movement and the political revolutions in America and France, a number of other revolutions occurred in the eighteenth century that impacted upon the possession and transmission of property, each providing occasion for anxious conjecture regarding property possession and loss. The impact of the Industrial Revolution (1750–1850), the companion to the Agrarian Revolution (in the service of which land was enclosed and consolidated to be more efficiently worked with advanced systems and technology of agriculture), was certainly tremendous.

H.L. Beales notes that the use of the term "Industrial Revolution," first employed by Arnold Toynbee in 1884 to describe the dynamics of the eighteenth century, appropriately denotes the overwhelming extent of the changes that constitute a proper revolution, in that one social system was replaced by another. Before the dual revolutions, agriculture was the economic basis of English life; afterward, industry was the basis (29–30). This shift, then, provides yet another source for the overdetermined trope of the destruction of Gothic property. Henri Lefebvre asserts, "A revolution that does not produce a new space has not realized its full potential" (54). Thus in the motif of the destroyed aristocratic castle, it is possible to identify the impact of the Industrial Revolution: the destruction of aristocratic space and the creation of commercial space as the locus of power. While the massiveness and mystery of the Gothic property gestures back, of course, to the castle and the cathedral, emblems of the dangerously encroaching aristocracy and the mysteriously authoritarian Church, the unpossessible massiveness of the Gothic property gestures forward, as well, to a new kind of property developing in the late eighteenth century. Mary Poovey notes that "modern industrial capitalism was characterized by a new organization of space and of bodies in space" (*Making a Social Body* 25). Poovey's comment recalls Foucault's observation in *Discipline and*

Punish that the eighteenth century saw the development of "great manufacturing spaces" (142) and that the "factory was explicitly compared with the monastery, the fortress, a walled town" (142). Thus in the eighteenth century the sublime "manors, monasteries [and] cathedrals" (Lefebvre 53) were joined and, in time, replaced by the sublime factory, the dark power of the aristocrat and clergy equaled and surpassed by that of the capitalist.

Kayman remarks upon the impact of these economic and social revolutions on literature, arguing that "under pressures from new economic phenomena concepts of fiction shifted in literary narrative as it sought to respond to and participate in the new commercial reality" (375). James Thompson notes that contemporary writers were well aware of this phenomenon: "To conservative social critics, Augustans such as Alexander Pope, Jonathan Swift, and Henry Fielding, a cash economy threatens social revolution ... for it is the cash nexus which can ... transform the master into a servant and the servant into the master" (37). Here, too, it is possible to see the Gothic tendency to reflect and valorize the kinds of social change that elicit anxiety in proponents of the *status quo*. The transformation that Thompson posits as a source of anxiety is figured and endorsed in the conventional Gothic narrative in which the peasant is revealed as the owner and the seemingly aristocratic owner is displaced.

Another significant result of the Industrial Revolution, leading to further Gothic anxieties, was that inheritance lost its status as the primary mode of acquiring property; the social impact of this is evident in Gothic anxieties regarding transmission of property. Richard M. Smith notes "it is implicit in so many studies of pre-industrial societies that the most important method of acquiring property is by the process of inheritance" (1). McKendrick posits a corollary to the Industrial Revolution, what he calls the Consumer Revolution, marked by the shift from inheritance to buying as the prime mode of acquisition. *Otranto* and *Baron* both set the anxiously ambivalent tone toward inheritance that dominates the Gothic text centuries after the disturbances of the eighteenth century. In each text, the conventional structure of inheritance based on primogeniture[10] is disrupted only to be reinstated with variations at the conclusion. In *Otranto*, the line of inheritance is disrupted when Ricardo appropriates the property from Alfonso. Ricardo, in addition to appropriating Alfonso's property, appropriates the conventions of orderly inheritance based on primogeniture—he inappropriately bequeaths the appropriated property to *his* son and through him to Manfred, his grandson. Thus the usurped property, once again, is transmitted in an orderly sequence that reflects the rules of primogeniture. But this illegal manifestation of primogeniture devolves into primogeniture with a vengeance: a saint appears to Ricardo in a dream and promises him that his family will own Otranto "as long as issue-male from Ricardo's loins should remain to enjoy it" (109). The economic structure that Ricardo misappropriates to ensure the smooth transition of the appropriated property becomes the path that leads to the downfall of his dynasty as Conrad his great-grandson is killed and Manfred is unable to furnish a new heir. The ambivalence of the text toward inheritance and primogeniture manifests itself in the re-instatement of Alfonso's family line of inheritance. For Theodore, announced by the ghost of Alfonso as his legitimate heir (108), is the heir through his mother's line. At the conclusion of the narrative, Father Jerome, the priest of Otranto, confesses that Alfonso had secretly married and that his only child, a daughter, was the wife of Jerome and the mother of Theodore. In this too, then, Walpole subverts the seeming security of his Gothic closure by calling into question the legitimacy of primogeniture, showing primogeniture in the service of the villainous usurper of property and proposing the radical possibility of an alternate, feminized, means of legitimate inheritance of both property and identity. Walpole further feminizes inheritance in his text by deploying the motif of the union of the two competing families through marriage. The marriage of Theodore to Isabella, previously thought to be the Alfonso's closest heir (hence her attraction for Manfred), further solidifies Theodore's claim through the feminine line and further subverts the primacy of primogeniture.

Clara Reeve's depiction of disrupted patterns of inheritance provides a more tempered version of the radicalism of Walpole's text; although she wholeheartedly endorses the restoration of the usurped property to the noble aristocrat, her text also reveals skepticism about the dependability of primogeniture. In this, Reeve anticipates her successor, Ann Radcliffe, whose texts, while also conservative, offer a female-centered critique of primogeniture. Reeve's villain, Sir Walter Lovel, disrupts the order of primogeniture when he kills Sir Arthur Lovel and suppresses the identity of Sir Arthur's son; Sir Walter further disrupts orderly inheritance of aristocratic property by selling the Castle to the husband of his sister. (Sir Walter's subsequent punishment is suited to his crime; he is forced to surrender "his own lawful inheritance and personal estate into the hands of [the Baron]" [122]—that is, he is removed from the line of inheritance, his property passing on not to his own son but to his nephews.) In this, Reeve reveals the conservatism of her stance in comparison to Walpole's radicalism. Whereas the legitimacy of Walpole's heir is substantiated through the female line, the illegitimacy of Reeve's usurper is revealed though his reliance on the female line for the transfer of property. Yet there is an echo of Walpole's radicalism in Reeve's dénouement. Edmund's rights of aristocratic primogeniture are ultimately restored through supernatural and legal means; however, Reeve further strengthens his claim by closing the narrative with the marriage of the Baron's daughter and Edmund. The property is thus doubly held and transmitted—by Edmund through his father's line and by Emma through her father's line. The necessity to support the inheritance through marriage reveals a subtle skepticism in Reeve's text about the power of primogeniture alone and also suggests that female inheritance conveys a certain legitimacy.

Yet another transformative effect of the Industrial Revolution upon patterns of inheritance may be traced in the conventional Gothic motif of family dysfunction. The breakdown of the structure of inheritance, with children no longer dependent on the wealth generated by the parent, brought a breakdown in parental authority: "One consequence of industrial capitalism, then, was a marked decrease of parental control over children. Within families, at all social levels, new tensions of power and allegiance rose" (Webb 167). One particular area in which the family was losing control was in the choice of a spouse for the child as new ideas of marriage with a romantic rather than an economic basis began to emerge. "One of the most dramatic causes of tension was the demand for love as a basis of marriage" (Webb 167).[11] "Although the dominant development in marital relations at the end of the eighteenth century was toward love as the basis for marriage, economic developments strengthened the demand for familial allegiance among the upper class" (170). This tension is visible in Manfred's villainous insistence on manipulating the romantic and sexual couplings of the members of his family in order to support his dynasty. He matches Conrad and Isabella to support his claim to Otranto; when Conrad dies, Manfred plans to divorce his wife, Hippolita, so that he can marry Isabella and through her engender his line and legitimize his claim. The closure of *Otranto* is remarkably pessimistic about the possibilities of romantic love; although the power of the patriarch is deposed, the younger generation fails to engender its own happiness. Theodore, whose true love, Matilda, has been killed by her father, is left to marry Isabella "with whom he could forever indulge the melancholy that had taken possession of his soul" (110).[12] The impact of the Industrial Revolution on family relations is, of course, only one of the various sources of the motif of family dysfunction that, like the motif of the destruction of the castle, is engendered by a variety of social pressures of the eighteenth century. It is important to remember that the motif of the demonic patriarch (which will be discussed more fully in the next chapter) can also be productively read as a reaction to the French Revolution and as an expression of Romantic anxieties toward authority.

3

Fantasies of Return

Property Restoration Imagined

The eighteenth century, then, was a period marked by revolutionary changes, many of which were apparent in the new means of acquiring, possessing and transmitting property as well as in the changing definition of property. The rise of Gothic literature may be productively read as a response to these transformations. Typically, Gothic property is restored to the original owner, one way or another. The commitment of the Gothic text to the restoration of property to its pre-narrative owner together with the belatedness of the Gothic moment—the conventional Gothic narrative begins at a time far later than the originating events of usurpation—reveal the nostalgia of the Gothic, the yearning for a return to the pre-narrative moment when property and identity were securely possessed by the proper (aristocratic) owner. The Gothic masterplot traces the attempt to recapture the integrity of the past, framed as the restoration of property. This mode of nostalgia represents an understandable response to the rapid changes that accompanied the political and economic revolutions of the eighteenth century.[1] Gothic nostalgia for a past free of economic tension anticipates Marxist nostalgia for a pre-industrial, pre-capitalistic society. Both the Gothic and Marxist text desire the return of property to the proper, original owner. Marx, of course, envisions the return of property to the people who preceded the aristocrats and capitalists; whereas Gothic property is invariably returned to the aristocrat. Yet the Gothic, too, reveals a yearning to return the property to the proletariat in the restoration of the castle to an aristocrat who *appears* to be a peasant. And both the Marxist and the Gothic imaginations anticipate the destruction of a hierarchal economic system: Marx in the downfall and destruction of the expanding and encroaching capitalist system; the Gothic in the destruction of the Gothic castle and the usurping aristocratic dynasty that engenders it.

Indeed, Marx reveals an affinity for the Gothic in the opening line of *The Communist Manifesto* (1848), "A spectre is haunting Europe—the spectre of Communism." In Marx's formulation, the ghost of Communism is to perform the typical Gothic ghostly function (enacted by the ghosts of Alfonso in *Otranto* and the Lovels in *Baron* and by many other ghosts in the tradition): the discovery of the repressed rightful owners of property and the restoration of their usurped property.[2] Both systems also share the inability to imagine the idyllic time that presumably lies beyond the restoration of property and the destruction of the structures of oppression. As Robert Heilbroner notes, it is the destruction of capitalism that is the focus of *Capital*: "In all of Marx there is almost nothing that looks beyond the Day of Judgment to see what the future might be like" (161). Similarly, the Gothic text closes at the moment of destruction of the new usurping order and restoration of the old, leaving unresolved the appearance of the next stage.

Another question left unanswered by the Gothic text: what exactly is the Gothic attitude toward property possession? Does the Gothic reflect fantasies of stability or anxieties of instability? Does the restoration of the castle represent a conservative endorsement of the *status quo*? Does the restoration to a seeming peasant represent subversion? And what exactly does the conventional destruction of the Gothic building suggest? As these questions indicate, the political ambivalence of the Gothic is most apparent in the conclusion of the narrative, the part in which restoration is typically accomplished. That is, in the formulation of D.A. Miller in *Narrative and Its Discontents*, the closure in which a text typically achieves stasis in achieving the state that the narrative endorses. Yet the typical Gothic closure resists a clear and definitive statement of purpose.

The Ambiguous Politics of Restoration in Walpole and Reeve

Both Walpole and Reeve close their works with the restoration of the appropriated property, as well as with the conventional marriage between the families who have been competing for the property. Theodore marries Isabella, whose father, Frederic, is thought to be the legitimate inheritor of Otranto before the identity of Theodore is revealed; Edmund marries the daughter of the Baron. Moreover, each text ends pointedly in the sunny world of realism and order after spending much narrative time in the realm of dark supernatural chaos. Yet despite the narrative similarity, a closer look at each text reveals the differing attitudes of the two writers: Reeve's fear of disorder and immorality, as opposed to Walpole's anxious yearning for change.[3]

The conclusion of Walpole's novel certainly gestures to order and stability: with the restoration of property and identity, and the performance of the stabilizing marriage. The final transfer of the castle of Otranto, whose earlier history has been marked by theft, murder and haunting, is effected through the orderly signing of legal documents. The last night of the dark, irrational narrative is followed by a morning in which the cold light of reason prevails, a world in which the pen is indeed mightier than the sword (including the giant sword of the ghostly Alfonso): "In the morning, Manfred signed his abdication of the principality" (110).

However, this conservative ending is only superficially stable: Walpole undermines the solidity of the restoration of property by introducing the motif of the destroyed castle, to be re-enacted in countless Gothic narratives. Theodore is indisputably identified as the true owner of the Castle of Otranto only after it has been cast down into rubble:

> The moment Theodore appeared, the walls of the castle behind Manfred were thrown down with a mighty force, and the form of Alfonso, dilated to an immense magnitude, appeared in the centre of the ruins. Behold in Theodore, the true heir of Alfonso! said the vision [108].

In destroying the property as it is restored to Theodore, Walpole suggests again that property is unpossessible and unrestorable. Walpole also subverts the normalization of the ending marriage between Theodore, the heir, and Isabella, the closest heiress. Unfortunately Theodore's true love, Matilda, has been murdered by her father Manfred. At closure, Walpole's aristocrat, Theodore, remains insecure and abject, less in possession than possessed— by "the melancholy that had taken possession of his soul" (110). Walpole thus ends his novel with a subversive undermining of his seemingly conservative closure.

Reeve presents a more stable conclusion than does Walpole. Indeed, *Baron* reveals Reeve's eagerness to move from an immoral world in which ownership is dictated by theft and murder and indicated by ghosts, to a moral world in which possession is effected through the signing of legal documents. Edmund, whose only previous allies were the ghosts of his murdered parents, is now embraced by the substantial and powerful members of the ruling class, to which he rightfully belongs. As in Walpole's text, this moment of restoration takes place in clear daylight: "The next morning Sir Philip entered into consultation with the two Barons, on the method he should take to get Edmund received, and acknowledged, as heir of the house of Lovel" (107). As in *Otranto*, the final righting of order is accomplished in the realm of law. After a lengthy and orderly inquiry replete with witnesses and commissioners, the Baron arranges a thoroughly legal transfer of property and title, calling upon the institutions that represent the highest level of civil order: Sir Philip is "to go to the King…[to] request that he may be called up to parliament by a writ, for there is no need of a new patent, he being the true inheritor; in the meantime, he shall assume the name, arms, and title" (148).

Moreover Edmund's stabilizing dynastic marriage is a happy one: "the new Lord and Lady are "examples of conjugal affection and happiness. Within a year from his marriage she brought him a son and heir" (151)—future primogeniture thus firmly guaranteed. As Kate Ellis remarks on the conservative nature of Reeve's ending: "For Reeve [the] radical vision stops at the institution of marriage" (64). "By ending her novel on an unequivocally happy note, Reeve transformed Walpole's Gothic experiment into a vehicle for domestic optimism" (68).

Yet the closure of Reeve's text reveals an undercurrent of anxiety and instability. To celebrate the marriage of his daughter Emma to Edmund, the Baron, having voluntarily relinquished his illegally acquired property to Edmund, "ordered the doors to be thrown open, and the house free for all comers" (148). The Baron's gesture calls into question the integrity and ownership of the property that has been opened to all, its boundaries transgressed. Edmund further muddles the clarity of Reeve's normalizing denouement by calling in his peasant foster parents, publicly acknowledging his debt to them, and declaring that his foster mother "should always be received as his mother" (149–150). So, although Reeve's castle does not literally fall, some aristocratic walls are figuratively broken down.

Neither text, then, manifests an unambiguous response to eighteenth-century anxieties of property. *Otranto* and *Baron* each unfold a struggle between law and fantasy, between validation and subversion of the possibilities of possession. Neither text ends in the satisfyingly static moment that D.A. Miller sees as being the endpoint of the narrative, the moment when the text endorses the situation that it posits as ideal. The orderly restoration of property and identity to the legal and authentic owner appears to be a satisfyingly conservative move, unless we recall that to effect this restoration the property has been seized from the apparently rightful aristocratic owner (Manfred, the Baron), the seeming representative of hegemony, and returned to an apparent outsider whose identity has been previously unknown. The seeming stability of the Gothic ending is disrupted by the randomness with which the proper owner is discovered as much as it is by the frequent destruction of the restored property.

Literary Heirs of Walpole and Reeve: Ambiguous Fantasies of Restoration

In subsequent Gothic narratives, influenced by Walpole and Reeve, the subversive ending and the conservative ending continue to co-exist and compete as two possible alternatives for Gothic closure, resulting in an ambiguously tense struggle that endures beyond the closing frame of the narrative. The inability of the Gothic text to arrive at the moment of stable stasis—or the resistance of the text to this state—is emblematized by yet another of the myriad conventions of the Gothic narrative, the deferred ending, the conclusion that participates in a refusal to attach stable meaning to the closure of the text. This narrative strategy accommodates competing models of closure by providing more than one ending for the narrative, deferring the final ending longer that is narratively necessary. Ann Radcliffe, who, like Reeve, represents herself and is generally seen by critics as a proponent of the conservative, moral Gothic tendency toward restoration of the *status quo*, makes use of the deferred ending in *The Mysteries of Udolpho* (1794)[4] to resolve the political inconsistencies of her text. Radcliffe's conservative tendencies are visible in her use of the normalizing Gothic closure and the return of her narratives to the world of domesticity and realism; however, Radcliffe reveals the ambiguity of her political stance in deploying a series of false endings, thus deferring the final ending of the text and resisting the safety of the normalizing domestic closure to which her narrative finally accedes. After escaping from the clutches of the evil Montoni who seeks to appropriate her property, Emily St. Aubert is informed by her rescuer DuPont[5] that "the estate, of which Montoni had attempted to defraud her, was not irrecoverably lost" (131). The narrative could easily end here with all major problems resolved. Yet the final settlement of property on Emily is delayed for many pages—by shipwreck, by the apparent treachery of her lover Valancourt, and by the mysteries at the superfluous Chateau-le-Blanc. Not until these problems are resolved is the final closure, including the conservative disposal of the estates, achieved.

The central problem of Radcliffe's narrative as of Walpole's and Reeve's, is the disposal of property.[6] In Radcliffe's text, too, the villain seeks to misappropriate property. However, Radcliffe, in keeping with the conservatism of the 1790s that arose in response to the excesses of the French Revolution, attempts to control the extremes indulged in by her predecessors. Her villain Montoni, although capable of imprisoning his wife and her niece (behavior not quite illegal, as the next chapter reveals), works through quasi-legal means. Rather than killing Emily for her property, he appropriates the property by forcing her to sign a document ceding her estates to him. Here is a villain who works through law and reason and who comes prepared: "In a very solemn manner he ... immediately laid before her a paper, which was to transfer the right of those estates to himself" (2.106).

The denouement of Radcliffe's novel is generally read as a moral model of domestic normalization. Montoni is punished and all that he stole is restored. Moreover, Radcliffe endorses a return to realism in her deployment of the strategy of the explained supernatural, whereby each ghostly manifestation is explained through rational means at the end of the text (a strategy that locates Radcliffe as a precursor of the detective story): the ghostly noises are explained by pirates; the ghostly music is the work of human hands; the horrible vision of decay behind the black veil is revealed to be a wax creation. In the absence of any real ghosts, the possibility of rational, legal ownership is apparently solidified and valorized.

Yet a reading that focuses on the movement of property in *Udolpho* reveals the implicit subversiveness of Radcliffe's conclusion. For, although Radcliffe's narrative ends with a stable and secure restoration and consolidation of property, the property is restored to and consolidated by a young woman. Radcliffe counters the system of primogeniture by positing a female line of inheritance: Emily inherits the property that belonged to her two aunts, the Marchioness and Madame Cheron (333) and ends in full possession of a number of estates. Emily is further enriched by her husband's good fortune. In a move that further disrupts the conventions of primogeniture, Valancourt's older brother "resigned to him a part of the rich domain, the whole of which, as he had not family, would of course descend to his brother [Valancourt] on his decease" (344). Radcliffe further subverts the orderly restoration of property and consolidation of property ownership by providing a competing, subversive outcome for the eponymous property. Although Emily is the heir of her aunt, Montoni's wife, Udolpho, the eponymous, darkly mysterious, epistemologically unpossessible central property, eludes Emily and is inherited by a marginal, impoverished character "who was the nearest surviving relation of the house of that name" (344).

The distribution of property at the end of Radcliffe's *Sicilian Romance*

(1790) provides an even more compelling illustration of her conservative tendencies, in that the conclusion of that earlier novel features a single consolidating inheritor. While she reforms the system of primogeniture, by feminizing it, Radcliffe does not modify its inequity in any way. In *A Vindication of the Rights of Men* Mary Wollstonecraft focuses on the inequity that lies at the root of primogeniture: "Property ... should be ... more equally divided amongst all the children of a family; else it is an everlasting rampart, in consequence of a barbarous feudal institution, that enables the older son to overpower talents and depress virtue" (23). Once again we see the limits of the Gothic imagination as Radcliffe's reversal ends with one sibling, albeit a sister, consolidating all power and property.

Yet, even in the presumably conservative *Udolpho*, competing models of closure allow unresolved tensions to surface, disrupting the seemingly normalizing tendency of the Gothic closure to restore order and rule and to return the Gothic text to reality and realism. In Radcliffe's deployment of competing modes of closure, it is possible to see the sustained Gothic struggle against the imperatives of legal reality and realism. The conventional normalizing ending that accedes to the pragmatic legal and economic realities of the eighteenth century is subverted by the last gasp of Gothic excess and disorder.

4

Nineteenth-Century Expansions

The preoccupation with questions of property and the struggle between subversive and normalizing solutions continue to haunt the Gothic; this preoccupation and struggle inform the set of recurring motifs that define the mode. Yet even in the conventional Gothic, repetition yields to variation. Nineteenth-century texts that evoke the Gothic tradition, like Emily Brontë's *Wuthering Heights* (1847) and Charlotte Yonge's *Chantry House* (1886), revise the familiar Gothic preoccupations with property and possession to reflect the particular concerns of their times and of their authors.

Emily Brontë carefully sets her novel in the late eighteenth century, the era of the high Gothic, and revisits Gothic concerns regarding property and inheritance. The narrative of *Wuthering Heights* traces the pattern of appropriation and restoration of Thrushcross Grange and of the eponymous property that is suitably located in a desolate setting and appropriately identified with medievalism: Lockwood detects the date 1500 engraved at the front door (4). As Sanger delineates, Brontë carefully constructs the legal means by which Heathcliff appropriates and consolidates the estates of the Earnshaws and the Lintons. Like Montoni in Udolpho, Heathcliff is a Gothic villain who observes the letter of the law. He wrests Wuthering Heights from his adoptive family the Earnshaws when Hindley Earnshaw, the only son, dies of dissipation after mortgaging the property to him. Similarly, Heathcliff deploys property law to acquire Thrushcross Grange. Echoing Manfred's manipulation of Isabella in *Otranto*, Heathcliff imprisons Cathy Linton and forces her to marry his son, Linton. When Cathy's father dies, having been prevented by Heathcliff from changing his will to displace the Heathcliffs from the line of inheritance, the Grange passes to Cathy and thence to her husband, Linton, a legal minor; upon Linton's death the property passes to Heathcliff.

This narrative thus establishes Heathcliff as a literary heir to Manfred, the prototypical Gothic villain. Like Manfred, Heathcliff attempts to deploy the structures of primogeniture in the cause of usurpation and tries desperately to perpetuate his line, using his son as a pawn at the service of dynastic imperative. In her narrative, Brontë emphasizes the psychological dimension of her hero-villain, thus tempering his villainy much more than does Walpole.[1] In seeking to perpetuate his dynasty through the union of his son and Cathy Linton, Heathcliff seeks vicariously to consummate his passionate union with Catherine, Cathy's mother, and to establish himself as an insider rather than the outsider he is. But Linton, like Manfred's son Conrad, is sickly and dies, dashing Heathcliff's hopes of perpetuating the line of inheritance. From the perspective of the movement of the property, the closure of *Wuthering Heights* is a comfortable and normalizing one. The disruptive and subversive Heathcliff is displaced from the line of property transmission. The usurped properties revert to Hareton Earnshaw and Cathy Linton, the descendants of the proper owners; the legitimate line of inheritance will be reinstated through their children.

It is evident that, although *Wuthering Heights* is clearly indebted to the conventions of the Gothic tradition, Brontë revises these traditions in a number of significant ways. Reflecting the shift of money and power in the nineteenth century, Brontë removes her novel from the aristocratic settings of her precursors. Neither the original owners nor the usurper are members of the aristocracy: the Earnshaws are farmers; the Lintons are members of the landed gentry. In a significant shift that relocates the source of economic anxiety from the entrenched, grasping aristocratic class to the marginalized lower class, Heathcliff, the usurper, is an authentic member of the lower classes and, as H.L. Malchow suggests, also a racially-hybrid encroaching outsider, feared by the post-revolutionary, imperialistic society that engenders him. In *Baron* and *Otranto*, the peasants are ultimately comfortably identified as noble-hearted aristocrats in disguise. Heathcliff's origins are never identified; he remains a threatening enigma. In addition to betokening a new kind of class fear, the continued mystery of Heathcliff's origins reveals that Brontë's nineteenth-century world is less well-ordered than Walpole's and Reeve's, more random and thus more frightening and realistic.

The presence of ghosts in *Wuthering Heights*, however, reveals that Brontë's text does not move unilaterally toward realism. The narrative is framed by two ghostly encounters experienced by Lockwood. In accordance with the conventions of the trope, these ghosts have been dispossessed of their earthly place. The first encounter is framed safely within the dream of a fool, no danger to the tenets of nineteenth-century realism. Lockwood—who has already unwittingly identified himself as a timid prig, the kind of man who shrinks "icily into myself, like a snail" (5) at the first sign of interest by a young woman, and thus likely to be susceptible to foolish imaginings and fears of contact—dreams that, as he stretches out his arm to silence a scratching branch, "my fingers closed on the fingers of a little, ice-cold hand," the hand of Catherine Linton "come home" (20). The ghostly encounter that provides the end frame of the novel, however, is not confined by the rationality of realism. This time, Lockwood encounters not a ghost in a dream but a little boy (in the outside world) who is frozen in fear, as are his sheep, because they see "Heathcliff and a woman." In this second manifestation then, these ghosts are freed from the confines of Lockwood's imaginings, floating free in the world visible to boys and sheep. Even the practical Lockwood admits that, although "he probably raised the phantoms from thinking, as he traversed the moors alone ... yet, still, I don't like being out in the dark, now" (255). Whereas in her first manifestation Catherine is struggling to get into Wuthering Heights, a conventional ghost anchored to property, at the end of the narrative the ghosts of Catherine and Heathcliff are freed of the anchors of property and of literary realism.

Critics have long noticed the seemingly paradoxical and unique co-existence within *Wuthering Heights* of mundane legal concerns of property possession and Gothic excesses and hauntings. Both Charles Piercy Sanger ("The Structure of Wuthering Heights" 1926) and Nancy Armstrong ("Emily Brontë In and Out of Her Time" 1982) persuasively argue for the co-existence in *Wuthering Heights* of the realism of property ownership and the imaginative fantasy of the supernatural and Gothic excess. Sanger's essay, a painstaking study of the narrative structure of Brontë's novel, reveals that the fantastic narrative is set against the backdrop of her "considerable knowledge of the law" (333); he delineates each aspect of property law that Brontë employs to facilitate the consolidation of the Earnshaw and Linton property by Heathcliff. Expressing admiration for Brontë's mastery of complicated property laws, Sanger enthuses "so far as I know, no other novel in the world" (335) demonstrates the same respect for the structures of the law. In this, Sanger implies, Brontë distances herself from her Gothic influences: "German romances can hardly have been the source of her knowledge of English law" (336). Yet, as we have seen, the significance of property law in earlier English narratives serves to connect Brontë firmly to the English Gothic Romantic tradition.

Armstrong also sees in *Wuthering Heights* a unique blend of the ideologies and concerns of the Romantic Gothic and the utilitarian Victorian. Writing of the "politically and philosophically hostile positions [that] coexist in [the] novel" ("Emily Brontë In and Out of Her Time" 366), including the conflict between the literary realism of utilitarianism "coming into vogue during the 1840's" (365) and the fantasy of Gothic Romanticism, Armstrong argues that "all the Gothic devices ... are engineered by common law... [bringing] Gothic devices in the service or realism instead of romance" (372). Yet, as the earlier discussions of *Baron* and *Otranto* indicate, the tension that Armstrong locates uniquely within *Wuthering Heights* marks each text written within the Gothic tradition. Armstrong's reading obscures the conventionality of the paradoxical excesses that inform Brontë's text. Her comment that "the persistence of forms of Romantic supernaturalism in the novel disturbs the otherwise conventional ending" (374) ignores the long tradition of the conflicted Gothic closure in which the consolidating ending is typically disrupted by a last instance of Gothic excess.

Armstrong's reading, which locates Brontë on the cusp between subversive Gothic fantasy and normative Victorian realism, falters because it falls into the critical stereotypes of Gothic and Victorian fiction. Clearly, despite the stereotype, English Gothic fiction is not oblivious to the contingencies of property and of the law; conversely, even the most staid Victorian fiction is not immune to the temptations of Gothic excess, especially in texts that deal with matters of property possession, stereotypically identified as a Victorian concerns.

Charlotte Yonge is another Victorian writer who deploys the fantastic methods of the Gothic to address realistic concerns regarding property possession. Yonge is generally considered by critics to be the exemplar of conservative Victorian domestic fiction, representative of the middle class reaction to nineteenth-century upheavals: the political turmoil that swept Europe in 1848, the outbreak of the Crimean War, the Indian Mutiny of 1857, the crisis in the cotton mills of Northern England that followed the American civil war, the publication in 1859 of Darwin's *Origin of Species*, the emergence of historical-critical approaches to the Bible, the ongoing problem of Ireland and, beginning in mid-century, the movement for women's rights. Yonge, who was an enormously popular influence on middle-class women readers, writes novels driven by virtue and morality. In this Yonge demonstrates allegiance to the female Gothic of her precursors, Reeve and

Radcliffe. In writing of Yonge's politics, June Sturrock states, "Yonge was no feminist; her response to the possibility of social change is invariably conservative" (15). "Her novels show an endless engagement with the subject of proper feminity" (27).[2] And yet, as Sturrock also notes, Yonge's "religious convictions, formed, first by her father's High Church teachings and later by John Keble's Tractarianism, drove her to reject certain 'worldly' values" (16); her conservative religion paradoxically led her to discard certain Victorian conventions, for example, "to see that respectability was not the supreme moral virtue" (25).

Thus Yonge's seemingly settled and staid position reveals the kind of ambivalent thinking that finds expression in the eternally tense and unsettled Gothic mode. And indeed, Yonge does seem very much at home writing in the genre.[3] A striking and sustained invocation of the Gothic narrative, couched within a conventional Victorian narrative of domestic life, may be found in Yonge's *Chantry House* (1886). Yonge's affinity for the belated, nostalgic, Gothic text that yearns to return to the idylls of the past, can be partially explained by her stance as a conservative novelist. Yonge, too, is driven by nostalgia, the desire to return to simpler, better times. In *Chantry House*, Yonge personalizes Gothic nostalgia, revisiting her own childhood experience of Otterbourne, the site of the Yonge family home in the 1820's before the time when "church restoration was settling in" (*Chantry House* 2.120).[4] But *Chantry House* is not only an outburst of nostalgia for a lost past. Within the Gothic mode, always susceptible to tense struggle, Yonge discovers a vehicle suited to her attempt to reconcile conflicting narrative strategies and ideologies of possession, resulting in a text that evokes the typical Gothic struggles in order to settle them. *Chantry House* is quite firmly located within the Gothic tradition, evincing the familiar, and by the late nineteenth century, clichéd trappings, that began as eighteenth-century conventions. In Yonge's novel, however, Gothic excess and fantasy are mitigated by Victorian realism and reason, and Gothic horror is contained by language and by law.

Chantry House, the home of the Winslows, is clearly located in the Gothic landscape. Erected upon an ancient abbey that had been built in 1434, the house reveals a telling blend of modern and Gothic architecture. Although built in Queen Anne style, it features a "Gothic porch ... and a flagrantly modern Gothic porch it was, flanked by two comical little turrets ... there was [a] modern addition ... in Gothic taste, i.e. with pointed arches filled up with glass over the sash-windows" (1.73). In this early description of the house, it is possible to see an emblem for the strategy of Yonge's narrative, her tactic for balancing the competing demands of conservative domestic realism and the subversiveness of the Gothic mode. For, rather than present a dark, tension between conflicting styles, she negotiates them with humor: the porch, in which Gothicism is tempered by the influence of Victorian architecture, becomes a comical image of synthesis rather than a tragic image of struggle.

Chantry House reveals its Gothic credentials in being suitably haunted. The rooms in the older end of the house, with "deep mullioned windows … and very handsome groined ceilings" (1.74), are regularly visited by the ghost of a previously dispossessed inhabitant, Margaret Fordyce. Margaret, as the Winslows discover, had lived at the turn of the eighteenth century and had been the second wife of a Winslow ancestor. After the death of her husband, her stepsons imprisoned and killed her. Margaret makes a series of appearances, generally to Clarence, the second son of the Winslows, who is himself displaced by the dictates of primogeniture. These appearances culminate in the ghostly re-enactment of Margaret's imprisonment and death. But here too, Yonge's text mitigates Gothic excess and tension. Margaret's appearances are governed by the rule of order: her ghost appears in a regular, predictable way, always around the New Year.

The course of Yonge's narrative follows the typical pattern of the Gothic text, tracing the Winslow family's discovery of Margaret's buried story. Not until the conclusion of the novel is the last piece of evidence, Margaret's body, uncovered. In the course of preparing for one of the weddings with which the novel conventionally concludes, workers, digging in the foundations of the house discover "an old chest, and within lay a skeleton, together with a few fragments of female clothing, a wedding ring … ghastly confirmation … to connect the bones with Margaret (2.224). On "the ensuing night there was a strange, quiet funeral service at Earlscombe church" (2.225); the narrative is safely laid to rest with the burial of Margaret's bones. This disinterment and reburial is typical of the Gothic.[5] The trope lends itself to a psychological interpretation, as representing the return and suppression of the repressed; and indeed that reading is quite satisfactory. However, Yonge's religious tendencies suggest that the trope of the restored and reburied body discloses Christological roots. In the Gothic text, as in the New Testament, the restoration of the dead body leads to the re-establishment of order, rather than instating Gothic horror. Yonge's deployment of this typically horrifying trope, then, portends Christian salvation, denaturing its power as a horror-inducing image.

The unearthing of Margaret's history reveals yet another case of misappropriated property.[6] The Winslow brothers have killed Margaret to steal her property, Chantry House. Suppressing a will that bequeaths the estate back to Margaret's family of origin, the Fordyces, the brothers renew an earlier, invalid will to legitimize their claims. The descendants of these murderers, the Winslows, encounter the convergence of fantasy and law as they learn from an old witch-like woman that because of their ancestor's appropriation of Chantry house, there is "a curse on you all! The poor lady as was murdered won't let you be!... It's well known as how the curse is on the first-born. The Lady Margaret don't let none of 'em live to come after his father" (1.153–1.154). The reality of the curse is confirmed by legal documentation: the Winslows consult "the registers" (1.154) and discover a remarkable, and even radical disruption of primogeniture, surprising perhaps in a writer aligned with conservative politics. In every branch of the Winslow family, including their own, the first-born son has died, although in each case the cause of death was ascribed to natural rather than supernatural causes.

Throughout the novel Yonge develops the theme of disrupted primogeniture and interrupted property transmission. Margaret's curse is directly responsible for the Winslows' surprising inheritance of Chantry House, having eliminated family members more directly in the line of inheritance. But this is just the last in a long line of disruptions that have broken the line of orderly property transmission. The original abbey built as a chapel in 1434 "was granted to Sir Harry Power" (1.65). This neutral "granting" suppresses the stark significance of this event: the appropriation of Catholic property during the Reformation. The narrator, Edward Winslow, acknowledges that the family cherishes "the broken bits of wall and stumps of columns, remnants of the chapel" as charming garden elements, never "troubl[ing] ourselves about the desecration" (1.75). The retrospective awareness of Edward, who tells the family story as an old man, that the neutral "granting" was accompanied by destructive "desecration," discloses Yonge's endorsement of the passage of time to balance two competing views: the placid conservative acceptance of the young Edward and the more skeptical awareness of the abuses of power of the older, wiser Edward.[7]

In proper Gothic fashion, the various matches that are proposed to unite the competing families and consolidate the claim to property in *Chantry House* are consistently interrupted. The earlier engagement of Griff, the eldest surviving son of the Winslows, to Ellen, the daughter of the Fordyces, is initially interrupted due to Griff's dissipation (also the cause of the deferral of the marriage in *Udolpho*); the match is ultimately prevented by Griff's ill-judged marriage to another, and by Ellen's subsequent death. The plan by Clarence, the second Winslow son, to marry the younger Fordyce daughter, Anne, is deferred by a particularly nineteenth-century obstacle: Clarence goes off to Hong Kong, "which was then newly ceded to the English and where the firm wished to establish a house of business" (2.184). The narrative does manage to end with the typical Gothic closure of the consolidating marriage: the two youngest children of the Winslow and Fordyce families marry. In arranging her marriages, Yonge adheres to a convention that appears in the female Gothic from Radcliffe on: although the marriages effect dynastic goals and reconcile feuding families, they are based on love, not economics. Martyn and Anne marry because they realize that "what they had felt for each other all their lives was love" (2.221).

Yonge, then, deploys all the Gothic conventions to unfold her story, while also allowing the Victorian and domestic context of her narrative to soften Gothic horror. The story she thus constructs is an appealing, comfortable and ultimately safe re-enactment of the mode. In this it is possible to see the appeal of the Gothic to Yonge; her synthetic text allows her to endorse her conservative worldview. Yonge succeeds in appropriating a typically unstable mode, a mode whose power derives from its instability, for stable ends. Her text so closely follows Gothic convention that it lacks any suspense or surprise. In her careful re-enactment of the myriad conventions of the Gothic mode, a catalog of conventions that are more than a century old when deployed in *Chantry House*, murder and theft become comfortingly familiar, domesticated in the cause of domestic realism. In this, Yonge taps into a central paradox of the Gothic: the essential narrative strategy of this shocking and suspenseful mode is internal and external repetition. The Gothic is defined by a set of recurring conventions; horrifying and excessive though these conventions may be, the very nature of their unchanging repetition serves to contain and dissipate their impact. Echoing the moral tradition of Reeve, Yonge returns her characters to the totalizing stability of the moral plane in which competing ideologies of possession are reconciled. As the Winslows come to discover the origins of their inherited property, their Victorian propriety dictates that they ignore the realities of legal possession, and the fantasies of supernatural possession, turning to their Christian morals to determine the proper owner of the property.

Even the potentially radical nature of the transmission of the property through the female line is absorbed by Yonge's totalizing morality. The Winslows discover that the last rightful owner of the property was Margaret Fordyce and that it thus belonged by rights to the Fordyce family. Significantly, Margaret acquired her property by inheriting it from her own family, not through marriage. Moreover, Margaret inherited her property from another woman. It becomes clear that the real crime of the Winslow brothers is that they have disrupted a female line of property succession, making Margaret's curse, which blasts the male line of primogeniture, a particularly apt vengeance and a notably horrifying instance of the power of female speech. Yonge's indictment of primogeniture in the instance of Margaret's curse and Clarence's struggles reflect a legal struggle of her times. Avner Offer explains that primogeniture was condemned in the Free Trade in Land literature of the 1870s because it led to concentrations of large estates held by a small minority of the population. Indeed, this legal struggle took on a moral cast as the inequity of the system led to primogeniture being identified as "the root of evil" (Offer 40); certainly the moral undertones of this legal struggle would have appealed to Yonge. Indeed, Yonge constructs a character who explicitly emblematizes herself to make a direct pronouncement on the issue. The Winslows are visited by Miss Selby, a kind "elderly spinster" (1.104) much like Charlotte Yonge. It is she who declaims to Edward: "Margaret Fordyce ... was the heiress, and had every right to dispose of her property" (1.105). By the lights of tradition and law[8] this is patently untrue; by the lights of feminism, couched as morality, this is indeed right and this is, in fact, the resolution that the narrative endorses.[9] Feminism, law and tradition are all reconciled, then, by the simple moral statement of the author's stand-in.

Moreover, the larger claims of Christian morality supersede even Margaret's legal and feminist claims; the property, the source of struggle and discord, as is all Gothic property, is disposed of in a particularly harmonious (and anti–Gothic) way. In her reconstruction of the trope of the destroyed Gothic property, Yonge introduces an important variation on the theme. The ultimate solution to the conflicts surrounding Chantry House is accomplished, not through the conventional destruction of the property but with a very unconventional and moral disposal of the property. In Yonge's formulation, the family is finally dispossessed of the House not because it is destroyed but because they willfully give it up to be used as an orphanage, a cheerfully Victorian version of the conventionally disruptive Gothic ending.

Yonge's revision of the Gothic is amplified by a conversation with a family friend, Henderson, who "had some very interesting talks with us two over ancestral sin and its possible effects." In one significant conversation, Henderson recalls "the 18th of Ezekiel as a comment on the Second Commandment" (1.155). In this Henderson evokes that famous motto of the Gothic, the Second Commandment threat to visit "the iniquity of the father upon the children" (Ex. 20.5). But in a typical move of Yongeian mitigation, Henderson counters these vengeful words with the more temperate words of Ezekiel: "The son shall not bear the iniquity of the father with him" (18.20). Yonge reconciles two ideologies that compete within the Bible as well as within the Gothic text: irrational vengeance and rational justice. Here too Yonge reveals her faith in the organizing, rationalizing powers of the written word, and most particularly, the Word.

The central conflict in Chantry House becomes, then, not the struggle of the conventional Gothic text: the question of who will win, whether possession will be legally effected or dispossession imaginatively accomplished. Yonge's text struggles to effect the moral approach that will erase all questions of possession or dispossession.[10] The central quandary for the Winslows becomes how to restore the usurped property to the Fordyces, not how to keep it for themselves. Even the possessiveness of imperialism is subsumed under the umbrella of morality. In Hong Kong Clarence's actions serve to conservatively endorse the ideology of empire, or at least empire as practiced with a moral religious sensibility; he achieves great success and wealth "without soiling his hands with the miserable opium traffic" (2.192). Moreover, Clarence's enterprises in Hong Kong are revealed to be inspired by his moral and anti-imperialistic desire to earn enough money to pay the Fordyces for the appropriated property. Thus, in Yonge's Victorian vision, morality solves all the typical Gothic tensions regarding property possession, resulting in a text that provides a comfortingly stable, if static and unexciting, conclusion for her largely proper female audience. Her Gothic narrative is, then, Gothic in form only and, as Ruskin says of Gothic architecture, "It is not enough that it has the Form, if it have not also the power and life" (159).

Not surprisingly, Modern writers of the early-twentieth century rediscover the dynamic potential of Gothic anxieties of possession. Virginia Woolf's *To the Lighthouse* (1927), is meditation on the gendered interfamilial struggle for control over property and children: the decay of the family house that follows Mrs. Ramsay's death echoes the motif of the destruction of contested property and Mrs. Ramsay returns at the novel's end in the form of a ghost. As the painter Lily Briscoe regards the house, she sees "some wave of white [go] over the window pane" (300) and then Mrs. Ramsay appears, rekindling in Lily a feeling of "old horror." It is the feeling of horror that haunts every Gothic text: "to want and want and not to have" (300), an old horror, indeed.

Part II

Ghosts

Possession of Person in the English Gothic

5

Self-(Dis)Possession in *The Woman in White*

Personal possession, the ability to possess one's own body and mind (to be self-possessed), or to hold proprietary rights over the bodies of others, is, like the right of property possession, a cornerstone of modern Western culture. Indeed Irene Tucker evokes Locke to indicate that self-possession is a prerequisite for possession of property: "self-possession is ... the ground for possessing the world" (17). And yet, the concept of personal possession is even more unstable and anxiety-provoking than is the concept of property possession, inviting the interventions of the Gothic text.

Since the advent of the Enlightenment, Western philosophy has valorized a powerful liberal ideology that promotes freedom for each individual; that is each person is empowered to own his own body and the fruits of his labor.[1] And yet, the foundational idea of self-possession was contradicted in the eighteenth century by economic and legal systems that allowed human beings to be possessed by others: marriage allowed husbands to own the bodies (and property) of wives and children; slavery allowed Europeans to own Africans; the newly-developing penal system allowed the state to control the body and mind of the criminal.

The tense and anxious Gothic mode provides a fertile ground for playing out the anxieties that result from the competing notions of self-possession and self-dispossession: the ideological and theoretical representations of the self as unalienable that counter and are countered by the material commodification of the person in commerce and in law. The Gothic interrogation of personal possession unsettles both the Enlightenment reliance on the powers of the rational mind to apprehend both reality and itself,² and the opposing economic assertion that the person may be possessed through marriage or slavery. While showing in excessive detail the susceptibility of the mind to dispossession and the susceptibility of the body to ownership, the Gothic seems to yearn for dispossession of the self, as it yearns for dispossession of property, repeatedly demonstrating that, in fact, the person cannot be owned. The Gothic self is constantly slipping the economic and epistemologic bonds constructed to contain it.

※

One way in which the Gothic interrogates the stability of self-possession is in the trope of recovered identity, leading to the recovery and restoration of property, as in the cases of *Otranto*'s Theodore and *Baron*'s Edmund. As the recovery of property implies the instability of property ownership, so too does the recovery of identity suggest the essential unreliability of personal identity. With the random restoration of the hidden identity of the "real" owner, hauled from the margins to suit the exigencies of the Gothic plot, identity becomes a mere function of plot, drained of any essential meaning. The trope of the random discovery and recovery of the true identity of the legitimate heir also destabilizes the certainties of social hierarchy. In the eighteenth century, class-identify was as important as individual identity; if identity is unclear, so too is class affiliation, resulting in a double destabilization of self.

In the eighteenth-century texts *Otranto* and *Baron*, the reinscription of personal identity and class affiliation is—narratively, if not thematically—a function of the comic ending, happily resulting in the upward mobility and restoration of the truly noble heroes. In the nineteenth century a number of factors work to amplify the significance of individual identity and hence diminish the comic possibilities of class identity redefinition. The influence of the Enlightenment valorization of the individual human, as well as the greater economic and class mobility of the nineteenth century that allowed the meritorious individual to transcend class categories dictated by the randomness of birth, resulted in an increased estimation of the value of the individual, defined by personal attributes rather than by categories of class. This estimation emerges in the Romantic and Victorian valorization of individual experience and imagination. In the nineteenth-century Gothic, then, loss of individual identity in itself (as opposed to loss of property and social position) is of great import.

The Woman in White

The horror of lost identity is at the center of *The Woman in White* (1860). Wilkie Collins deploys a number of the obligatory Gothic conventions, including the invocation of the biblical text that informs the Gothic canon, beginning with Walpole's Preface to *Otranto*: "'The sins of the fathers shall be visited on the children'" (497). Collins resurrects the iconic demon-husband, Sir Percival Glyde,[3] and in doing so invokes the trope of marriage as death; in referring to the union of Sir Percival and Laura, Walter, the narrator, confesses that "writing of her marriage [is] like writing of her death" (161). Sir Percival seems the typical evil aristocrat, "a man of the rank of baronet, and the owner of property in Hampshire" (64); his ancestral home is suitably named Blackwater Park. Appropriately, "one wing of it is said to be five hundred years old ... it had a moat round it once" (171). The other two villains, Mr. Fairlie and Count Fosco, are also, as dictated by convention, members of the ruling classes. Mr. Fairlie, Laura's uncle, an effete aristocrat, is too involved with his own illnesses to save his niece from her villainous husband. (His brother, Laura's father, although dead before the narrative begins, is also implicated by the text for arranging the match with Sir Percival before his death.) In the representation of the Italian Count Fosco, Collins taps into the conventional depiction of the Gothic villain as the racial and religious other, originally deployed by Walpole in the description of Manfred, the Catholic Italian, in *Otranto* and by Ann Radcliffe in her representation of the villainous Catholic Italians, Montoni (*Udolpho*) and Schedoni (*The Italian* 1797). Fosco too is an apparently demonic husband. His wife, Laura's aunt, who used to be a giddy girl, is after marriage to Fosco subdued into submission; she "sits speechless in corners" (188), in the words of her husband, "self-immolated on the altar of [my] life" (551).[4]

As in *Udolpho*, the conflict for the possession of property is entwined with troubling questions about identity. The narrative of the lawyer, Gilmore, explains the extent of the wealth Laura will inherit by virtue of her identity: "Miss Fairlie's expectations ... were of a twofold kind; comprising her possible [but likely] inheritance of real property, or land, when her uncle died and her absolute inheritance of personal property, or money, when she came of age" (128). Sir Percival marries Laura in an attempt to appropriate her property; when his attempt to force her to sign away her wealth fails (213),[5] he resorts to means only seemingly less sensational than murder. Sir Percival and Count Fosco plot to steal Laura's property by stealing her identity, in the words of Fosco's chilling confession, by effecting "the complete destruction of Lady Glyde's identity" (550). They succeed in placing her in a madhouse, an "asylum," in the place of Anne Catherick, a feeble-minded young woman who looks remarkably like Laura. Substituting the sickly Anne for Laura, Sir Percival uses Anne's subsequent death as the opportunity to appropriate Laura's property through her presumed death. In doing so, Sir Percival also steals Anne's identity since she is buried under Laura's name.

The physical resemblance between Laura and Anne is reinforced by their mental inadequacy; both are feeble-minded, displaying a grotesquely exaggerated feminine passivity that borders on insanity. When Walter meets Anne, as she is escaping from the asylum, she is confused and lacking self-possession; her mind is vacantly available for appropriation by other ideas and individuals. As they near London, "the idea of shutting herself in [to a cab] ... had now got full possession of her mind" (19). By the end of the narrative, Laura, too, having been subjected to the asylum, is reduced to simple-minded childishness. Walter takes her "out for her walk as usual, and ...see[s] her quietly settled at her drawing" (390–391). Walter and Marian put her safely to bed before they discuss plans to reassert her identity; in order to make her feel useful, Walter pretends to sell her "valueless sketches" (429). Indeed it is this shared feebleness of mind, as well as their physical resemblance, the "ominous likeness" (64), "the fatal resemblance" (497), that renders Anne and Laura susceptible to loss of self-control and thereby fair game for Sir Percival's carceral plots.

Collins ironically develops the theme of unstable identity and self-possession by stripping his villains of their identities as well. As in the eighteenth-century Gothic, aristocracy is no proof of fixed identity; the "Secret" that looms over Sir Percival is his own illegitimate birth. Walter discovers that since Percival's father never married his mother, "he was not Sir Percival Glyde at all ... he had no more claim to the baronetcy and to Blackwater Park than the poorest labourer who worked on the estate" (456). Although he came to England and "took possession of the property" (474), "a word from me [Walter]: and house, lands, baronetcy, were gone from him for ever—a word from me, and he was driven out into the world a nameless ... outcast" (457). The instability of Sir Percival's identity is reinforced by his actual namelessness. In telling Walter of her connection to Sir Percival, Anne Catherick's mother refuses to name him—"I shall not call him by his name," because it is, in fact, not his name: "He never had a name" (473)—and refers to him as a "nameless gentleman" (482). Count Fosco too is deprived of his identity, dying anonymously. After he is assassinated in Paris, his body is discovered without identification, "nothing being found on him which revealed his name, his rank, or his place of abode" (562). Moreover, Walter discovers that the name Fosco is an alias and even the Countess's biography of her husband "throws no light whatever on the name that was really his own" (562).

There is a crucial distinction between the namelessness of Fosco and that of Sir Percival. Sir Percival is born into namelessness; adopting his aristocratic name is necessary for him to achieve all that he desires: property and prestige. For Sir Percival, seeking to identify with the aristocracy, namelessness is powerlessness, a ceding of self-possession to others. Fosco explicitly articulates the extent of Sir Percival's loss of power, his vulnerability due to his secret: "Two women in possession of your private mind—bad, bad, bad, my friend!" (293). Conversely, Fosco, whose power derives from his association with a mysterious Italian Brotherhood, deploys his namelessness as a source of power. His unidentified body lies in the Paris morgue "unowned, unknown" (561). In refusing the confining label of his actual name, he refuses categorization and epistemological possession by others; he alone knows and owns his actual self. Indeed, the competing models of the anonymity of Percival and Fosco reveals the recurring struggle in Collins's text and in the Gothic mode: the yearning for identity and stability of self and the wish for the freedom and power that destabilizing namelessness brings.

Collins thus constructs an overwhelming pattern of namelessness in his novel, a pattern of lost identity and self-possession. Characters representing a range of classes as well as both genders experience a destabilization of identity that is engendered by a variety of causes: illegitimacy, madness, the will of the self or the will of another. And yet there are two characters who largely manage to sustain their own identities, their self-possession: Marian and Walter. In fact, these two become the anchors by which the identities of the other characters are restabilized.

One explanation for Marian's continued self-possession is her forcefully unfeminine character: she is assertive, reasonable and confident in her own abilities—daring to oppose the two villains, even climbing on a roof to overhear their evil plans—in contrast to the far more self-effacing and conventionally feminine Laura and Anne. Marian's deviance from female patterns is indicated by the infamous description with which Collins introduces her. Walter describes her "swarthy" complexion and unfeminine appearance: "The dark down on her upper lip was almost a moustache. She had a large firm, masculine mouth and jaw; prominent, piercing, resolute brown eyes ... altogether wanting in those feminine attractions of gentleness and pliability" that Walter deems essential to female beauty (24–25).

Marian's "masculine form and masculine look of the features" (25) denote that she will be a female character assertive enough to defy villainy. Her "piercing" brown eyes—Collin's appropriation of the trope commonly used to denote the aggressive sexuality of the Gothic villain—signify that hers is a reasoning intelligence that ensures that she, unlike Anne or Laura, will maintain possession of her mind when faced with adversity. Yet Walter's unappealing description of Marian reveals another explanation for Marian's ability to sustain her self-possession. She is empowered to possess herself because her lack of physical attraction or personal wealth renders her safe from appropriation by others. In this description, Collins highlights the sad situation of nineteenth-century women; the only way to maintain self-possession is to be undesirable. This point is emphasized by the ironic attraction of the villainous Fosco to Marian. Only he can see that she is a "sublime creature" (539); only he displays a "fatal admiration" (550) for her intelligence and fortitude,[6] proving that, in a world populated by husbands like Fosco and Perceival, she is fortunate that the otherwise astute Walter Hartright persists in preferring the vapid and feeble-minded Laura over her splendid self.

Despite his dense blindness to the charms of Marian, Walter stands as her equal in maintaining his possession of self throughout the novel.[7] Significantly, Collins alters the identity of his particularly nineteenth-century hero, who is neither aristocrat in peasant disguise like the heroes of Walpole's or Reeve's texts nor sufficiently tamed aristocrat, like Radcliffe's. Collins's hero is an authentic member of the middle class, earning his living as a drawing master. Yet he demonstrates his true nobility of character by rescuing Laura from the ruling classes. In fact, his class status is an asset; in a text and in a mode in which aristocracy is synonymous with villainy, his class is a sign of his true nobility. Anne Catherick, the other besieged woman in white, says about Walter, "Not a man of rank and title.... Thank God! I may trust *him*" (18). Collins thus asserts the stable and stabilizing identity of his middle class hero.

Yet Walter's heroism is not dependent upon mere personality; despite his own self-possession, he is aware of the slipperiness of identity and repeatedly turns to the stabilizing power of the written word,[8] in the form of legally admissible documents, to fix the identity of Laura Fairlie. After the death of Sir Percival, Walter realizes that "all present hope of establishing Laura's identity had suffered" (471). He implicitly acknowledges the tenuousness of personal identity, realizing that "recognition of Laura by the people of [her] village" and "the practical test of her handwriting" would be shaky refutation of "the evidence of her aunt [who has been involved in the plot to steal her identity] ... the evidence of the medical certificate ... the fact of the funeral and the fact of the inscription on the tomb" (503). Walter knows that to refute the power of the deceptive written documents—the medical certificate, the tomb inscription—he needs opposing written documents to support Laura's claim. Seeking the evidence that will prove that Laura arrived in London "one day after the date of her (assumed) death" (534), he demands of Fosco "plain proof, which does not depend on your personal asseveration of the date at which my wife ... traveled to London" (530). Fosco understands that Walter requires a text: "You call a letter from my late lamented friend, informing me of the day and hour of his wife's arrival in London, written, signed, and dated by himself, a proof, I suppose?" (531). This is finally the proof that Walter offers to reestablish Laura's identity: "I reminded my audience of the date of Lady Glyde's death, recorded on the inscription in the churchyard ... and confirmed its correctness by producing the doctor's certificate. I then read from Sir Percival's letter announcing his wife's intended journey ... dated on the 25th—the very day when the certificate asserted her decease" (557).

Conversely, Walter turns to textual documentation to invalidate the identity of Sir Percival. Although the record of the marriage of Sir Percival's parents is to be found in the church register, "the entry ... compressed into a smaller space than that occupied by the marriages above" (448), Walter discovers that the entry is a forgery. Turning to a second document, the "copy of the Marriage Register of Welmingham Parish Church ... compared, entry by entry, with the original" (455), Walter discovers "nothing! Not a vestige of the entry which recorded the marriage of [Sir Percival's parents]" (455–456). Thus in comparing the two copies of the church registries, Walter discovers that Sir Percival's father never married his mother; this discovery invalidates Sir Percival's legitimacy, depriving him of "the name, the rank, the estate, the whole social existence that he had usurped" (456–457), depriving him, in fact, of his (false) identity.

Yet the method whereby Walter stabilizes Laura's identity and destabilizes that of Sir Percival's is itself flawed. Although words can validate, they can also mislead. When Laura is confined to the asylum, mistakenly identified as Anne Catherick, the nurse insists, "'Look at your own name on your clothes ... in good marking-ink.... Anne Catherick, as plain as print'" (382). As the forged church register indicates, documents can be forged and so are not entirely reliable. Of even greater consequence, the meaning of Sir Percival's lost identity lies within neither of the two conflicting registers that Walter consults; neither document reveals an essential truth. Meaning, rather, is deferred and is, in fact, generated within the gap created between what J. Hillis Miller calls the "repetition" of the two documents. As Miller suggests in *Fiction and Repetition* the gap created by the repetition of the two documents invites interpretation. In this case, it is Walter's interpretation of the two registers that indicates to him Sir Percival's illegitimacy. Thus interpretation of language, itself idiosyncratic and unstable, is the only stabilizing strategy that Collins affords his hero.

Collins's text thus ultimately subverts the very strategies of fixing identity that it proposes. Although Marian seems to sustain her self-possession through her personal power, Anne and Laura lack the necessary fortitude to do so. Even more significantly, Marian briefly forfeits self-control when her mental strength is assailed in the delirium of typhoid fever. The observation of a housekeeper upon her recovery indicates the extent of her momentary dispossession: "her mind [is] recovering itself" (337). Walter's method of relying on the interpreted written word is undermined by his own flawed interpretative history. Earlier in the novel when he reads the writing on the tombstone, "'Sacred to the memory of Laura" (365), he accepts that she is dead, an interpretation that is disproved by the appearance of the presumably dead woman: "Laura ... was standing by the inscription and was looking at me over the grave" (367). As in the case of the forged register, the misleading tombstone inscription indicates that the written word is unreliable and is therefore a flimsy scaffold upon which to found identity. Ultimately, then, *The Woman in White* unravels the possibility of securing fixed identity, disabling the various strategies of self-possession that it seems to endorse.

Collins 1860 novel of a husband attempting to steal his wife's identity is a clear reminder that coverture was still in place until the passage of the Married Women's Property Acts of 1870 and 1882, meaning that, in fact, every married woman ceded her identity and property to her husband under law. The conclusion of the book amplifies the legal reality of male control in marriage and property in a less horrifying and more realistic manner. Laura marries the primary narrator, Walter Hartright, who has restored her identity, and thus her property to her. Collins conservatively moves from any hint of a female line of inheritance by re-instating primogeniture in the last words of the novel, the announcement of the birth of the son of Laura and Walter: "*the Heir of Limmeridge*" (564).

5. Self-(Dis)Possession *in* The Woman in White

As a text preoccupied with the problems of possession of person, *The Woman in White* manifests the complex of motifs that underpin Gothic anxieties of self-possession. During the course of the novel, the hapless Laura is subject to tropes that interrogate the ability of the self to possess the mind, especially in her madness, the insanity imputed to her by her husband. She is also subject to a number of conventions that dispute her ability to possess her body: enclosure and the associated motif of (premature) burial—her incarceration in a mad house and her supposed entombment. The chapter that follows focuses closely upon these tropes as they appear in *The Woman in White* and in other texts.

6

Dispossessions of the Mind and the Body

A Gothic Tropology

Madness

Laura's imputed madness places her in a large company within the Gothic universe. The Gothic presents a broad spectrum of mad characters whose powers of self-possession are destabilized in a variety of ways. Indeed, it could be argued that within the nightmare realm of the mode, madness is the defining personal quality that manifests itself in every character in some degree. In his "Preface to the Second Edition" of *Otranto* Walpole states that his experiment with his characters is "to make them think, speak and act, as it might be supposed mere men and women would do in extraordinary positions" (8). Since the action of the Gothic is so far from rational, the response of the characters too is removed from the realm of the rational.

The prevalence of mad characters in the Gothic is yet another instance of Gothic resistance to modern strategies of containment. As the Gothic expresses an anxious resistance to new forms of property and property possession that were developing in the eighteenth century, revealing, as indicated in the previous chapter, that it is quite simple to lose property, so does the recurring trope of madness show the ease with which one may lose one's mind, despite the categoric certainties of the Enlightenment.[1] The ideational shift precipitated by the Enlightenment, from valorization of the epistemologic authority of church and state to promotion of the powers of the rational human mind, suggests Foucault's description of the eighteenth century as "the age of reason confined" (*Madness and Civilization* 65). The age of reason worked to redefine and then confine all those who did not fit its categories and ways of thinking: "the debauched, spendthrift fathers, prodigal sons, blasphemers, men who 'seek to undo themselves,' libertines" (65). Foucault asserts that any approach deemed unreasonable, apprehending the universe in terms outside the limits of the Enlightenment, was defined as conclusively and inescapably mad. The abstract construction of madness as a separate social category was then paralleled by the material construction of confining madhouses and asylums to ensure that this newly distinct population was kept apart. Those who enacted the "scandal of madness," the "example of transgression and immorality" (81) that threatened to disrupt the categories of the Enlightenment definition of the human, were thus redefined as a distinct type of monster and animal appropriately contained within walls to space dedicated to them.

The English Gothic inverts and subverts the categorization and containment that Foucault identifies with the redefinition of madness as a separate human category in the eighteenth century. In the world of the Gothic, madness does not exist as a distinct category of the human, to be contained within a separate space. Instead, the walls of the asylum are permeable and all are mad, as demonstrated by the predicament of Anne Catherick in *The Woman in White*.[2] She is confined to a "Private Asylum, where a sum of money which no poor person could afford to give, must have been paid for her maintenance as a patient" (93). She is confined, not because she is mad, but because she has access to a secret that threatens the rich monomaniacal Sir Percival who pays to have her defined and confined. Laura Fairlie too is later confined to the asylum, subsumed by the identity of Anne, not because she is essentially mad but because her husband, the personification of hegemony, declares her mad; her madness is the result of an arbitrary application of unbridled power, the strategy deployed by her husband to deprive her of her identity and thereby her wealth. In this Collins anticipates Foucault's assertion that far from being an essential and distinct state, madness is understandable as deviance from the desires of authority—"the old rites of Order, Authority, and Punishment"—as determined, diagnosed, by the Enlightenment scientist, the physician, in his role of "Father and Judge, Family and Law" (*Madness* 272). Collins highlights the alignment of the husband and the aristocratic with this order, as Percival pays off the physicians to attain the diagnoses that advance his ends.

Walter speaks for Collins in resisting this malevolently and autocratically imposed definition of madness. Even after he hears that Anne has been diagnosed and institutionalized, he says of her, "the idea of absolute insanity, which we all associate with the very name of an Asylum, had, I can honestly declare, never occurred to me in connexion with her. I had seen nothing ... to justify it at the time" (22). In discarding the label and associations of insanity, attested to by the powerful and domineering Sir Percival and his medical allies, and basing his judgment upon his own experience, Walter illustrates Collins disdain for the forces of diagnosis.

Yet Collins does not dismiss the social power of Sir Percival. Instead he amplifies the power of diagnosis to create as well as to construct madness: Laura's confinement in the asylum actually results in a real loss of self. She says, "'They have tried to make me forget everything, Walter" (369) and indeed "they" succeed in stealing part of Laura's self: "her memory of [some] events ... was lost beyond all hope of recovery" (499). In highlighting the dangers of those who define and confine, Collins demystifies the abuses of power that Foucault delineates, alerting his readers to a very real threat in their midst.

The Madness, or Sanity, of the Wife

In reflecting a real social danger in his novel, Collins gestures to a venerable literary tradition of husband-induced or -imputed madness in the Gothic, a motif that interrogates the reliability of male science to define female mental instability. Perhaps the most famous victim of husband-imputed and -induced madness is Bertha Rochester in *Jane Eyre* (1847). It is revealing to read Collins's text as a response to Brontë's novel. Like Sir Percival, Rochester invokes the power and authority of the medical profession to support his diagnosis of his wife's madness, confirming Foucault's contention that the "absolute authority" of the physician is a "complement to the old rites of Order and Authority" (272). In his confession to Jane, made only after his plan to commit bigamy has been uncovered, Rochester tells Jane, "the doctors now discovered that *my wife* was mad—her excesses had prematurely developed the germs of insanity" (334). The "discovery" of Bertha's madness signifies that it is not readily discernible, that it needs to be diagnosed and defined by the authorities, who are empowered to observe a woman who is "coarse and trite" (333), displaying "giant propensities," and redefine her as "mad" (334), suited to the asylum; in the context of these terms, Rochester does Bertha a kindness in keeping her at home.

It is significant to note that Rochester describes the madness of his wife by deploying distancing strategies that Foucault observes in the social construction of madness as a distinct category of being. Foucault notes that "Until the beginning of the nineteenth century ... madmen remained monsters—that is, etymologically, beings or things to be shown" (*Madness and Civilization* 70). Although as a citizen of the nineteenth century, Rochester does not display his mad wife—in fact, he hides her away—he does construct her as monstrously inhuman. Bertha is, in his words, a "goblin," a "thing" (337), "a demon" (342). Rochester further establishes the nonhuman status of Bertha by evoking the images that evoke what Foucault calls the "animality of madness" (78). In Rochester's words, she lives in "a wild beast's den," guarded by a "keeper" (336–337).

In his construction of Bertha's non-human status, however, Rochester reveals more than he intends. For, in the course of his confession to Jane, Rochester repeatedly aligns Jane too with the nonhuman, the animal. He calls her a "ewe lamb" (326), a "bird" and "a linnet" (337). Moreover, Rochester locates himself in the same non-human, animalistic category; he says to Jane, "you recoil from my touch as if I were some toad or ape" (330). What Rochester accomplishes in the course of his speech, in effect, is to deconstruct the barriers that he has so carefully constructed with the assistance of Bertha's physicians. By the end of the speech both he and Jane have joined Bertha in the realm of the non-human. And indeed, Jane recognizes that nothing separates her from Bertha other than Rochester's will, the categories that he chooses to draw. When Rochester asks her, "If you were mad, do you think I should hate you?" (328), she responds, quite chillingly and (given his history with women) accurately: "I do indeed, sir" (329).

In responding thus to Rochester's speech, Jane explicitly locates herself within Bertha's category, in confirmation of Sandra M. Gilbert and Susan Gubar's reading of Bertha as the double of Jane, in *The Madwoman in the Attic*. Jane further articulates her alignment with Bertha in declaring, "I am now" mad (344), revealing the permeability of the boundaries of the category. At this moment also Jane demonstrates the radical independence that endears her to feminist critics. Rather than passively allow a man to determine her mental status, Jane seizes for herself the power of self-diagnosis and self-definition, asserting her right to self-possession. She asserts her rights to possess and define herself when she says, "I am insane—quite insane, with my veins running fire" (344). Seizing upon madness as a means of self-definition, self-possession and resistance to the social category role—the mistress—that Rochester attempts to impose, Jane uses her statement of madness to maintain possession of her body, of her mind and of her moral self. Her statement of madness allows her to counter the unreliable voices of her "conscience and reason" (344), the dual voices that represent the authority of Society and the Enlightenment. These internalized voices of conventional authority urge her to submit to Rochester's will: "Who in the world cares for *you*? or who will be injured by what you do?," the voices ask. Jane provides an "indomitable reply," a reply that is irrational in its disregard for convention and material realities and in its assertion of self-possession by an impoverished female: "*I care for myself. The more solitary, the more friendless, the more unsustained I am, the more I will respect myself*" (344). Jane's speech act, whereby she seizes self-possession in declaring her madness, thus anticipates the now-conventional feminist reading that locates subversive resistance within female madness.[3]

Maria, the protagonist of Mary Wollstonecraft's *The Wrongs of Women or, Maria* (1798), is a literary precursor to Bertha and Laura, in that she too, is declared mad and institutionalized by her husband in collusion with medical authorities. Maria is deprived of her child and of her freedom through "the selfish schemes of her tyrant—her husband" (76). Indeed, Wollstonecraft's novel provides a fictional example of the consequences of the inequity against which she rails in *Vindication of the Rights of Men*. Maria and her eventual lover Henry are the victims of a system in which property is not distributed equitably, where only "the strong gained riches, the few have sacrificed the many to their vices" (*Vindication* 8).

Maria is incarcerated in a madhouse; the poetic punishment for her attempt to escape her marriage with her baby—to possess herself and her child—is to be cast into a situation in which she loses all, including possibly her mind. Wollstonecraft's initial description of the madhouse explicitly refers to the conventions of the Gothic that by the time of her novel had already been concretized as clichés: "Abodes of horror have frequently been described, and castles filled with specters and chimeras … what were they to the mansion of despair [the asylum]" (75).[4]

Yet, although Maria's situation is Gothic indeed, she resists the loss of her reason by staying sane, thereby managing to sustain her identity. Nancy E. Johnson asserts that Maria's enduring sanity illustrates faith in the tenets of the Enlightenment: "Wollstonecraft's advocacy of reason … derived from her awareness that the ability to function as a rational person is a requirement for authority in civil society" (110). Despite being in a madhouse, Maria consistently represents herself as sane. When Maria meets her attendant, later her ally, Jemima, she calmly asks her, "'Do you really think me mad?'" The circuitous logic of Jemima's response—"'Not just now. But what does that prove?—only that you must be the more carefully watched, for appearing at times so reasonable'" (77)—reveals the power of patriarchy. For despite the empirical evidence of Maria's sanity, Jemima accepts the label imposed by husband and physician. Maria also resists this definition in engaging in intellectual work in the asylum. She reads the books passed to her from Henry Darnford, and writes a lucid narrative of her life for him to read. By insisting on defining herself as sane, she asserts her self-possession. Thus Maria in her sanity and Jane in her madness are subversive not because of madness or sanity but because each refuses to relinquish self-possession, to allow her identity to be appropriated and defined by another.

The question of madness is completely factored out of the equation of self-possession in George Eliot's story of mental appropriation in marriage, *The Lifted Veil* (written 1859; published 1878). Although Eliot does deploy Gothic strategies in other works, this is her most fully developed venture into the Gothic form, drawing on Gothic tropology in alluding to the supernatural and focusing on the central gendered contest between good and evil. Yet Eliot's narrative too, shows how susceptible is the mind of the wife to the possession of the husband.

The early part of Eliot's narrative appears to subvert the paradigm of the appropriating male. Latimer, who exerts narrative control in telling the story, is "sensitive, unpractical" (8) and effeminate, "half-womanish, half-ghostly" (20), a marginalized, unfavored second son. His enhanced capacity to penetrate and to possess the minds of others, in apprehending their thoughts, is feminized, denoted as an "abnormal sensibility" (18–19), "like a preternaturally heightened sense of hearing, making audible to one a roar of sound where others find perfect stillness" (26). As Gilbert and Gubar note, heightened sensitivity is "an extension of the woman's traditional role ... she is taught to develop her sensitivity to the unspoken needs and feelings of her family" (449). Latimer represents this ability not as a masculine power whereby he invades others but as a force that is thrust upon him. His mind is occupied by the thoughts of others, as he experiences "the obtrusion on my mind of the mental process going forward in first one person, and then another" (19).

Conversely, in the early stages of the narrative, Latimer's future wife, significantly named Bertha, exerts the mental power more conventionally associated with the male figure. When Latimer first meets her, he sees that her "face had not a girlish expression." Instead, a "fatal-eyed woman," she exerts the typically male power of visual penetration. When Latimer feels her eyes "fixed on me.... I felt a painful sensation as if a sharp wind were cutting me" (16).[5] The power of "Bertha, the self-possessed" (59), initially enables her to resist mental rape by her husband, his "abnormal power of penetration" (51). Before they marry, he finds that "Bertha, the *girl*, was a fascinating secret to me" (30); her "present thoughts and emotions were an enigma to me amidst the fatiguing obviousness of the other minds around me" (44). After marriage too "Bertha's inward self remained shrouded from me" (46). Only when Latimer takes on the mantle of patriarchy—becoming the head of his family upon the death of his father, which has been preceded by the death of his older brother—do his powers of penetration overcome Bertha. "It was the evening of my father's death. On that evening the veil which had shrouded Bertha's soul from me ... was first withdrawn" (47–48). Once her inner self is revealed to her husband, Eliot's Bertha, like Brontë's Bertha,[6] becomes an object of distaste to her husband. Once Latimer can read Bertha's being, he "saw all round the narrow room of this woman's soul—saw petty artifice and mere negation" (49).[7] The narrow attic room within which Bertha Rochester is confined is transformed into the internalized confinement of Bertha Grant's consciousness. Yet each place of confinement—room and mind—is the construction of the husband. Whereas Mr. Rochester designs a room to confine his Bertha's body, Latimer's apprehension of his Bertha's essence, enables him to imagine a metaphoric room that contains her mind.

The true depth of Bertha Grant's mental resources, however, is indicated in her success in eluding Latimer's attempts to possess her mind. As Gilbert and Gubar argue, "if we wrench ourselves free from Latimer's perspective to consider Bertha's point of view" (464), we see that she needs to kill him to reclaim her own life and her own self. Bertha, succeeds in re-possessing herself: she escapes from her marriage ("Bertha and I have lived apart"), retaining her wealth ("the mistress of half our wealth") and manipulating the perceptions of her society, living "pitied and admired; for what had I against that charming woman" (66). Bertha, in maintaining her self-possession, resisting the intrusions of Latimer and of the reader—we too never penetrate her consciousness—also succeeds in securing possession of her body and of her property. It is telling that Eliot turns to the subversive and unrealistic Gothic form to present a woman who succeeds in undermining and escaping the constraints of patriarchy, perhaps a reflection of Eliot's skepticism of the possibility of such an occurrence in her actual society.

Confinement/Imprisonment

In his chapter on "The Great Confinement" in *Madness and Civilization*, Foucault argues that the creation of the new distinct social category of madness was paralleled by the construction of walls of containment to maintain a physical separation between the newly distinct social categories. "The seventeenth century created enormous houses of confinement" (38) by the end of the eighteenth century (the time of the flowering of the Gothic) "an entire network had spread across Europe" (44), including England. The madhouse in *Wrongs: Maria*, the attic in *Jane Eyre* and the asylum in *The Woman in White* are all representative of this network. Yet imprisonment is not limited to madwomen within the Gothic text.

Indeed, a vast array of walls of containment were constructed at the end of the eighteenth century to confine the newly-defined non-normative. From the perspective of Foucault's insights, these walls literally concretized the newly-distinct developing categories of the human in the eighteenth century. The Gothic preoccupation with confining walls reveals an anxious response, and even resistance, to the walls of containment and to the evolving categories that they protect.[8] In the Gothic world, a variety of non-normative, socially marginalized types, are enclosed within a variety of structures of containment, dramatizing dispossession of their own bodies. Almost every Gothic heroine, mad or sane, is locked up at some point during the course of her adventures. In *Otranto*, Isabella is trapped in the labyrinthine bowels of the Castle of Otranto. In *Udolpho*, Emily and her aunt, Madame Montoni, are confined within the eponymous castle by the villainous and aristocratic Montoni, in his attempt to get them to sign over their property to him.

Those objects of confinement who are not women, are marginalized, non-normative in some other way. In *Otranto*, Manfred imprisons Theodore, the presumed socially inferior peasant—he is "kept prisoner under the [giant] helmet itself" (19). In Reeve's *An Old English Baron*, the hero, Edmund, like Theodore, presumed to be a peasant, is confined to a haunted room; he discovers that his mother too, socially weakened by the death of her husband, had been confined by her villainous brother-in-law. Manfred's ultimate self-confinement—he and his wife, Hippolita end their lives immured within the walls of "neighboring convents" (110)—represents his surrender of social power.

Radcliffe's *A Sicilian Romance* demonstrates an array of marginal characters threatened by loss of physical self-possession through imprisonment. The usual types of women are subject to enclosure: the young girl, the nun, the wife and the mother. Both young daughters of the evil marquis are imprisoned by their father. Emilia is "ordered to confine herself to her apartment" (80) when she is suspected of helping her sister Julia escape her confinement. Julia has been imprisoned by her father because she refuses a proposed match; after a foiled escape, she is "confined in a small room in a remote part of the castle" (73). Julia is later mistakenly locked in "a large ruinous mansion" within what "had once been a chamber" (111) by the Marquis Murani who is looking for his own runaway daughter. Eventually, Julia is confined to a convent, as is Cornelia, the sister of Hippolutus, Julia's beloved. Cornelia's story reveals the lack of personal and economic mobility, that is reflected by imprisonment: because there is not enough family wealth to support both herself and her brother—her "father's fortune was unsuitable to his rank"—"it was necessary for me to assume the veil," living within "the cold walls of a monastery" (119).

The young, powerless, imprisoned man is represented by Ferdinand, the brother of Julia and Emilia. When he attempts to help his sister escape, he is "confined in a dungeon by order of the marquis" (69). As a token of his social impotence, Ferdinand spends an inordinate amount of time struggling with unwieldy keys and locks. Exploring the vaults beneath his father's castle, he encounters "a small door ... a lock withheld his passage" (39). When he is struggling to help his sister escape, he finds "a door that obstructed their way. He applied the different keys and at length found the proper one; but the lock was rusted, and refused to yield." (67). The failure of the phallic key further encodes Ferdinand's impotency: the rusted key breaks in the lock. Yet each time, Ferdinand does manage to break through the containing barriers, asserting both his self-possession, his freedom to control the movement of his body, and his masculinity. The first door yields to an alternate phallic implement: when "Ferdinand applied a knife" (40). The second yields to Ferdinand's brute strength: he makes "a desperate push at the door ... it seemed to yield, and by another effort of Ferdinand, burst open" (67). In Ferdinand's successful attempts to escape, then, we can see the uses of masculinity in effecting self-possession even in situations of social impotence.

Servants, too, reveal social impotence through their inadequacy in the face of locked doors. In a comedic enactment of the locked door motif, the servants of the marquis attempt to obey his orders to open a series of locked doors. When the marquis commands his servant, Robert: "'Unlock that door'... Robert applied the key, but his hand shook so violently that he could not turn it" (77). The marquis turns to his servant Anthony with the same order, "'Please you, my lord,' replied Anthony, 'I never was a good one at unlocking a door in my life, but here is Gregory will do it'" (77). Needless to say, Gregory, too, is incapable.

Conversely, the marquis demonstrates his own potency in opening difficult doors. He appears "with the keys of these buildings in his hands

... a pair of iron gates were unlocked" (76). The great door to the southern part poses "some difficulty, for the lock, which had not been turned for many years, was rusted" (76). However, "at length the lock yielded ... the door ... creaked heavily upon its hinges" (76–77). Yet eventually, the servants, too, reveal their masculine capability. Upon a shouted order from the marquis, they "applied their strength to the door" (77) which opens, leading to another series of doors that the servants fearfully unlock. Thus in each case, the impotent character eventually breaches the barrier—revealing the Gothic tendency to recast real problems of social inequity and impotence in a fantastic way that can then be surmounted.

Premature Burial

The trope of premature burial, an extreme form of physical enclosure, is yet another Gothic strategy that appears to offer escapist fantasy while actually addressing serious social concerns. This motif too appears in *The Woman in White*. As Tamar Heller suggests—writing of "the carceral world" constructed by Collins—"the novel's most central symbolic site is the grave of Laura and Marian's mother, which functions as an image for women's lack of identity" (113). Moreover, as Heller indicates, "the inscription that falsely identifies Anne as Laura, cause[es] Laura to be symbolically buried alive" (114). Mary Wollstonecraft's use of the trope suggests that confinement in the madhouse, as experienced by Collins's heroine as well as by her own, also figures a form of early interment. Like Laura Fairlie, Wollstonecraft's Maria is "buried alive" (85) in the madhouse by her husband. Numerous other Gothic figures also undergo this type of enclosure. Louisa, the mother in *A Sicilian Romance*, is subject to a double premature burial. Upon being confined to a dungeon, "I had been buried in effigy at a neighboring church, with all the pomp of funeral honor due to my rank ... my days passed in a dead uniformity" (177). Earlier in that novel, Hippolutus and Julia, escaping bandits, run into a large vault, but it is "the receptacle for the murdered bodies of the unfortunate people who had fallen into the hands of the banditti" and "the lock was so constructed that it could be moved only on the other side ... they were enclosed in a vault strewn with the dead bodies of the murdered" (166). Of course, these figures, like most Gothic protagonists who are buried alive, do eventually manage to return to world of the living, reflecting the fantastic re-appropriation of the Gothic body, and the even more fantastic refutation of death.

Internalized Boundaries

In fact, there is only one form of confinement for which the Gothic offers little hope for escape: the self-confinement that results from internalization of social regulation, like that posited by Foucault.[9] This pattern of internalized morality and self-imposed confinement is present in the actions of both of Radcliffe's young protagonists, Julia and Ferdinand. When Ferdinand is confined to his father's dungeon, he prevails upon a servant to spend the night with him in the presumably haunted space. Yet Ferdinand suppresses his self-interests and yields to his internalization of his father's law, in refraining from overpowering the servant and escaping; he "disdained to involve an innocent man in destruction, and spurned the suggestion from his mind" (98). Julia too, indicates that ultimately her confinement, too, comes from within. While still safely established in her family castle, Julia chooses to confine herself: "she loved to retire in an evening to a small closet" (5). Once she has escaped the castle, she finds refuge in "a solitary cottage ... deeply sequestered" (105) "a safe asylum" (106). Julia voluntarily[10] enters the monastery of St. Augustin "where she could find a secure retreat" (109) and she is "sheltered in the obscure recesses of St. Augustin" (116).

Radcliffe affirms the dangers of such self-imposed confinement in highlighting how quickly the walls of the sanctuary become the walls of the prison. Although Julia chooses to enter the convent, she rapidly becomes a prisoner there, a pawn between her father and the malevolent abate, each of whom wants to subject her to his particular institution of containment: the father wants her to marry a suitable aristocrat; the abate wants her to become a nun, to be "immured for life within the walls of a convent" (141), "condemned for life to the walls of a monastery" (144). Radcliffe's representation of the internalization of social control—the readiness with which her characters relinquish their self-possession to authority—reveals a form of confinement that is less easily transgressed even in fantasy than is the wall of the castle or the dungeon. After all, how does one breach a self-constructed barrier?

7

The Double and the Ghost
Refusals of Self-(Dis)Possession

The Double

The trope of the double arises in response to fears of the self being dispossessed of agency through enclosure and imprisonment. The figure of the double arises to escape the confinement of the primary self; the strange appearance of the double in the outside world suggests the ability of the self to escape confinement, physical or social. Yet, this capacity for liberation poses its own set of problems: the fear that the doubled self can also refuse self-control. The paradoxical figure of the double thus works to escape repression and imprisonment, while simultaneously introducing the possibility of loss of self-control, evoking fears of madness and alienation.

The Woman in White provides ample evidence of the dual nature of the double. In *The Woman in White*, the liberating nature of the double is visible in Laura's escape from the confinements of the asylum and of death. Walter discovers that Laura has eluded death and that it is her double, Anne Catherick, who has been buried under her name. The doubled relationship of Anne and Laura is confirmed throughout the novel[1]; Walter notices that Laura and Anne are "the twin-sisters of chance resemblance, the living reflexions of one another" (82). Only later do Walter and the reader learn that this is no chance resemblance: Anne is revealed to be the illegitimate daughter of Laura's father.

Collins's deployment of the double is just one example of this frequently recurring Gothic trope.[2] Although doubling may be found in Walpole and Reeve, Radcliffe takes the trope to new heights of excessiveness.[3] Radcliffe's affinity for doubled characters is prefigured by the patterns in

A Sicilian Romance (1790), her second novel: the two wives of Mazzini, the good Louisa and the evil Maria; the two good mothers, Louisa and her friend Madame de Menon; the two good brothers, Ferdinand and Hippolitus; the two evil fathers, Mazzini, representing unbridled secular power and the Abate, representing unbridled religious power. Julia, the protagonist is doubled in a number of ways by characters whose presence does nothing to advance the narrative, whose sole function is to mirror Julia: her sister, Emilie, whose existence within the novel is limited to serving as her sister's double; Sister Cornelia, who, like Julia, is consigned to the convent following an unsuccessful romance and who is revealed as a quasi-sister to Julia as the sister of Hippolitus, Julia's eventual husband.

Radcliffe furnishes Julia and her family with yet another set of even more seemingly superfluous and random doubles that reveals significance upon closer inspection. When Julia escapes from her father's castle to avoid a forced marriage to the Duke de Luovo, the narrative traces his pursuit of her. Beset by banditti, the duke is surprised to discover, "in the person of the principal robber his own son! who, to escape the galling severity of his father, had fled from his castle some years before, and had not been heard of since" (86). No less surprised than the duke is the reader who has never heard of this son, Riccardo, and who, once the scene concludes, will hear of him no more. But this scene, while doing nothing to advance the narrative, does serve a purpose in Radcliffe's text. Through mirroring, it reinforces her description of the relationship between Ferdinand, Julia's brother, the hapless son and his father Mazzini, the harsh father. This episode also establishes a paired relationship between Mazzini, Julia's father, and the duke, her intended husband. The duke, like Mazzini, is a father "whose heart was a stranger to the softer affections [of] parental feeling" (87). In establishing the duke within the mold of Mazzini, Radcliffe foreshadows Julia's fate if she marries him.

Julia herself is also doubled in the course of the pursuit. The duke pursues a woman through the mountains. Seeing her from a height—"in her air he thought he discovered…. Julia"—and he sets off "on full speed over the plains" (83). When the duke finally apprehends the object of his pursuit, he discovers that the lady with "the very air and shape of Julia" is "a stranger!" This unnamed stranger is, in fact "the younger daughter of a Sicilian nobleman, whose avarice, or necessities, had devoted her to a convent," leading her to flee with her lover (94). The dangers of the patriarchy are reinforced in the narrative of the unnamed lady. Julia's family situation is further mirrored (to inadvertently comic effect) when Julia, fleeing the duke, is captured by a cavalier who announces, "'Wretched girl! I have at least secured you!'" before exclaiming, "this is not my daughter" (112). It is established that this pursuer is, in fact, the "Marquis Murani, the father of the fair fugitive whom the duke had before mistaken for Julia" (112). Murani becomes then another seemingly superfluous echo of Julia's father, Mazzini; his presence too serves the function of reinforcing the prevalence of despotic fathers.

Indeed, Radcliffe provides two entire families to mirror the structures of the Mazzini family. The convent family is a fairly exact mirror of Julia's family: the sororal nuns support each other, calling themselves by "the affectionate appellation of sister" (113); the autocratic malevolent father, the controlling Abate re-represents the authoritarian model of the Mazzini patriarch. Radcliffe also provides a positive version of the Mazzini family. After Ferdinand and Julia are shipwrecked while trying to escape from Sicily to Italy, they are taken in by the inhabitants of a beautiful villa (as opposed to a less domestic castle or abbey). The villa is inhabited by a "young cavalier [of] pleasing and intelligent countenance" (154) and his "wife and sister ... ladies of a very engaging appearance" (155). This family is the benevolent version of the Mazzini family. Since the evil father is absent,[4] the good brother is empowered to be patriarchal head; the mother is happily present. Freed of paternal repression, the figure of the sister sustains her integrity, unlike the doubled Mazzini daughters.

The bifurcation of the Mazzini sisters illustrates the double-bind of the double as an image of freedom. Julia manages to escape from her father's control, but in escaping, she also slips the social bonds that protect and define her; in escaping her father's control, she loses her self-control as well. It is possible to identify in Radcliffe's eighteenth-century construction of the self and its confusions two complementary models of the eighteenth-century self, those posited by Philippe Ariès and by Foucault in *The Hour of our Death*. Ariès's notion of the newly configured eighteenth-century self focuses upon the Romantic valorization of the unique properties of the individual that distinguish the individual from others. These individual properties compel the individual to resist systems of authority created and imposed by others. Thus Julia, who escapes from her father's castle and from the abbey, is the newly defined and liberated individual, resisting the bonds of State and Church. However, Julia's double, the lady whose path she crosses, to universal confusion, destabilizes the sense of Julia as a unique individual, possessing her own distinct "air" and demeanor. In her construction of Julia's double, then, Radcliffe presents and interrogates the newly valorized sense of the individual promoted by Romantic ideology. In *The Order of Things*, Foucault notes this instability of the modern self, positing that the sense of bifurcation, of doubling, is yet another manifestation of the early modern age: "Before the end of the eighteenth century, *man* did not exist" (308). With the instatement of "man" as an object of study, an instatement necessitated by the mysterious novelty of the individual, the human consciousness was divided into two: the object and the subject. Since each individual is unique and new, then, the individual is unknown and mysterious even to its own consciousness. This enigma, too, is identifiable in Julia and her permutations. Upon escaping the bounds and definitions of authority, Julia's escaping self mutates into a new mysterious, and no longer recognizable lady, exhibiting the Romantic fear articulated by Nina Auerbach that "the self with whom we live in intimacy can become deformed and a stranger" ("Jane Austen and Romantic Imprisonment" 15).

This doubled transformation of self recalls Castle's "The Spectralization of the Other in *The Mysteries of Udolpho*." Castle argues that Radcliffe's characterizations reveal that in the age of sensibility and sentimentality the subjectivity of the other becomes unsubstantial, the other becomes the ontological and epistemological ghost, spectralized in a way that eliminates the need for supernatural sources of horror and mystery. Thus, to Castle, the Radcliffean other becomes like Freud's uncanny—itself the figure of the transmuted double—"a hidden familiar thing that has undergone repression and then emerged from it" (51) in an altered and unrecognizable form. But Radcliffe's double moves beyond the spectralized other that Castle posits; for Radcliffe's double represents the spectralized *self*, the self that has been rendered mysterious and uncanny through the process of bifurcation noted by Foucault. Radcliffe's self is not only haunted by others, it is haunted by itself, destabilizing the self in a frightening way by presenting the subject with a self that is unrecognizable; in fact, Gothic characters virtually never recognize their mirrored selves.

Radcliffe's deployment of the uncanny trope of the double—a trope that evokes a very real and justifiable horror of her time, the fear of losing one's self, of losing self-control—is productively read within the context of the strategy that frequently typifies her narratives: the explained supernatural. That is, Radcliffe's narratives tend to evoke and imply a supernatural presence that is rationally explained by the closure of the novel. This strategy is evident in *A Sicilian Romance*; the three Mazzini children are alarmed by lights and a variety of groans and hollow sounds that emanate from the southern part of the castle. The evil Mazzini resorts to supernatural—and false—explanations to account for these manifestations to his son. Displaying his affinity for the art of Walpole and Radcliffe, Mazzini invents an inveterate hatred between our family and that of della Campo.... My grandfather seized Henry della Campo ... confined [him] in a close chamber of the southern buildings, where he expired. A rumor ...prevailed ...that the southern buildings of the castle were haunted.... One night.... I had such strong and dreadful proofs of the general assertion, that even at this moment I cannot recollect them without horror [53].

The effect of these words upon Ferdinand—in addition to dissuading him from exploring the southern regions of the castle—is to force "upon his belief, that he was the descendant of a murderer" (54). The irony of that realization and the rational explanation for the seeming supernatural manifestations in the castle are revealed with the disclosure that the source of the ghostly lights and sounds have a rationally explicable source: the wife of Mazzini, the mother of Ferdinand, who has been declared dead and held captive in the castle for fifteen years. Radcliffe's rational and plausible explanation for the lights and sounds, then, is no less horrifying then Mazzini's supernatural account. However, horrifying as the explanation is, it also reaffirms the powers of the rational mind to apprehend the universe, consolidating Radcliffe's commitment to realism and to a world void of supernatural specters.

Seen within the context of the explained supernatural, Radcliffe's use of the uncanny double serves to introduce psychologically realistic terror, that fear of losing possession of ones's self into her text without disabling its commitment to realism. This strategy is concordant with the imperatives of realistic fiction and, as E.J. Clery suggests, with the imperatives of gender: "a woman wishing to publish fiction in a supernatural vein needed to be prepared to negotiate" (*Rise of Supernatural Fiction* 106)—meaning that her writing could not veer too scandalously from the world that she and her peers were expected to inhabit. Radcliffe's representation of the spectalized self, the double, reveals an early instance of the movement of the Gothic toward the psychologized and interiorized supernatural.

The Ghost

As a reading of Radcliffe through the lens of Freud and Castle suggests, the figure of the quasi-supernatural double arises from the same psychological depths as the figure of the ghost. Although the uncanny double arises from internal psychological realism and the supernatural ghost operates externally in the fantastic Gothic world, both work to unsettle certainties of self-possession. As we have seen, Radcliffe evokes the supernatural figure of the ghost only to lay it to rest, choosing instead the realistically acceptable figure of the uncanny double to emblematize anxieties of self-possession. Collins follows this strategy in a more focused manner, showing in a more direct way the relationship between the double and the ghost. In his text, a single figure, that of Anne Catherick, suggests the supernatural and then, when the supernatural is explained, serves as the double who unsettles Laura's personal identity.

Anne Catherick, the apparent title character, first appears to Walter and to the reader as a ghostly "extraordinary apparition ... dressed from head to foot in white garments" (14). A schoolboy who sees her reports that she is "arl in white—as a ghaist should be" (73). The schoolboy's sighting affords another instance of doubling; he thinks that Anne is the ghost of Mrs. Fairlie. The rational explanation for Anne's dress is that she emulates Mrs. Fairlie, who "often wore white herself; and she always dressed her little daughter [Laura] in white" (87). Mrs. Fairlie serves as Anne Catherick's good mother, the double of her real mother, the cold and unfeeling Mrs. Catherick.

Of far greater import is that the white clothing of the three women—Mrs. Fairlie, Laura, Anne Catherick—works to destabilize the identity of the title character. Moreover, Collins's direct association of the figure of the double with the figure of the ghost reveals that the figure of the ghost is always a double, the supernatural and insubstantial counterpart of the previously living and materially substantial person.

❧

We have seen that the Gothic ghost works to dispute and dispel certainties of legal possession of property. Individuals, too, like structures, are susceptible to ghostly (dis)possession. In fact, ghostly tropology interrogates philosophical and legal certainties of personal possession—possession of body, self, mind—by the individual and of the individual. Like Terry Castle, Peter Buse and Andrew Stott recognize within the Enlightenment the necessary precondition for haunting: "With the advent of the Enlightenment, a line was drawn between Reason and ... magic and witchcraft, irrationality, superstition and occult" (3). As the presence of the Gothic ghost indicates, haunting does not simply arise in contrast to the Enlightenment perspective, it rises in opposition to it. The Enlightenment promise that the rational mind can sustain self-possession and can epistemologically possess a universe governed by natural law is unsettled by the irrational, inexplicable and incomprehensible supernatural ghost.[5] Similarly the possessing Gothic ghost rises up to oppose the certainties of the English legal system that give certain individuals the right to possess others. Emblematizing the self that is not subject to the rule of natural law or civil law, the ghost thus refutes legal principles and institutions of personal ownership and certainties of the Enlightment.

The Bleeding Nun of Matthew Lewis

A variety of Gothic ghosts possess bodies and minds (as opposed to merely haunting spaces) and thereby dispute certainties of personal possession. A memorably horrifying example of a ghost who moves from possessing space to possessing the body is the Bleeding Nun who haunts the narrative of Raymond in Matthew Lewis's *The Monk*. Indeed, the entire spectrum of personal possession and its attendant anxieties is evident within this brief narrative.[6]

Within this web of dispossession of self, we encounter the Bleeding Nun, "a Female of more than human stature.... Her face was veiled.... Her dress was in several places stained with the blood which trickled from a wound upon her bosom. In one hand She held a Lamp, in the other a large Knife" (138). Agnes tells the story of the Nun's haunting, using the language of spatial appropriation: "She made bold to seize upon the Castle ... took her abode in the best room of the house and [became] established there" (139). Her haunting, then, typically refutes the rights of the legal owners of property: "The Castle became scarcely habitable" (140). The displacing powers of the Nun are, however, ultimately subdued by a "cunning" Baron. Employing a "celebrated Exorciser" (140), the Baron subdues the Nun and subjects her to the regular and regularizing rule of law: "She was now grown much more tractable and well-behaved. She walked about in silence, and never made her appearance above once in five years ... on the fifth of May of every fifth year" (140–141).

The Bleeding Nun's suppressed powers of spatial possession find expression in personal possession; she takes possession of the identity of Agnes, who has attempted to possess the Nun's identity, in a narrative that succeeds in destabilizing the identities and individuality of both. Raymond and Agnes devise a plan for elopement; in a variation of the theme of the double, Agnes, a nun, plans to appropriate the identity of the Bleeding Nun. At the usual haunting time, she is to dress "in the same apparel as the Ghost is supposed to wear" (148) and to escape with Raymond while the inhabitants of the castle cringe in fear. The plan goes awry when the Bleeding Nun, orchestrating her own escape, appropriates Agnes's identity, or to be more precise, re-appropriates her identity from Agnes.

The Nun also succeeds in effecting possession (and here the word takes on sexual overtones) of Raymond's body. Raymond thinks that it is Agnes, "the lovely Ghost" (155) disguised as the Bleeding Nun, who is escaping with him and pledges himself to her, declaring, "Agnes! Agnes! Thou are mine!/Agnes! Agnes! I am thine!" (155). He later discovers, to his horror, that he has mistakenly eloped with the authentic Bleeding Nun. His declaration of commitment results in a hellish honeymoon of several months' duration; every night at one the Nun enters his room, unveils her face, that of "an animated Corse" (160) and succubus-like seats "herself at the foot of the Bed" (160), fixes him with her gaze, and touches him "with her rotting fingers" (163). She "grasp[s] with her icy fingers my hand … and pressing her cold lips to mine … [she] repeat[s,] "Raymond! Raymond! Thou art mine!" (161)—thereby appropriating his language in order to appropriate his body.

Although the sexual nature of Raymond's possession is quite clear, the exact form of this sexual possession is uncertain. The sexuality of the Nun is notably ambiguous. The blood that stains her dress does gesture to the female figure; it is evocative of the menses that Julia Kristeva locates as a source of repulsion to patriarchal culture (*Powers of Horror*), and that William Veeder[7] identifies as the perceived cause of intellectual inferiority in early modern scientific thought, as influenced by Aristotelian biology ("The Nurture of the Gothic"). Yet the blood also gestures to the male; the bleeding bosom evokes Catholic representations of Jesus and the Bleeding Heart. The masculinity of the Nun's gender is also suggested by her large physical size and in the phallic nature of her sexual possession of Raymond. As he lies in his bed, "her eyes were fixed earnestly upon mine: They seemed endowed with the property of the Rattle-snake's for I strove in vain to look off her. My eyes were fascinated, and I had not the power of withdrawing them from the Spectre's" (160). The Nun thus takes possession of Raymond through the phallic, serpent-like gaze.[8]

The figure of the sexually ambiguous and horrifying Nun may also be seen as emblematizing the misogynist anxieties of Lewis, illustrating his fear of the ability of the female body to dispossess male agency. Significantly Lewis's vision of the female body also includes the mangled corpse of the prioress, and the seductive (also sexually ambiguous) Matilda, ultimately revealed as a demonic representative of Satan. Re-enacting Adam's fall, this demon disguised in female form seduces Ambrosio, the eponymous Monk, with the assistance of a snake and propels him upon his decadent journey.

The story of the Bleeding Nun reveals that in this case the figure of the ghost, like the figure of the double, is a paradox: the simultaneous emblem of possession and dispossession. For, whereas the Bleeding Nun possesses the identity of Agnes and the body of Raymond, she is doubly dispossessed of her own identity and body. Ultimately, the machinations of a mysterious Exorciser restore her name and identity; Raymond discovers that the Bleeding Nun is, in fact, Beatrice, the great-Aunt of his Grandfather. Beatrice, like all ghosts, and indeed like all mortals, is dispossessed of her own body through death. She is doubly dispossessed because, having been murdered by her lover, "my bones lie still unburied" (172) and so "the restless soul of Beatrice continued to inhabit the Castle" (175). By burying the dispossessed bones of his ancestress, restoring them to their rightful place, Raymond appeases her ghost and takes back possession of his own body.

Like other forms of the double, then, the spectral figure is a literary mechanism that confronts real anxieties of self-possession; like other forms of the double the ghost is a paradoxical figure, expressing both aspirations for freedom from restraint and fears of attendant loss of self-control. The presence of the ghost that possesses the self, instead of the space, demonstrates that, even in its early stages, the English Gothic moves toward an interiorization of the supernatural, an interiorization more typically[9] associated with the twentieth century when the haunted mind is more representative of post–Freudian twentieth-century anxieties than is the haunted castle.[10] Yet, as the Bleeding Nun illustrates, the move inward begins at the moment of origin of the Gothic; the haunted twentieth century is the literary heir of the interiorized haunting that begins with ghosts and uncanny doubles in the turn of the nineteenth century.

8

Resurrection Fantasies

Defying Death's Dispossession

English Fears of the Confining Catholic Church

The many instances of imprisonment by the Church demonstrate the place of the Catholic Church in the English Gothic imagination as a source of danger, an institution that imprisons bodies (in Church structures) as well as minds (through Church doctrine), limiting physical as well as spiritual movement. In Radcliffe's *The Italian* (1797), Ellena is imprisoned within a convent administered by a demonic abbess; Julia is held hostage in an abbey in Radcliffe's *A Sicilian Romance* (1790). In Lewis's *The Monk* (1796), Agnes is confined in an ever-worsening series of Catholic prisons; first confined to the convent as a nun, she is later cast into the dungeons of the Inquisition with her dead baby. Powerless young men too, are confined within the structures of the Catholic Church. Vivaldi in *The Italian* and the Spanish monk in Maturin's *Melmoth the Wanderer* (1820) are both sons out of favor with their families who find themselves trapped within the labyrinthine walls and dungeons of the Inquisition.

Most moments in which the innocent subject is physically imprisoned by the Church also gesture toward premature burial, as the evil minions of the Church threaten to entomb the subject before its time. In Radcliffe's *The Italian*, Ellena, imprisoned within a convent, encounters the possibility of premature burial as she is confined to "stone chamber secured by doors of iron.... This condemnation admits of no reprieve; the unfortunate captive is left to languish in chains and darkness ... till nature ... obtains refuge in death" (126). Similarly, Ellena's mother is presumed dead but discovered to be a cloistered nun. Agnes, the nun in *The Monk*, also endures premature burial; her death is falsely announced when she is buried alive in the tomb-like bowels of the Church. In a plot that perverts the narrative of *Romeo and Juliet*, Antonia (also in *The Monk*) ingests a potion that renders her "dead to the world" (329) although alive to the depredations of the eponymous character. The fearful and irresistible powers of the Church to dictate life and death, and the anxieties that kind of power provokes, are also evident in the narrative of the Spanish monk in *Melmoth*. Like Agnes, the brother of the monk is declared to be dead by a representative of the Church when he is, in fact, entombed alive. In each instance, then, the power of the Church dictates that the actuality of the victim's animation cannot be verified even though it is suspected; each narrative evinces Protestant fears in response to the mysterious, quasi-supernatural and seemingly irrational powers of the Catholic Church.

Secular Fears of Premature Burial

An examination of the trope of premature burial reveals that it also responds to actual, secular, anxieties of personal possession. The fear of live burial was widespread and, to a degree justified, in early modern Europe and England. The fear manifested itself, as Philippe Ariès indicates, in the 1660s: "precautions [to avoid live interment] became frequent in wills" (399). The anxiety peaked in the late eighteenth and early nineteenth centuries, coinciding with the originating moment of the Gothic mode. Ariès, citing the "'universal panic' [that] had taken hold of people's minds at the idea of being buried alive, of waking up in the bottom of a grave" (396), locates "around 1740" as the time "that doctors seized upon the issue" (399). Alexander Altmann notes that on April 30, 1772, Duke Friedrich of Mecklenburg-Schwerin issued an order to Jewish subjects prohibiting the religious custom of rapid burial and requiring a waiting period of three days to ensure that no living person was buried (288). Jan Bondeson adds that

> in the 1790's, as concerns about apparently dead people grew widespread in the German states, a new literary genre was born ... several "amusing" collections of anecdotes and short stories about apparently dead people either fortuitously awakening in their coffins or suffering superlative torments in their premature tombs were published and had no difficulty in finding readers [93].[1]

Clare Gittings quotes from a letter written by Lord Chesterfield in the late eighteenth century expressing this fear: "All I desire, for my own burial, is not to be buried alive.'" Gittings adds that "the fear of being buried alive ... was still common throughout the eighteenth century" (205).[2]

Amplified Fears of Death in the Early Modern World

The pervasive anxiety of premature burial is associated with a heightened fear of the death of the individual, representing the ultimate loss of self-possession and self-control; this fear too was a product of early modern transformations. Both Gittings and Ariès locate the eighteenth century as a time when the fear of death began to loom large in the modern imagination. In pre-industrial England, death was less fearful because more common. Gittings argues "death was ever-present and could strike at any time" (8); death was accepted as a natural part of earthly existence. As Ariès indicates, this dominant attitude "expressed a naïve and spontaneous acceptance of destiny and nature" (29). With the waning of the theological comforts of an afterlife, and a heightened awareness of the "uniqueness and importance of the individual" (9), as "the sense of individual destiny" (xvi) and the danger of individual loss was heightened, the sting of death was amplified. This sense of despair was exacerbated by eighteenth-century skepticism regarding the promises of a compensatory afterlife.[3]

One early manifestation of anxieties of mortality, the ultimate loss of self, endures in Gothic tropology. Ariès notes that the "macabre iconography of the fourteenth to the sixteenth centuries, [including] the 'transi,' or half-decomposed corpse ... reflects a new sensibility toward death and the threat of personal destruction" (caption for picture between pp. 204–205). This fearful response to individual death is quite visible in Lewis's *The Monk* and is, in fact, an important source of the spectacular horror that distinguishes Lewis's mode of excessively outrageous Gothic from Radcliffe's more discreet terror.[4] *The Monk* is replete with instances of grotesquely macabre death. As the evil Prioress is ripped apart by an angry crowd, Lewis describes the destruction of her body with undisguised gusto, "the Rioters still exercised their impotent rage upon her lifeless body. They beat it, trod upon it, and ill-used it, till it became no more than a mass of flesh, unsightly, shapeless and disgusting" (356). Agnes's dead baby is also reduced to decayed flesh; "It soon became a mass of putridity, and to every eye was a loathsome and disgusting Object; to every eye, but a Mother's" (412).[5] The body of the evil Monk is also destroyed, but in this instance disintegration precedes death. Cast into a hell on earth for his sins, he is pierced by rocks, his body "bruised and mangled" (441), "broken and dislocated" (442), insects "drank the blood that trickled from Ambrosio's wounds.... The Eagles ... dug out his eye-balls" (442) until, at last, he is reduced to a "corse" (442). But even more (seemingly) natural forms of death disgust Lewis, or his characters, revealing the anxiety that even the most uneventful death aroused. The freshly dead and intact body of Elvira evokes in her loving daughter a "movement of disgust" (307), even though the daughter is unaware that Elvira has been murdered. In this, Lewis confronts the horrors of death that are repressed by Radcliffe when, for example, in *Udolpho* she creates the figure of death and decay behind the black veil, "the face ...partly decayed and disfigured by worms...," and then, in an analogue to the explained supernatural, explains it away as being "formed of wax" (334), not really horrid, not really death.

The complex of Gothic tropes associated with the loss of self-possession reveals a varied response to the very actual fear of death, which represents the ultimate loss of self. Indeed, in *The Ghosts of the Gothic*, Judith Wilt, who convincingly argues that theological concerns of the early English Gothic are important in themselves and are not simply disguised sexual and political concerns, locates the fear of death, represented by the prevalence of ghosts, as the central fear of the fearful Gothic. Yet Wilt, correctly, does not discount sexual and political concerns within the Gothic mode. In fact, the sense of fear and dread that permeates the mode is overdetermined: a response to authentic theological, social, legal, historical, sexual and philosophical anxieties.

❧

Significantly, the trope of live burial also reveals a subversive response to the very real anxieties of death it illustrates. For the prematurely buried undead body, has the ability to return to life in a realistically plausible enactment of resurrection. The trope of quasi-resurrection appears memorably in *The Woman in White*. When Walter visits Laura's presumed grave, the site of her presumed burial, he sees an unknown veiled woman who "had possession of me, body and soul[6]... the woman lifted her veil.... Laura, Lady Glyde, was standing by the inscription, and was looking at me over the [her] grave" (367). Laura is looking not just "over" the grave but "from" the grave; presumed dead, she is delivered from the grave back to life. Variations of the trope of resurrection abound in the Gothic, in which bodies are repeatedly buried in order to be exhumed. Wollstonecraft's Maria escapes the asylum with her lover; Agnes is released from her dungeon by her lover. Louisa, the mother, is rescued from the dead by her daughter Julia in *A Sicilian Romance*, and Julia's lover Hippolitus returns from the dead as well.[7]

A related trope, the living dead, also works to reflect and deflect real anxieties by subverting the newly amplified cultural distinction between the dead and the living. As Gittings indicates, actual instances of premature burial "possibly account[ed] for the origin of stories about vampires" (30). Ariès too sees the literary consequence of this fear; "the living corpse became a constant theme, from baroque theater to the Gothic novel" (396), including, of course, the servant in *The Lifted Veil*, Frankenstein's monster and the figure of Dracula.[8] In the fantasy of reversal of enclosure, of premature burial, and of death, the Gothic tropes of resurrection and of the living dead subvert the boundaries, physical and social, that Foucault and Ariès identify with the early modern era. By breaching the confining walls of madhouse and dungeon, the Gothic body resists the institutional control of the madhouse and of the prison that Foucault identifies in *Madness and Civilization* and in *Discipline and Punish*. In transgressing the boundaries between death and life and reversing the progression from life to death, the resurrected or undead figure violates the newly defined boundaries between the living and the dead that Ariès detects during the time of the origins of the Gothic.

9

Slavery and Marriage

Gothic Reflections of Political Rhetoric

As we have seen, many of tropes and strategies manifesting anxiety of personal possession appear in Collins's *The Woman in White*. In fact, the title of the novel suggests two important contexts for this anxiety. In designating the "woman" (and it is useful to remember that the specificity of this woman is obscured so that ultimately the woman becomes a generic "Woman"), Collins gestures to one segment of the population whose self-possession was consistently threatened from the early times of the Gothic to his own time, largely through the institutions associated with marriage. A Morrisonian reading of the whiteness within Collins's title and text suggest, as Toni Morrison discovers in "Romancing the Shadow," a repressed preoccupation with racial blackness lurking within the textual obsession with whiteness. This reading is advanced by the physical fairness of the two women, Laura and Anne, who are threatened by the darkly foreign Fosco and the villainous Sir Percival whose seat is Blackwater Park. In wrapping his besieged woman in white clothes and skin, Collins gestures toward another institutional threat to self-possession, based on skin color, and long-linked in the liberal English imagination with the issue of women's rights: slavery.

Slavery

Slavery is, of course, an institution that vexes categories of Western liberal thought and notions of the right of the individual to self-possession. The existence of slavery destabilizes contentions like those made by Locke in his essay "Of Property" that the self is an unalienable possession of the individual. Hegel too suggests that there is a conceptual as well as a moral impropriety involved in slavery, in that men are figured as objects of possession instead of possessors: "The argument for the absolute injustice of slavery ... adheres to the concept of man as mind, as something inherently free" ("Property" 57, p. 48). Yet the slave trade, of vast economic importance to the financial existence of Britain and a source of revenue that helped finance the Industrial Revolution, presupposed a displacement of the subjective self—the viewing of the African as a primitive subhuman creature was necessary to the whole enterprise of slavery.

By the period of "classical Gothic" literature, conventionally defined as the period between *Otranto* (1764) and Maturin's *Melmoth the Wanderer* (1820), slavery was well-established in the British Empire, as were the political forces in support of abolition.[1] In addition to the anxieties generated by the institution of slavery in the form of unsettling questions of personal possession and unsettling political debates, the presence of the slaves themselves served as a cynosure for anxieties. Fear of slaves, in the form of slave rebellion, was part of the anxious cultural backdrop during the time of the flourishing of the Gothic.[2] Slavery and abolition had long haunted the British literary imagination,[3] as when Horace Walpole, an outspoken advocate for abolition created "An Account of the Giants Lately Discovered," a thinly veiled indictment of colonialism and slavery. In his letters Walpole mounts a more explicit attack on slavery. In a letter of 1750 he writes that the "horrid traffic of selling negroes ... chills one's blood" (cited by Trevelyan 92). It is important to note that this letter links slavery to horror.

The response to slavery of Matthew Lewis, who was even more directly involved in the slave trade, is more muted. Lewis's firsthand experience as a slave-holder is recorded in the *Journal of a West India Proprietor 1815–1817* in which Lewis represents himself as the benevolent slaveowner who believes that his slaves love him as "a dog grows attached to the person who feeds and makes much of him" (105) and who expresses "anger and surprise" (102) at hearing of the mistreatment of his slaves at the hands of an overseer. In telling language, Lewis narrates, "The property was nearly ruined and, absolutely in a state of rebellion ... at length he committed an act of such severity that the negroes, one and all, fled" (103). The reader of *The Monk*, in which every imaginable horror is vividly expressed, is left to wonder at the uncharacteristic repression in that vague phrase: "an act of such severity." Railo cites a poem of Lewis's in which Lewis does condemn slavery, albeit in more abstract terms: "the slave trade" appears in the Heavenly book of human sins read by the Angel of Judgement (Railo 127). Thus Lewis like Walpole thinks of slavery in terms of horror, and sin.

❧

The impact of slavery and the dark slaves upon Gothic tropology is noticed by a number of critics. Markman Ellis, writing of the figure of the zombie, sees slavery as the source of a number of Gothic tropes, including tropes referring to the dual anxieties of personal possession: the fear of external control and the fear of loss of self-control. The fear of external control manifests itself in the responses to "slave societies and the slave plantation system [that] appeared to contemporaries as gothic institutions, vast prisons ... with chains" (*History of Gothic Fiction* 208). The fear of the loss of self-control results in "descriptions of rebellions [that] typically retailed examples of slave depravity indicating how slaves acted without restraint" (209). Ellis notes that descriptions of the atrocities included rumors, certainly influencing and influenced by Gothic tropes, that rebel slaves drank the blood of vanquished white overseers (209). Malchow traces the continuing influence of slavery and slaves upon the Gothic imagination. In his important work, *Gothic Images of Race in Nineteenth-Century Britain*, Malchow proposes that "the Other, the outsider, the racially foreign is probably buried in the whole genre of gothic horror" and locates within Mary Shelley's ambiguous stance toward the monster she creates a displacement of sympathy tinged with fear that manifests itself in much anti-slavery writing. Malchow locates the figure of the slave in a number of dark outcasts in addition to Frankenstein's monster, including Bertha Rochester, the dark West Indian of mysterious origins. Joan Baum sees Heathcliff as the encoded slave, brought from Liverpool, a center of slave trading (58–59); this trade resulted in " a growing black population in villages and seaports all over the country" (59).

Rhetorical Linkage of Slavery and Marriage

The prevalence and power of anti-slavery rhetoric rendered it a readily available code for another political movement espousing the rights of self-possession: the women's rights movement.[4] The beginning of modern feminism in England was synchronized with the period of anti-slavery organization. As Clara Midgely notes, "The personnel involved in the two movements overlapped." This early period of women's rights activity also coincided with the rise of the Gothic.

In *The Politics of Sensibility*, Markman Ellis provides a rhetorical explanation for the conflation of abolition and women's rights activism. He suggests that the figure of the slave is frequently deployed "transferentially" to discuss something else, for example "notions of national identity, incarcerative punishment or even existential melancholy" (55). And indeed there is a strong tradition of rhetorical conflation in the literature of the two movements. In "Remember Those in Bonds," Clare Midgely writes, "The woman/slave analogy tended to surface at high points in the popular antislavery campaigns" (93) and cites the work of Mary Wollstonecraft in the 1790's. Wollstonecraft's declaration in *Wrongs of Woman: or, Maria* (1798), "Women [are] born slaves" (79) echoes an early and influential instance of rhetorical conflation, Mary Astell's famously stirring rhetorical question, "If all men are born free, how is it that all women are born slaves?" (*Some Reflections Upon Marriage*, cited by Wiesner, 288).[5] Yet, a solipsism of sorts presupposes this conflation: comparing the lot of the English wife to that of slaves comes dangerously close to minimizing the situation of the slave. These writers displaced anxieties about their own assumed powerlessness and inferiority onto their representations of slaves without actually considering the subjective experience of the slaves.

Certainly, as Markham Ellis points out in *The Politics of Sensibility*, there were legal as well as emotional contexts for this conflation; the association of the two states did, in fact, buttress the legal structures that determined women's status. Legal writing represented slavery and marriage as typologically related—the one explained or illustrated the other—and both Montesquieu and Blackstone sequentially discuss chattel slavery and marriage. In *The Spirit of the Laws* (1748) Montesquieu follows his discussion of the laws of civil slavery with a chapter on "domestic slavery" or marriage (cited by Markman Ellis, *The Politics of Sensibility* [112]). Ellis further notes that the first volume of Blackstones's *Commentaries on the Laws of England* (1765) considers the rights and duties of persons in their private and economic relations as consisting of three great relations: master and servant; husband and wife; parent and child—in that order; after his discussion of slavery, Blackstone moves to discussing the husband and wife.

There are also valid material justifications for the rhetorical conflation of the situation of women and slaves. In "Remember those in Bonds," Midgeley argues for the validity of the conflation: "For behind the rhetoric of female privilege and male protection lay the reality that in early nineteenth-century Britain married women lacked any independent legal rights, making them defenceless against domestic violence and sexual abuse, and giving their husbands total control of their children and their property"

(91). As Ferguson notes in *Subject to Others,* "The same people who enslaved Africans forced middle-class women into marriage" (108). Furthermore, under English common law marriage, like slavery, denoted civil death. Wives, like slaves, owned neither their own bodies nor the products of the labor of their bodies, in the case of the women: their children.[6]

Zofloya; or, the Moor: The Missing Subaltern

The rhetorical conflation of the state of the woman and of the slave suffuses the text of Charlotte Dacre's *Zofloya; or, the Moor* (1806). Dacre's novel, set in Venice[7] at the "end of the fifteenth century" (3), recounts the story of the demonic possession of the body of a slave and the final displacement of a quite insistently self-possessed woman. Dacre works diligently to create a web of relationships that interrogate questions of personal possession, evincing the twin fears of being controlled by another and losing self-control. Everyone in this novel is possessed by someone else. The body of Zofloya the slave is possessed by his owner and then by Satan, who occupies the body of the slave after he is killed. The soul of Victoria, who is previously possessed by Henriquez, the object of her obsessive love also ultimately falls under the control of Satan. Victoria's mother is possessed by her evil lover Ardolph. Victoria's brother, Leonardo, is possessed by his evil lover, Megalena. The relationship between Leonardo and Megalena is remarkable in that it sets the stage for the subsequent appearance of the slave Zofloya, establishing an equation between love and slavery. Leonardo calls himself "'your unhappy, guilty slave'" (113). The narrator calls him "the enslaved Leonardo" (114) and, invoking the colonialism that was a precursor to slavery, tells of "the fatal empire that a worthless wanton had acquired over a young and susceptible heart" (115). This prefiguring is strengthened by the racial overtones of Dacre's language. In describing Megalena's influence upon Leonardo, she writes, "thus darkly colored became the future character " of Leonardo" (115) whose "dark hue of ... character [made him] slave of an artful worthless wanton" (124).

Berenza, Victoria's husband, is possessed by his wife; after she murders him, his corpse is appropriated to further underscore his dispossession. (Satan in the guise of Zofloya[8] removes the body to hide the evidence that Berenza was poisoned.[9]) Henriquez, Berenza's brother, is dispossessed through a drug administered by Satan/Zofloya that results in delusion, "his possession" (215). Henriquez also provides the only example in the novel of benevolent passion, in the form of his pure love for the pure Lilla. Yet

Dacre represents even this relationship in terms of possession: Henriquez's "soul was enslaved by the simplicity and innocence of the youthful Lilla" (194). In this pattern of possession, Dacre indicates that no one is able to resist personal dispossession, to sustain self-control, and that the only recourse is to choose one's possessor wisely, something all of her characters fail to do.

Dacre reinforces her message through excessive metaphors of possession. In the novel minds or hearts or bosoms are possessed by "ideas" (67, 70); "delights and pleasure" (69); "gloom" (77); "jealousy" (111); "passion" (106); "horrible images" (135); "loathing" (149); "hatred" (158); "feelings" (179); drug induced delusions (215); "calm" (222); "the madness and confusion of hell" (226); "horror" (232). Indeed, as this litany indicates, the course of the narrative may be delineated by the progression of possession. In turn, as they wend their way through the novel, various characters possess their own soul (67, 78); the "affections" of a beloved (80); a "bed" (97)[10]; "tender and ... exalted sentiments towards a lover"; a "cause of melancholy" (138); a "secret" (142, 143); "grace and majesty" (145); the souls of others (150); power (151); the hearts of others (152); a "claim" on another (240).

The pattern of the language of proprietorship in Dacre's text highlights the journey of an initially self-possessed woman toward dispossession. In the early stages of the novel, Victoria is a model of self-possession. True to her name, she resists the conventional role of the imprisoned Gothic heroine. When she is "deceived and entrapped" (45) by her mother's evil lover, she engineers her escape from the isolated country house of her aunt. In a walled garden, she discovers a "small wooden door, formed in the wall, and secured by two rusty bolts, and a heavy iron lock" (53). She charms her attendant into getting the key so that she may escape to the outside wood where "she beheld no boundaries, nothing to retard her" (57). Upon her escape to Venice, Victoria reverses the conventional paradigm. She resists possession by her lover and eventual husband, Berenza, who realizes that "'I never possessed either the heart or the mind of this girl'" (71). Instead, Victoria possesses Berenza; after she courageously rescues him from a murder attempt, "so complete and powerful a dominion had the act of Victoria obtained over his mind" (125) that he offers "to her the unworthy gift of himself" (126), although he still resorts to the language of patriarchal appropriation. In his proposal he asks, "'And thou wilt be mine—honorably and solemnly mine, then?'" (127).

Although to post-feminist eyes Victoria's self-possession appears a remarkable and laudable trait, Dacre's narrative voice condemns her powerful personality. In an early description the narrator states that Victoria is of a "violent and overbearing disposition" (15). Victoria was a girl of no common feelings—her ideas wildly wandered, and to every circumstance and situation she gave rather the vivid colouring of her own heated imagination, than that of truth" (28). Oddly, Dacre thus condemns her female protagonist for the very qualities of imagination and narrative control that Dacre expresses. Dacre's narrator condemns her protagonist's force, wit and self-possession throughout the narrative. Imprisoned by her aunt, Victoria realizes that she may exert the power of her personality as a weapon of resistance: "Was it intended she should remain for ever a prisoner in this gloomy abode ... she determined to ... betray no vexation, but to act precisely as events might shew necessary" (46). Victoria's early deployment of passive resistance works. "She conquer[s] her emotions" (50) and in sustaining her self-control she is able to bide her time until an opportunity for escape arises. Yet the narrator unkindly condemns her for this strategy, saying, "thus ... did she learn the most refined artifice, which, by practice, became imbued into the mass of her other evil qualities" (50). Seemingly Dacre, or her narrator, cannot accommodate the idea of a powerful woman, capable of possessing herself and dispossessing others. When Victoria kills her husband, the narrator attributes this to "the masculine spirit" (189). And yet, even if her creator cannot fully appreciate this powerful, transgressive and self-possessed woman, the modern reader is awed by the grandeur of her personality; this woman is so strong that only Satan can possess her.

It is through the snare of love, the paradigmic source of dispossession in this novel, that Victoria becomes vulnerable to Satan/Zofloya's overtures. After five years of marriage to Berenza, Victoria becomes obsessively enraptured by his brother Henriquez; he is "the unconscious possessor of her soul" (150), a turn of phrase that ironically foreshadows Satan's triumph. This obsession allows Satan/Zofloya to subvert Victoria's self-possession. Victoria dreams of her beloved and *his* beloved, Lilla; suddenly a new figure enters her dream, colonizing her brain: "a Moor of a noble and majestic form" (136). With Victoria's assent the dream figure of Satan/Zofloya interrupts the dream wedding of Henriquez—Lila becomes a specter; Berenza is killed; but Victoria's plans are thwarted as Henriquez is inconveniently transformed into a skeleton. The pattern of mental appropriation of Victoria by Satan/Zofloya recurs; he continues to colonize Victoria's brain by penetrating her dreams: "he haunted her dreams" (143). Additionally, as Victoria comes to notice, he is able to discern her thoughts. When she asks, "'How is this Zofloya?...You seem to read'—," he completes her sentence, "'Your thoughts!... Have I not always read them?'" (248), and adds for good measure, "'You are mine'" (248).

Despite Victoria's resistance—she demurs: "It [Zofloya's assistance] gave thee my *friendship* ... not *myself*" (160; italics added)—Satan/Zofloya comes to possess her body as well, ultimately possessing "'your friendship—your trust—your confidence—yourself'" (200). As the novel climaxes, Satan/Zofloya spirits her unconscious body from the palazzo to save her from the retribution of the Inquisition for her crimes; as she loses consciousness Victoria realizes that "she was no longer mistress over herself or her faculties.—Chill horror took possession of her" (232). As this episode reveals, the trope of female fainting in English literature and culture may be productively read as suggesting dispossession of the female mind and body. Victoria ultimately cedes her rights of self-possession to Satan/Zofloya: "'how completely I am in your power ... possessing no earthly friend or protector'" (234).

Of course Satan/Zofloya's possession of Victoria displays overt sexual overtones with attendant undertones of miscegenation. Satan/Zofloya: "'The Signora is not my wife ... neither is she my mistress—she will be mine'" (239) and Victoria concurs, "Zofloya—I am thine ever'" (239). Needless to say, the unorthodoxy of this sexual relationship distresses Leonardo who, although living the debauched life of the bandit, has an appropriately white mistress; "the chief became visibly agitated" (240) in response to Satan/Zofloya's statement of possession. The final episode of the book, in which Victoria and Satan/Zofloya gradually retreat from the world, is enacted in a crescendo of statements confirming Victoria's dispossession. Satan/Zofloya: "Ah, Victoria.... I will not claim thee yet—but when I do, then thou wilt be wholly and compleatly mine'" (240); "'Then art thou mine—for ever!'" (243); "'Thou will be mine!... to all eternity!'" (244); "'Victoria is mine,' he cried in a voice of thunder" (263), leading to Victoria's requisite statement of relinquishment of self. Satan/Zofloya demands, "say then at once—wilt though unequivocally give thyself to me, heart, and body, and soul ... thou must first swear to abide by what thou hast now said'" (266)[11]; culminating in Satan's final statement in his own "fierce, gigantic and hideous" self: "'the glory of thy utter destruction is mine!'" (267).[12]

The idea of losing one's soul to Satan is unsettling enough, yet a more horrifying fear (because more pervasive and actual) lurks beneath this tale of demonic possession, the fear of losing oneself to one's husband. To recognize this fear at the heart of the narrative, it is important to understand the message encoded in the description of Satan/Zofloya, who is, on first appearance, the quintessential Gothic suitor: tall, dark and handsome, with penetrating eyes: "His dark but brilliant eyes ... pursued her with their strong imperious rays" (191). The power of Satan/Zofloya's eyes is associated with his ability to invade her mind. He looks at Victoria "with a piercing eye" (178) as he tells her that he can read her mind. And as Satan begins to reveal his true self, "the terrible eyes of Zofloya shot fire, as they turned their burning glances on Victoria" (229); true, there is damnation in that fire, but this is also the language of sexual passion.

Satan/Zofloya who, for good measure has a compellingly seductive voice, "the silver tones of the Moor penetrated to the very heart of Victoria" (198), succeeds where Victoria's husband, Berenza, fails. Berenza's plaint, "Oh could I but penetrate her thoughts" (71) clearly denotes his inadequacy. In fact, the relationship of Satan/Zofloya and Victoria is powerfully encoded as the relationship of husband and wife, more so than is that of Victoria and Berenza. The wedding of the latter couple is anti-climactic, occurring off-stage. Berenza proposes; Victoria evasively responds: "'I most ardently desire to become thy wife,'" and then we are told that "a very short period from this beheld Victoria de Loredani the wife of Il Conte Berenza" (127). Conversely two powerful enactments of marriage frame the encounters of Satan/Zofloya and Victoria. When Satan/Zofloya enters Victoria's mind at the dream wedding of Lilla and Henriquez, he whispers in her ear: "'Wilt thou be mine ... and none shall oppose thee ... and the marriage shall not be'" (136); Victoria's response, "'Oh yes, yes'" (136) echoes the wedding vows. The last meeting of Satan/Zofloya and Victoria is similarly marked by a sworn commitment on the part of Victoria, at Satan's insistence. He says: "'say then at once—wilt thou unequivocally give thyself to me, heart, and body, and soul?'" Victoria voices her acceptance: "'Oh, yes! yes, forever!'" (266). The message is clear: there is little distinction between handing oneself over to the Devil or handing oneself over to a husband.

In typical demonic-husband style—like Sir Percival, Mr. Rochester and countless other Gothic husbands—Satan/Zofloya reveals his true character the moment the woman is irrevocably committed. "Look again,'" he taunts "'and—see to whom thou hast sworn!'" (266), revealing at last Satan divested of the body of Zofloya. This is a novel that does not lack for models of excessively possessive lovers. Berenza *wants* to possess Victoria: "My mistress ... must be mine exclusively, heart and soul" (75), he declaims. Ardolph, the lover of Victoria's errant mother, comes close to approximating the demon lover, "the skeptical, the cruel, the dangerous Ardolph ... employed these rare and fascinating qualities, as a demon would put on the semblance of an angel, to mislead and to betray" (8). He resolves "to possess her wholly" (12), seeking "undisturbed possession" (43) of her body and "mind" (44). But in the figure of Satan/Zofloya, Dacre outdoes herself and indeed the entire type by casting the quintessentially demonic, possessive husband as Satan himself.

⁂

Although Satan/Zofloya is exceptional in his deviltry and explicitly racial blackness, he belongs to a long Gothic tradition (starting with Manfred) of the darkly demonic male. The trope of the dark Gothic villain is embedded in the mode, although usually the darkness is only implicitly racial. The various Italian villains, who are defined as other by virtue of alien nationality and religion, are typically described as physically dark: Montoni in *Udolpho*, Schedoni in *The Italian* and the Spanish Ambrosio in the *Monk* are all physically swarthy. The darkly English Mr. Rochester also belongs to this tradition.[13] By emphasizing the darkness of the dangerous and inscrutable patriarch, the writers seem to tap into a readily available code for social danger; coloring the patriarch with dark tones, the Gothic writer appropriates racial shorthand to indicate that this character, too, is a threat. The figure of the Gothic male as racial other works then to highlight Anne Williams's observation that "a narrative organized around the female perspective ... necessarily views the male as "other" (141). The incomprehensible and anti-social behavior of the patriarch, indeed, the inhumanity of the male, becomes encoded in the most visual and most primal way, as racial otherness.

⁂

But a question remains: where is Zofloya, the Moorish slave, in all this? If this is a text that conflates the dispossession of slaves with that of wives, that invites a comparison of the two states, where is the second half of the equation? And the answer is that Zofloya quite simply is not there. There is no Moor—he is the empty space at the center of the novel, as the denouement reveals, a vacated body inhabited by Satan. Here is what we know of the slave Zofloya: he was "beloved by all.... He could dance with inimitable grace, and [had] skill in music" (138–139); he "was yet of noble birth" (141) and was held in high estimation by his superiors (139); he was not quite a slave because the "Spanish nobleman" into whose hands he had fallen and then Henriquez his master value him—he finds himself in "the service and guardianship of Henriquez" (141). And we know that Zofloya has been murdered by Latoni, a jealous fellow-servant who stabs him in the back and pushes him into the canal.

9. Slavery and Marriage

What little we know of Zofloya, then, we know because others narrate it. We do not know Zofloya's subjective self, what he felt about being a slave, or for that matter what his life of a slave was like. We do hear Satan's version of slavery; speaking as Zofloya, from within the body of Zofloya, Satan defines the state of the slave as chattel—"'I became the property of the Spaniard'" (153) and asserts Zofloya's nobility and presumed human pride, "Am I not thy equal?—Ay thy superior!—proud girl, to suppose that the Moor, Zofloya, is a slave in mind'" (242). Satan, having his own traditional problems with (divine) authority and dispossession, does seems to construct an empathetic voice for Zofloya, but he only approximates Zofloya's subjectivity as he appropriates his voice. This doubleness of voice becomes clear when Satan speaking as Zofloya faults Victoria for her presumed prejudice: "Does the Signora believe, then, that the Moor Zofloya, hast a heart dark as his countenance'" (151). Well, yes he does—he has the heart of Satan—and it is our awareness of this fact that makes us recognize that it is Satan speaking and that Zofloya's self is gone forever. Zofloya thus incarnates the reality of slavery; the body remains as a possession of others; the subjectivity of the self is erased.

Dacre presents this model of the slave as the germ for the ultimate failure of slavery; her novel presents not so much a critique of slavery as a warning to slaveholders of the need to consider the minds as well as the bodies they possess. Dacre shows that the masters' blindness to the subjectivity of the slave, their ignorance of the hostile power living in their midst, is the fatal flaw that leads to their destruction. The mistake of the masters, as articulated by Satan/Zofloya, is that they "suppose that the Moor, Zofloya, is a slave in mind" (242), when he is, in fact, a slave in body only. In ignoring the subjectivity of the slave, the masters provide him with the weapon he needs to overcome them; their lack of knowledge enhances the power of his knowledge, resulting in a slave with the power of the devil.

So, ultimately, Dacre's novel tells the story of slavery and the slave from the outside, from the perspective of the master's, or to be more precise, the mistress's experience. Perhaps Dacre's dramatization of the experience of the slave—in which the body is appropriated and the subjectivity effaced—tells the horror of slavery more than any slave narrative could. And yet the vivid presence of Victoria's self and Victoria's narrative of thwarted desire contrasted to the absence of Zofloya's self looks more like an illustration of the narcissism of white women writing sympathetically of slaves as an expression of their own displaced anxieties of powerlessness. Dacre also seems to corroborate Morrison's observation in "Romancing the Shadow," that white narratives of black and white experience tend to focus on what it feels like to be white in the face of blackness, what it feels like to be free in the face of slavery. Dacre's narrative plumbs the subjective depths of the dispossessed woman, but she invokes the narrative of the dispossessed slave only for contextual background. Victoria's attitude toward Zofloya reflects this stance. When Victoria tries to account for Zofloya's presence in her dream of Henriquez and Lilla she comes to the conclusion that it is irrelevant. She misinterprets the dream to mean "that every barrier to the gratification of her wishes would ultimately be destroyed. ... The frequent introduction of Zofloya she judged to be merely in consequence of her beholding him daily, sometimes attending behind the chair of his master at meal times, and on other occasions" (137). In other words, to Victoria, Zofloya has no meaning, no substance; he is reduced to scenery. A subsequent conversation between Victoria and Satan/Zofloya further emphasizes Victoria's obliviousness to Zofloya's subjectivity. The presumed slave attempts to relate his story to Victoria and—perhaps because his dispossessed situation resonates with that of Satan or because Satan omnisciently knows the facts of Zofloyas's life—the narrative of a sensitive, intelligent man reduced to captivity reveals a poignant immediacy:

> "I became the property of the Spaniard ... botany, chemistry, and astrology, were my favorite pursuits; this turn of mind was further encouraged and improved by an ancient Moor of Granada, who took pleasure in cultivating my taste.... While ... resident with the Spaniard.... I continued to have full leisure for the pursuit of my favorite branches of study, for he treated me as a friend and an equal, rather than as a miserable captive and domestic."

Victoria's response echoes the stance of the novel toward the subjective state of the slave. Insensitively interrupting his narrative, she impatiently cries, "'Zofloya! Zofloya! ... this is irrelevant'" (153).

And indeed this tale is irrelevant to the project that concentrates Dacre's interest and passion: the expression of the problems of the dispossessed woman, Victoria, who married to Berenza, finds "'that my energies are all enslaved, my powers fettered, by the hated name of wife'" (146), and who recognizes in contemplating a marriage to Henriquez: "'I will again sacrifice my liberty and offer to become his wife'" (195).

Marriage: The Covered Wife

The material world of eighteenth and nineteenth-century English law and culture was hardly a less horrifying place for the married woman than was Victoria's Inquisition-haunted Venice. Within the confines of the common law doctrines of coverture and primogeniture marriage put the woman at risk of losing possession of virtually everything with the possible exception of her soul.[14]

The eponymous protagonist of Wollstonecraft's *Wrongs of Women, or, Maria* is hardly overstating her case when she writes in her memoir, "the prejudices of mankind ... have made women the property of their husbands" (146). A principle of English common law, written into the Commentaries on the English Constitution by Blackstone in 1758, states that when a woman married, she became a *feme-covert* and ceased to exist as a separate legal entity. Under the system of coverture, the woman's legal identity was "covered" by that of her husband. She underwent a civil death and forfeited all rights to possess property, custody of her own children and, indeed, herself. Her husband could rape her or beat her—according to the doctrine of chastisement—by virtue of his legal possession of her body.[15] Through marriage, then, the husband gained legal possession of the body of the woman, any property she owned and the children she had with him. In Blackstone's formulation,

> By marriage, the husband and wife are one person in law: that is, the very being or legal existence of the woman is suspended during the marriage, or at least is incorporated and consolidated into that of the husband: under whose wing, protection, and *cover* she performs everything; and is therefore called in our law-french, a *feme-covert, foemina viro co-operta*; and is said to be *covert-baron*, or under the protection and influence of her husband, her *baron*, or lord; and her condition during her marriage is called her *coverture* [1: 442].

Or, in the words of a popular saying "ascribed to the great eighteenth-century jurist Sir William Blackstone, 'In law husband and wife are one person, and the husband is that person'" (Holcombe 18). Joan Perkin's rendering of this principle is somewhat less whimsical; quite correctly, she notes that under coverture, the wife became "a feme covert, a hidden person.... In Orwellian language, she became an 'Unperson'" (2).[16]

Not until the late nineteenth century was the hegemony established by the common law practices associated with coverture destabilized by the passage of a series of statutes in Parliament "recasting the laws governing divorce, married women's property, child custody, wife abuse and the action for 'restitution of conjugal rights' which in effect gave a husband custody of his wife's body by ordering an errant spouse to return home" (Shanley 3). The Divorce Act of 1857 ensured a woman's right to leave her marriage without "an extraordinarily complex and expensive procedure" (Shanley 9), although the wife could divorce her husband only if he "was physically cruel, incestuous, or bestial in addition to being adulterous" (Shanley 9).

Provisions for separation in the Divorce Act were subsequently broadened by the Matrimonial Causes Act of 1878 and the Summary Jurisdiction (Married Women) Act of 1895. The principle of coverture was fully undermined by the Married Women's Property Acts of 1870 and 1882 that "made it possible for every married woman to hold property in her own name" (Shanley 14). The Infant Custody Acts of 1873 and 1886 "gave mothers certain rights to appeal for custody of their minor children" (Shanley 14).

❦

Donna Dickenson, who notes that coverture "applied to married women with particular ferocity in Locke's time" (10) and that "in the doctrine of coverture the wife did indeed lose her agency and selfhood" (86), traces the consolidation of this principle:

> Coverture was the culmination and consequence of a long decline in women's civil rights, including their rights in property. [During the Middle Ages] women's economic activity and autonomy were substantial.... In the long run, the transfer of production from home to factory made the economic contribution of women appear less significant.... Women were restricted from public participation and civil rights.... The English property codes ... gave the husband all control over his wife's property and earnings ... as *The Lawes Resolutions of Women Rights, or the Lawes Provision for Women* (1632) enunciated in the seventeenth-century doctrine: "That which the husband hath is his own... that which the wife hath is the husband's." The situation of married women was worse in England and America during Locke's time ... than on the Continent ... because of the way the common law developed.... A married woman was effectively dead at law [81–83].

The principle of coverture, then, was based on a legal fiction, that is, the civil metaphorical, death of the married woman.[17]

Kayman, who draws on the language of literature to argue that eighteenth-century law did not "invent new plots" to reflect "new conditions and properties" but instead adapted old plots to new uses (380), cites Fuller who "points out that, in legal terms, a 'fiction' taken seriously, e.g., 'believed' becomes dangerous and loses its utility.... A fiction becomes wholly safe only when it is used with a complete consciousness of its falsity'" (Kayman 382). Taking the legal fiction engendered by coverture seriously is exactly what the Gothic does in literalizing the metaphor of coverture. The obsessive repetition of the motif of wifely imprisonment and husbandly murder in the Gothic masterplot represents the legal fiction of civil death in a literal form that proves the grave and real consequences of legal fiction. By amplifying the real horror of legal situations, the Gothic warns its readers not to dismiss seemingly mundane legal realities as mere, and acceptable, fictions.

Literalization of Coverture: Warning of Horror

The linguistic paradigm of literalization is delineated by Margaret Homans in *Bearing the Word* (1986). Reinterpreting the Lacanian account of the "myth" of language acquisition from the perspective of the female child, Homans discovers that "because difference does not open up between her and her mother in that same way that it does between mother and son, the daughter does not experience desire in the Lacanian sense" (5). For the daughter, the mother continues as a presence instead of becoming the necessary absence that Freud, Lacan and their predecessors locate as the precursor to the development of symbolic language. In Homans's formulation, the daughter thus "does not enter the symbolic order as wholeheartedly or exclusively as does the son," nor does she embrace the Law of the Father as enthusiastically. Her language remains more literal than men's, more grounded in literal presence and lacking the "gaps between signifier and referent" that typify symbolic language (11–14). Homans provides a specific instance of the appearance of literal language in literary texts that is useful to this discussion: "when some piece of overtly figurative language, a simile or an extended or conspicuous metaphor is translated into an actual event or circumstance" (30). Thus the Gothic representation of marriage as truly, literally, dangerous and confining to the wife literalizes the abstract metaphors of the legal fiction of coverture, warning its readers to take these metaphors seriously.

Indeed, the literalizing Gothic counters the legal abstractions that allow for horrors to be perpetuated under the guise of rational civil law. In writing of Blackstone's formulation of coverture, Dickenson states: "Blackstone presents this doctrine of coverture not as irrational, or anomalous ... but as the revealed truth of reason, in conformity with natural law" (83). The Gothic narrative interrogates and demystifies the abstract fiction, revealing the real horror that lurks beneath the neutral language of Blackstone's explication. The Gothic amplifies the blood-curdling reality that lurks within Blackstone's subtle acknowledgment of the retrograde nature of English law: "We inherit an old Gothic castle, erected in the days of chivalry, but fitted up for a modern inhabitant. The moated ramparts, the embattled towers, and the trophied halls, are magnificent and venerable" (Blackstone 3: 268). Clery extends Blackstone's Gothic metaphor to note that through marriage, the woman becomes a haunting ghost, resulting in the "haunting of the [structure of the] law by the spectre of the woman" (79). We have, indeed, encountered Gothic women spectralized by marriage: Louisa in *A Sicilian Romance*, Laura Fairlie, Bertha Rochester. Kayman makes a similar connection; he characterizes English common law as "a feudal story, a sort of legal romance" (378), with its "timeless ... plots" in which "a finite set of actions is performed by a stock cast of figures, and produces a fixed and predictable range of orderly conclusions" (378). Thus Kayman equates the conventions of English common law with those of the Gothic novel. The Gothic maneuver of literalization, then, builds upon the inherent Gothicism of English common law, demonstrating that the literal application of the abstract law results in situations that are irrational and unnatural, ultimately untenable in a society governed by law and reason.

※

The tendency of Gothic husbands to imprison or otherwise efface their wives thus literalizes the metaphorical legal fiction of coverture; the legal invisibility of the wife in civil law becomes literal (through death or imprisonment) in the Gothic text.[18] As the English Gothic begins, "The virtuous and tender Hippolita," wife of Walpole's Manfred and mother of his children, is threatened with divorce and immurement within the walls of a convent when her children are no longer adequate to support Manfred's dynastic plans. *Otranto*'s Manfred sets the pace for his many successors, men who attempt to make their wives quite literally disappear: Sir Percival attempts to steal his wife's identity and property and to bury her in an asylum (*Woman in White*); Maria's husband similarly plots to lock her away in an asylum where she is "bastilled" by marriage (*Wrongs: Maria* 155); Montoni imprisons Mme. Montoni (*Udolpho*); Mr. Rochester imprisons Bertha (*Jane Eyre*); and Mazzini imprisons Louisa (*Sicilian Romance*). In each of these instances the Gothic literalization of the legal metaphor effectively interrogates and demystifies the situation of the married women by showing the actual horrors implicit in symbolic civil invisibility. The Gothic representation of marriage, the literalization of coverture is, then, a reflection and demystification of the state of the married woman. Once the veil of legal mystification is removed, the reader can see for herself the realities of marriage.

The trope of the dangerous male relative demystifies the reality within the legal fiction of the civil death of the wife. In the Gothic, a long line of fathers and husband (beginning with Manfred) who promote marriage, whose economic plots and possession of the woman are supported by marriage, are revealed as frightening sources of death and danger, a reality under the law. Innumerable husbands threaten the death of their wives: Montoni's imprisonment of Mme. Montoni results in her death; Mazzini attempts to poison the wife whom he has imprisoned. Gothic fathers too are dangerous, literalizing the danger of the unbridled power allocated to fathers who have the power to impose marriage upon their daughters. In a literalization of the marriage plot, *Udolpho's* Montoni attempts to exert his paternal proprietorship and to "sell" Emily to his friend, Morani; Manfred mistakenly stabs his daughter Matilda to death at the end of *Otranto*; this murder anticipates the action of Schedoni, the quasi-father/priest, who narrowly escapes killing his brother's daughter (whom he later mistakes to be his own daughter) with a dagger in Radcliffe's *The Italian*.[19]

The recurring motif of paternal appropriation of the child (another instance of appropriation of the self of another) literalizes the absolute paternal rights within the system of coverture. In *A Sicilian Romance*, Louisa tells of a bitter moment of her imprisonment: her husband, the marquis, informs her, "I might see [her children] from a window near which they would pass.... I saw my children—and was [not] permitted to clasp them to my heart" (178).[20] Under coverture, not only does the husband have full control over the wife, additionally, "the father had the absolute right to custody of the children; the mother had no rights at all" (Holcombe 33). Joan Perkin adds, "The legal custody of children belonged to the father. During the lifetime of a sane father, the mother had no rights over her children ... and the father could take them from her and dispose of them as he thought fit" (14–15).[21] Thus, during the time that the conventions of the Gothic were being concretized, the mother was denied authority in the lives of her children, a reality that is also literalized in the trope of the missing mother, discussed below. A number of Gothic texts literalize, and thereby demystify, the horrors embedded within the legal principle of paternal possession. In Wollstonecraft's *Wrongs: Maria*, the father steals the baby after casting the mother into a madhouse; Maria is denied contact with the child and knowledge of whether the baby is alive or dead. The reader too is denied resolution; in an actual enactment of the motif of the absent mother (an instance of life imitating art), Wollstonecraft's writing was interrupted by her death at the birth of her daughter, Mary Shelley.[22]

A Complement to Literalization: Fantastic Refusals of the Power of the Patriarch

When the Gothic works to oppose legal structures by literalizing and thereby demystifying them, it deploys a strategy of heightened realism to interrogate material structures, and warn readers of their consequences. In a complementary maneuver, the fantastic conventions of the Gothic mode may also subvert legal reality in a ludic, fantastic maneuver. The power of the patriarch, the power that reflects legal realities, is almost always subverted in the Gothic narrative. The dangerous fathers and husbands of the Gothic, for all their threatening power, always ultimately fail; the women they torment persevere, endure and sometimes triumph. At the end of *Otranto*, Manfred is in despair, having mistakenly murdered his daughter and having been revealed as the descendant of a usurper. Stripped of family, property and dynasty, he signs an "abdication of the principality"; he and his wife take on "the habit of religion in the neighboring convents" (110). Isabella, whom Manfred has tried to use as his tool to perpetuate his dynasty and secure the property (she was the closest known heir to Udolpho), is empowered by her marriage to Theodore, the true heir of Otranto. Montoni, who has usurped Udolpho from its rightful owner Lady Laurentini, fails to appropriate Emily's property. His depradations finally come to the attention of the state[23] and troops are sent to capture him (192). He too, like Manfred, ends deprived of all power and property; the woman he has sought to oppress and dispossess ends in full possession of station and property. Schedoni, the evil and powerful monk in Radcliffe's *The Italian*, is, like Montoni, exposed in all his villainy. Brought to trial and condemned to die, Schedoni commits suicide in prison. Ellena, his prey, marries well and happily. The villainous husband of *A Sicilian Romance*, Mazzini, is poisoned; the demonic Ambrosio of *The Monk* is defeated by the Devil himself; Mr. Rochester is symbolically castrated and reduced to Jane's economic equal; Sir Percival loses his identity and dies in a fire. In addition to being defeated, disempowered and dispossessed, each of these patriarchs is unmasked during the course of the narrative; their secret calumnies always come to light. Thus, in each case, the closure that appears to be normalizing and conservative—good happily defeating evil—may in fact be read as subversively radical: the evil that is defeated is the evil of patriarchy. In the admittedly ludic and fantastic defeat of the dangerous, demonic, male, in the resistance of the female character to the threat of dispossession, the Gothic indulges in a fantastic refusal of the claim of the patriarchy to possess the woman, a claim that is readily supported by legal and economic realities of the eighteenth and nineteenth centuries.

Yet another Gothic convention—the interrupted wedding—also fantastically attempts to subvert, or avert, marriage, constructing a narrative resistance to the oppressing male and to the confinement of the woman that the patriarchy endorses. In a literary and legal world in which marriage denotes death for the wife, the motif of the interrupted wedding serves as a narrative strategy to defer the death of the heroine, to delay her dispossession. In deferring the marriage, the narrative struggles to sustain the heroine as an active agent, possessor of herself. This motif persistently recurs throughout the Gothic canon. *Otranto* begins as the wedding of Isabella to Conrad, Manfred's son, is interrupted when a giant helmet falls on the hapless groom, killing him; Manfred's plan to unite with Isabella is thwarted by the events of the narrative. In *Udolpho*, the marriage of Emily to Valancourt is prevented first by Montoni and then by Valancourt's supposed bad behavior. In *The Italian*, the wedding of Ellena and Vivaldi is spectacularly interrupted at the altar by officers of the Inquisition who carry off Vivaldi (186)—in a variation of the motif, Vivaldi dashes into the church to interrupt Ellena's vows committing herself to the church. In *Zofloya*, Victoria dreams of the interrupted wedding of Henriquez and Lilla, and Anne Catherick dreams of the interrupted wedding of Sir Percival to Laura in *The Woman in White*. Jane Eyre's wedding to Mr. Rochester is interrupted by the revelation of his intended bigamy. The fantasy of the interrupted wedding, however, like all ludic strategies, represents only a temporary deferral. Despite the struggles of the Gothic narrative against the legal and realistic structures of containment, the narrative of the eighteenth century moves inexorably toward the marriage of the heroine; her legal death is only temporarily delayed. Eventually, Isabella marries Theodore; Emily marries Valancourt; Ellena marries Vivaldi; Laura marries Sir Percival and, upon his death, Walter Hargrave; Jane Eyre marries Mr. Rochester. Thus the legal death of the Gothic heroine is only temporarily deferred. The fantasy of female power and resistance to containment cannot exist in the world of law and economy, the world of realism to which the Gothic ultimately returns. The closing fate of the Gothic heroine, paralleling the fate of the Gothic property discussed in the previous chapter, is the normalizing reinstatement to the proper owner, in this case the husband.

Yet, just as the closure of the Gothic text struggles to subvert normalizing restoration, in the motif of the destroyed property, so in the closing containment of the Gothic heroine through marriage it is possible to glimpse the Gothic struggle to sustain its ludic vision. For each heroine marries a man who appears to deviate from the line of powerful, demonic husbands—one who loves her for herself and not for her property, and who is reduced, diminished in some way as to render him less potent and dangerously patriarchal. Valancourt, for example, must be rehabilitated from his life of dangerous corruption before Emily (or Radcliffe) considers him suitable for marriage; Mr. Rochester is rendered safe through loss of property and physical injury; Walter is the safe and noble member of the middle class. Despite the tradition of a long line of demon-husbands, and the legal contexts that engender them, each Gothic narrative denies reality and fantastically manifests the hope that the closing marriage will be different. Yet here too the Gothic vacillates and struggles without providing a definitive vision: given the legal and literary contexts of the genre, the hope for the future seems far more ludic than plausible.

In addition to averting the death of the heroine, the deployment of the trope of the interrupted wedding (and the related strategy of the false ending) defers the death of the narrative, conventionally signaled in the Western canon by a resolving marriage. The deferred endings, and the competing endings discussed in the discussion of restoration of property, illustrate the internal struggle in the Gothic text between the central narrative, with its fantasies of dispossession, and the end of the text, which returns to the real world with the re-instatement of possession of property and person to the owners legitimated by law. D.A. Miller argues (in *Narrative and Its Discontents*) that the closure of the text represents the state endorsed by the author, and that the narrative attempts to sustain its existence by avoiding the state that it ultimately endorses. The ludic power of the central Gothic narrative and the presence of competing closures appear to disrupt Miller's paradigm. The subversive Gothic text, excessively reveling in the moments of dispossession, appears to valorize the deviant, utopian, state[24] that it cannot sustain because of the ultimate inability of the Gothic writer to resist the imperatives of the actual world of law and reason, and of realism.

The recurring Gothic tropes which address the reality of women in a patriarchy, dispossessed of property and of self, work then to demystify through literalization or deny through fantasy. Whichever strategy the Gothic text deploys, it serves as a warning to its young female readers of actual dangers: the astute reader cannot ignore the demystification of the real situation, and the practical reader cannot ignore the flimsiness of the fantastic denials of the dangers that lurk within the seemingly prosaic principles of common law. The Gothic works then as a counter-narrative to eighteenth-century romances that offer marriage, inextricably linked with love, as the best option for young women. The Gothic warns its romantic young female readers of the dangers of marriage—accounting perhaps for the suspicion with which Gothic literature was typically regarded, and the contemporary discussions of its dangerous influences upon impressionable young minds. Indeed the Gothic works assiduously to conflate possession of the woman with possession of her property and thereby to demystify the notion that romantic love is the prime cause for marriage.[25] The Gothic depiction of love and marriage reveals that the culturally promoted ideal of romantic love is simply a means to promote dynastic marriages that benefit the husband and the patriarchy. The various Gothic struggles over the possession of the woman through the bonds of marriage and the authority of fatherhood as a means to possession of property and dynasty literalize and thereby demystify the conflation of the woman's body and the property, as both a legal and a literary trope. Manfred seeks ownership of Otranto through union with Isabella. Montoni seeks marriage with Emily's aunt and guardianship of Emily as a means to appropriate their property. These situations remind their contemporary readers of the dangerous power of coverture in the eighteenth and nineteenth centuries.

Indeed, not only was the heiress endangered by the system of coverture, but (more importantly, perhaps) so was her property. Kate Ellis notes that "in 1753 Parliament was so concerned with the rape of rich heiresses as a way of forcing them into marriage (and thus gaining control over their fortunes and family connection) that it debated and finally passed a law, the Hardwicke Act, 'for the better preventing of clandestine marriage'" (xi). As Ellis observes, "the point of this law was not to protect women as such but to protect parents from having a valuable piece of their property carried off by a man of low birth" (51).[26] The Gothic thus de-romanticizes romance for its readers by reminding them that their status as heiresses, rather than their personal desirability, is what renders Walpole's Isabella, Radcliffe's Emily and her aunt, and Collins's Laura Fairlie desirable commodities; the struggle for possession of property is staged on the body of the woman, which is, ultimately, only the background for the struggle. In the conflation of the body and the property of the woman as objects of desire, the Gothic text reveals the motive of greed rather than romance on the part of the suitor and the husband. In clarifying that the suitor seeks the woman's wealth and not her charms, the Gothic text works to demystify the notion of romantic love and to show clearly the economic underpinnings of marriage as well as to demonstrate the dangerous nature of this state for women.

Foucault's insights regarding the social transformations within the institution of marriage in the eighteenth century demonstrate the significance of the cultural service that the Gothic provides in revealing the economic underpinnings of marriage to women readers. In Foucault's formulation, one of the many institutions changing at the time of the high Gothic was the family, of which the husband-wife dyad is the basic unit. Foucault envisions the older form of the family as a structure based frankly on the deployment of alliance: "a system of marriage, of fixation and development of kinship ties, of transmission of names and possessions" (*History of Sexuality* 106). With the changing conditions of the eighteenth century,

> this deployment of alliance ... lost some of its importance as economic processes and political structures could no longer rely on it as an adequate instrument or sufficient support. Particularly from the eighteenth century onward, Western society created and deployed a new apparatus which was superimposed on the previous one ... the *deployment of sexuality* [106].

That is, the economic foundation of marriage was obscured by the new notions of romance as the foundation of marriage. Foucault opposes the modern deployment of sexuality to the older deployment of alliance in a number of meaningful ways. The old system was based on strictly defined rules, rules that determined the link between partners; it visibly worked to perpetuate its own rules and structures and it was explicitly tied to the economy. The newer system, operating not by rigid and visible rules but by "mobile, polymorphous, and contingent techniques of power" (106), sustained itself by expanding its forms and areas of control, relied on sexual attraction to sustain itself and was linked to the economy in more subtle ways, not always visible to the eyes of girls blinded by love.[27] The new eighteenth-century form of the family is, then, as repressive as the old; its consolidation of power is simply more disguised and palatable. It is the Gothic demystification of this new system that is truly revolutionary, revealing the old system of alliance lurking beneath the new system of sexuality.

10

Missing Mothers and Suppressed Sisters

The Dangers of Primogeniture

The Gothic does not rest at warning young women of the dangers of marriage under coverture to themselves and whatever property they might own before the marriage. In the world of law the function of marriage is not limited to property acquisition; an even more important function is the transmission of property from father to son. The Gothic works to reveal the underpinnings of the system of primogeniture and its impact upon the women implicated in, or excluded by, its systems.

One consequence of the emphasis on the male line of transmission is the complete superfluity of daughters, especially if they are the sisters of male heirs. Although not the direct target of danger, their lack of status within the family structure, focused as it is on the transmission of property to the eldest son, subjects Gothic sisters to neglect that is sometimes fatal. In Radcliffe's *A Sicilian Romance*, the evil Marquis effaces his daughters, demonstrating their inutility within his patriarchal systems. An absent father, who abandons Julia and her sister Emilia, to be raised by a servant in the isolated Mazzini castle, the Marquis recognizes only the existence of his son: "the sole object of his pride" (10). The daughters, especially Julia, pay dearly for this neglect; the novel traces the course of Julia as, thrust on her own into the dangerous world, she must learn on her own to be an adult woman.

Indeed the daughter of Walpole's Manfred pays for her dispensability with her life. When she tries to comfort her father upon the loss of his son, Manfred casts off his loving daughter, Matilda: "'I do not want a daughter'" (21), he says,[1] because he values his dynastic imperatives above the bonds of family. Matilda's non-existence, her invisibility within the system of primogeniture is literalized when Manfred in his "blindness" (109) does not recognize her as his daughter. Coming upon Matilda with her lover Theodore, Manfred cannot identify her "by an imperfect gleam of moonshine" or by the "indistinct whispers" he hears. Only after he plunges his dagger "into the bosom of the person that spoke" (108), does he realize it is Matilda. And only as she is dying does he fully embrace her as "my child" (109).

❧

Yet, although all Gothic women are threatened, no woman is in greater peril in the world of the Gothic than is the mother. The typical Gothic mother is absent: dead, imprisoned or somehow abjected, to use the term Julia Kristeva applies to that which is "neither subject nor object" (1), that Kristeva associates with "our earliest attempts to release the hold of *maternal* entity" (13). The mothers of most Gothic heroines are dead long before the readers meet the daughters, including the mothers of Isabella (*Otranto*), Emily (*Udolpho*), Jane Eyre, Maria, and Laura Fairlie (*The Woman in White*). Those Gothic mothers who are not actually dead are effaced by their husbands in some other way; immurement being a favorite method. The trope of the missing mother is so prevalent in the Gothic that it invites a number of disparate overdetermined readings and interpretations, including the economic interpretation of the trope of the missing mother as a literalization of the system of primogeniture, the system that renders her unnecessary once she has become the mother of a son.[2]

Narrative Imperatives for the Effacement of the Mother

The absent mother, like the interrupted wedding, clearly benefits the needs of the Gothic narrative. The figure of the mother exerts normalizing social control and order, in texts and in life, providing a resistance to deviance that is beneficial to society but detrimental to narrative, especially the deviant Gothic narrative. In *Desire and Domestic Fiction* Nancy Armstrong suggest that the mother's surveillance within the family exerts a form of social control; to reframe this in Foucauldian terms, the mother plays the role of the surveilling panopticon within the family.[3] The mother's imposition of convention and quietude opposes the need of any novel for the deviance and instability that is identified by D.A. Miller as being necessary for plot and narrative. The mother, like the closing state of marriage, is the enemy of the "narratable."[4] Hence the problems posed by the figure of the mother to the excessive, plot-driven Gothic narrative.

The solution to this narrative problem is to exclude the oppressively suffocating figure of the mother. The absence of the mother from the Gothic text allows for a narratable deviance to flourish in the text, a deviance that allows the text to thrive. This reading suggests a Lacanian theory of narrative: as the absence of the mother is a necessary precondition for the development of language in Lacan's formulation, so is the absence of the mother a requirement for the narratable deviance necessary for narrative to occur. Indeed, if Walpole's Isabella, Radcliffe's Emily, Brontë's Jane Eyre, Wollstonecraft's Maria, and Collins's Laura Fairlie had mothers to protect them from their evil male relatives, their stories would end before they began.

The necessity of the mother's absence to allow for the narratable deviance upon which the Gothic thrives is made clear in an episode in Lewis's *The Monk*. The figure of the benevolent and powerful Elvira emblematizes the mother who suppresses deviant, and interesting, narrative. Elvira reveals the dangers of the maternal to the text, fulfilling the maternal mandate to provide wholesome, and deadening, normality to her daughter, by censoring Antonia's copy of the Bible. Elvira's interpretation of the Bible: "no reading more improper could be permitted a young Woman.... Every thing is called plainly and roundly by its name; and the annals of a Brothel would scarcely furnish a greater choice of indecent expressions" (259). Elvira responds to the biblical narrative by providing her daughter with a copy of the Bible in which "all improper passages [are] either altered or omitted" (260), a Bible drained of passion and excitement. No wonder the author of the equally exciting and equally deviant Gothic text feels threatened by the presence of the normalizing and censoring mother. And indeed, Elvira must be disposed of before the Gothic narrative can follow its course. The monk Ambrosio, who is unknowingly the son of Elvira and the brother of Antonia, must kill Elvira before he can perpetuate the quite deviant but also quite narratable rape of her daughter (his unknown sister, who is fully suppressed by her death at the end of the novel). Elvira hears her daughter's screams—"'Save me, Mother!'"—and discovers Ambrosio hovering over the drugged body of Antonia; "She reached Antonia's chamber just in time to rescue her from the grasp of the Ravisher" (301). To promote the plot (his and Lewis's), Ambrosio smothers Elvira with her daughter's pillow, a fitting end for a suffocating presence. However, even from beyond the grave, Elvira continues to exert influence upon her daughter, to the detriment of the narrative. The ghost of Elvira appears to Antonia and announces "three days and we meet again" (318), thereby informing Antonia of her fate and ruining the suspense of the novel for the reader.

※

Conversely in *Zofloya*, Dacre constructs Laurina, an evil mother who is bad for her children but very good for the narrative, and demonstrates that a mother may advance the deviant narrative if she is appropriately evil. In Dacre's novel, characters and narrator reiterate that the mother, who initiates the decline of her family by running off with a seducer, is "the primary cause" (258) of the unfortunate events that follow. Throughout the narrative, Victoria, the daughter, thinks reproachfully of her mother when things go wrong: "Victoria … cursed … the mother that first had weakly indulged, and then, by her own example, tempted and destroyed her … (244). 'Ah, mother, mother!' She cried, 'all this is attributable to thee'" (246).

The dying words of Laurina's husband, murdered by his wife's lover, set the tone: "on thy example will the life and conduct of thy daughter now be formed" (20). This prophecy (a revision of the familiar "sins of the fathers") turns out to be a curse for the characters (though a blessing for the narrative): "the curse of Laurina … entailed upon her daughter" (132). The ungrateful narrator, who owes her story to Laurina, also repeatedly denounces her for the influence that sets her children, upon the deviant course of Gothic narrative. "Example, a mother's example, had more than corroborated every tendency to evil" (133), the narrator declaims.

Like his sister Victoria, Leonardo quite correctly blames his mother for the narratable deviance of his life. He says to himself, "mother unkind! To thee, and thee alone, do I owe all this" (98). The narrative need for the mother to be evil if present is explicitly evident in an episode involving Leonardo. In an interlude during his usually colorful activities—attempting to stab his sister's lover in her bed; being seduced by the evil Megalena; declining into the role of a banditti chief—Leonardo takes a break in the forest with a different kind of maternal figure. Wandering hungry through the woods, he finds an old woman, a "good mother," who significantly gives him "a draught of milk" (96), and allows him to take the place of her dead son. Leonardo lives and works for her and nothing else happens; the narrative comes to a dead halt. In this pre–Oedipal place, Leonardo "felt no want" (99) until, fortunately for his narrative, Nina, the good mother, dies and Leonardo, despite owning the cottage and being free to stay in his peaceful life, "once more renewed his wanderings" (101).

The story of Lilla reinforces the narrative necessity of the absence of all but the most unnaturally deviant mothers. The victimization of Lilla, the beloved of Henriquez, lies at the sordid center of the narrative of *Zofloya*. Stolen from her lover, she is ultimately chained, half-starved and half-naked, in a cave and then finally she is murdered by Victoria who "covered her fair body with innumerable wounds, then dashed her headlong over the edge of the steep.—Her fairy form bounded as it fell against the projecting crags of the mountain" (226). Lilla's dismal but exciting end is to be expected in the light of her familial situation. Dacre makes a point of telling us twice on the same page that Lilla has no mother to prevent these colorful activities. She describes "the orphan Lilla" and then superfluously adds, "the blooming Lilla was an orphan" (133).

Cultural Imperatives for Abjection of the Mother

The narrative of Agnes, the prematurely buried nun in *The Monk*, indicates the categorical anxieties that lie at the roots of the motif of the missing mother. Discovered to be pregnant, Agnes is cast into the dungeons of the Inquisition where she becomes a mother. Laboring alone, "in solitude and misery, abandoned by all, unassisted by Art, uncomforted by Friendship, with pangs which if witnessed would have touched the hardest heart," she delivers her baby. Although the child "expired in a few hours after its birth," Agnes remains a devoted mother. Clinging to the rotting body of her "lovely Child" (411–412), Agnes relinquishes her child for burial only when she is freed. The repulsive description of the decaying body of the child, as well as the description of the battered body of the evil Prioress (the mother of her convent) previously discussed, reveals Lewis's misogynist discomfort with the body of the mother and with the product of her body, the child.

Additionally, the fate of Agnes sheds light on more generalized categorical anxieties that permeate the Gothic and the culture that generates it. The pervasive tendency in Western culture to perceive and represent the figure of the woman as absolutely good or absolutely evil, as either virgin or whore is reflected in the Gothic representation of women: the evil Prioress opposed to the innocent Agnes are but one of many doubled pairs in the Gothic that exemplify this duality. Yet the figure of Agnes resists these simplistic binaries; she is a nun whose virginity is belied by her maternity. Neither virgin nor whore, she subverts the categories that contain women and support the patriarchy as, in fact, do all mothers. In *Bearing the Word* Homans sheds more light on the categorical anxieties evoked by maternity. In the moment of childbirth the comforting integrity of the body is fragmented: one becomes two; what was internal and invisible becomes external and visible.

Psychological Imperatives for the Repression of the Mother

The cultural repression of the mother that is evinced by the Gothic clearly reveals a psychological foundation. In her essay "Professions for Women," Virginia Woolf argues that the figure of the mother, the oppressive Angel of the House (the figure that originates in Coventry Patmore's infamous and influential nineteenth-century poem), must be killed before the female author can write, hence the absence of the mother in the fiction of female writers.[5] Claire Kahane's important essay, "The Gothic Mirror," draws on this tradition of feminist scholarship. Building upon Adrienne Rich's insight in "Temptations of a Motherless Woman" regarding Jane Eyre, that "her separation from [a variety of mother figures] enables Jane to move forward into a wider realm of experience" (95), Kahane argues that the Gothic masterplot is the narrative of the individuation of the young woman, denoted by her escape from the mother who is constructed as the spectral Other, threatening to dissolve the boundaries of the daughter's identity. Kahane reads the conventional Gothic space, darkly empty and mysterious, as emblematic of the female body so that the young woman's attempt to get out of the enclosing castle, dungeon or attic emblematizes the attempt to separate from the mother.

Carolyn Dever suggests a psycho-biographical basis for the recurrent and powerful trope of the absent mother: the "epidemic status of puerperal fever" (12) in the nineteenth century. In "Dreaming of Children" Homans too observes that "in the nineteenth century giving birth was likely to be fatal to the mother or to the child or both and fearing childbirth or associating it with death would not have been abnormal" (262). Indeed, the biological and biographical realities of both the eighteenth and nineteenth centuries indicate a personal basis for the prevalence of this trope; in both the eighteenth and nineteenth centuries there seems to be an association between being a woman writer and being a motherless girl. Mary Shelley, Maria Edgeworth, the Brontës, to name but some examples, were all motherless.

The utility of a psychological approach is evident in Alison Milbank's

10. Missing Mothers and Suppressed Sisters 109

reading of the absent mother in Radcliffe's *A Sicilian Romance*. In this novel, the mother, Louisa, is believed to be dead; her son and two daughters have "lost their amiable mother in early childhood" (3). Milbank identifies the textual absence of the mother with Kristeva's notion of abjection—the mother's vacancy represents "the pre–Oedipal stage of one's first attempts to distinguish the 'me' from the 'not me'" (xxi)—and discovers Freudian and Lacanian meanings in the story of three children developing as individuals in response to the absence of the mother that has been imposed by the law of the father. In Milbank's reading the absence of the mother in Radcliffe's narrative emblematizes the maternal absence that lies at the center of the Freudian and Lacanian narratives of individuation.

And indeed the psychoanalytic reading that frames Radcliffe's narrative as the story of separation of the daughter from the maternal body is supported by the dominant image of childbirth that pervades the novel, evoking the first moment of freedom and escape from the female body. The terms and images that Radcliffe deploys to tell her story of imprisonment and escape pointedly evoke the narrative of childbirth. The place of enclosure is represented as "a large vaulted hall" opening "upon a narrow winding passage" (40), emblematic of the womb and the birth canal. The imprisonment is also described in terms of childbirth. Julia, the daughter, refers to her imprisonment as "my confinement" (106) and later refers to her mother's "confinement" (195).[6]

The most compelling and certainly the most enduring evocation of childbirth in the novel is found in the periodic groans and moans through which the abjected mother manifests her presence. Because the very number of instances, the repetition and accumulation of the periodically recurring groans, is evocative of the periodicity and duration of the sounds of distress emitted by the mother during labor, I will cite all the instances of laboring sounds that I have identified: "a low hollow sound" (35), "a low hollow sound" (39), "alarming sounds" (45), "a sullen groan" (46), "a groan was repeated more hollow and more dreadful than the first" (47). In some instances Radcliffe implies an association of the mysterious sounds with the groans of labor, defining the periodicity of the sounds and identifying them with distress: "a low and dismal sound. It returned at intervals in hollow sighings and seemed to come from some person in deep distress" (96–97); "the sound was repeated in moans more hollow" (97); "a hollow moan.... A groan longer and more dreadful was repeated ... the sounds were repeated, at intervals, for near an hour" (99). The long confinement and labor of Louisa culminates in a delivery.[7] Julia assures her mother that she has come to "deliver ... you" (181); "Let me lead you to light and life...[and be] the deliverer of my mother" (181–182). Julia's words unfold a strange inversion of the biological process whereby the child is freed of the maternal body. In *A Sicilian Romance* it is the mother and not the child who is confined and delivered. Radcliffe's reversal uncovers a social reality of pregnancy and childbirth in which the scandalous female body is abjected and confined, in which maternity is a prison, an excuse to dispossess the mother.[8]

Radcliffe's birth narrative disrupts Kahane's psychological paradigm as well as the biological paradigm; it is not the story of the daughter fleeing the engulfing mother, but the story of the mother subject to the social confinement of childbearing, dictated by the patriarchy, escaping her confinement toward individuation. Radcliffe's narrative also reverses a social paradigm: the mother manages to escape a prison that is a literalization of the confined situation of the mother in the eighteenth century. What is remarkable about Radcliffe's reversal is that although the mother is largely absent during the course of the narrative, her subjective experience of biological, psychological and social confinement and dispossession is foregrounded.

Rather than enacting the paradigm of the mother as enemy of the daughter, imagined by Kahane, the mother and daughter are allies in Radcliffe's text, united against the law of the father. Julia (like her brother Ferdinand) escapes *to* her mother within the castle, rather than escaping *from* her mother. Ejected from the castle because the absence of her mother allows her evil father to effect his marriage plots, Julia undergoes a series of circuitous journeys and escapes—from castle to abbey, to villa, to bandits' den—until she comes full circle and discovers her mother in the bowels of their own family castle. Escaping from the den through a labyrinthine cave, unaware of her proximity to the castle of her origin, Julia finds her way through a series of locked doors and passages (a reversal of childbirth) to discover in "a small room, which received its feeble light from a window above, the pale and emaciated figure of a woman" (174). This is her mother, long presumed dead, and she finds "to her inexpressible surprise, that she was now in a subterranean abode belonging to the southern buildings of the castle of Mazzini!" (175). In this scene, Radcliffe subverts the masculine psychological paradigms upon which Kahane bases her readings, the Freudian and Lacanian models of the development of speech and identity through the absence of the mother. As Milbank remarks, in fact, "these children are condemned to wander blindly until they rediscover their maternal origin" (xxiii). They are dispossessed of their own identity until their mother is restored to her own.

The relationship of Louisa and Julia exemplifies the feminist psychoanalytical model developed by Homans and Nancy Chodorow that posits a continuing relationship of closeness between mother and daughter. When Julia discovers that she must choose between forced marriage, subjection to the law of the father, and continued confinement with her mother, she throws her lot in with her mother: "Any fate is preferable to [marriage with the duke].... When I consider that in remaining here, I am condemned only to the sufferings which my mother has so long endured and that this confinement will enable me to soften ... the asperity of her misfortunes, I ought to submit to my present situation with complacency" (183). In casting her lot with her mother, Julia saves her; Julia's lover, Hippolutus discovers them both and frees them. The mother is "restored to the world and to happiness ... surrounded by her children and friends and engaged in forming the minds of the infant generation" (199). Louisa is established as an individual and a person of influence and her daughter Julia is established as her successor; Louisa sees "her race renewed in the children of Hippolutus and Julia" (199). Louisa becomes the matriarch and progenitor of a maternal line, the visibly present model for Julia, her savior and successor, who learns from the maternal model that individuation is accomplished not in escaping but in establishing female structures. Here too, in the representation of a family re-established upon the maternal line, Radcliffe reverses eighteenth-century paradigms, delineating instead a feminist dream of matriarchy.

Of course, the closure of Radcliffe's Gothic narrative is typically unstable: Julia, the successor of the female line, physically resembles her malignantly patriarchal father. We know this because the two sisters are dissimilar in appearance: Julia is dark and her sister Emilia is fair. When Julia first encounters her mother she thinks that "she discovered the resemblance of Emilia!" (174); by default, Julia must resemble her father, an unpleasant imperfection in the perfect maternal line established by Radcliffe's narrative.

Economic Imperatives for the Exclusion of the Mother: The Literalization of Primogeniture

Radcliffe's reversal of the model of the patriarchal family goes beyond a subversion of psychological models; in positing a matriarchy that perpetuates itself through the matriarchal line and through the younger of the two daughters, Radcliffe subverts a powerful contemporary economic and legal paradigm as well, the paradigm of primogeniture. Primogeniture is the common law doctrine that limits the rights of the mother to possession, determining that all of the father's property is bequeathed to the firstborn son: "The common law only allowed [women] to inherit land if they had no brothers, under a system of primogeniture" (Erickson 3). This system, intended to preserve large estates, and to keep capital within the family, effectively erased the female presence from the line of property transmission. As Erickson points out, this also effectively limited a woman's right to accumulate wealth since "land was the basis of wealth in an agricultural society" (18). The eighteenth century, the time that saw the rise of the Gothic, also saw the effect of strengthened imposition of primogeniture: "In the period up to and including the seventeenth century, with the centralization and consolidation of states into absolutist monarchies, inheritance through the female line was barred" (Dickensen 82). In fact, "the legal provisions for the maintenance of landed inheritance were actually strengthened in the eighteenth century, notably by introduction of the device of 'strict settlement'" (Clery *Supernatural Fiction* 76).[9]

As the figure of the imprisoned or murdered wife literalizes the female experience of coverture, so does the figure of the absent mother literalize and thereby demystify the situation of the mother within the system of primogeniture. Under primogeniture the mother of a son is legally absent and unnecessary; the sonless mother is an obstacle, with potentially dangerous consequences. This horror is amplified in *Otranto*: Manfred's ambition for dynasty—"'my fate depends on having sons,'" he declares— leads him to seek to divorce his wife, "the virtuous and tender Hippolita" (23), and to immure her within the walls of a convent so that he can re-engender his dynasty on the reluctant body of Isabella, the intended of his dead son.

❧

As a consequence of primogeniture anxieties, the idea of women inheriting property is particularly fraught in the Gothic, with its ongoing preoccupation of property ownership. Ann Radcliffe makes a specialty of ending her novels with the, albeit, unstable female inheritance of the contested property. The possession and appropriation of physical space in the form of real estate is an early preoccupation of Radcliffe's *A Sicilian Romance*; before Julia is completely ejected from the castle there is much inter-familial maneuvering for space. Early in the narrative, Julia stakes out her own territory within "a small closet" within her father's castle. Within this room Julia safeguards "her favorite authors" and "her musical instruments" (5).

10. Missing Mothers and Suppressed Sisters 113

This closet is later the site of the declaration of love by Hippolitus, who demonstrates his worthiness by apologizing for invading Julia's space: "forgive this intrusion, so unintentional" (51), he begs. The malignancy of Julia's presumed stepmother becomes apparent when the Marchioness appropriates her stepdaughters' space: she claims "the chambers of Emilia and Julia" and leaves to "Julia only her favorite closet" (27). But Radcliffe reverses the appropriation by the stepmother—whose rights of property derive from her usurping relationship with the evil patriarch, Mazzini—in an appropriately feminist manner. In their new rooms near the sealed-off southern section of the castle, Emilia and Julia hear the apparently ghostly sounds that, unbeknownst to them, emanate from their mother. Ultimately their fear of the apparent supernatural outweighs their fear of their father's civil powers. Although the marchioness refuses the girls' request for "a change of apartments" (47), the sisters turn to their brother, their ally within the patriarchy. Ferdinand is able to persuade the marquis to grudgingly allow the girls to move. "They were accordingly reinstated in their former chambers, and the great room only … was reserved for the marchioness" (54). Thus the intervention of the mother (operating on the irrational and quasi-supernatural plane) gives the girls the impetus to oppose their displacement by the rational law of the father and to reappropriate their rightful place from the usurping marchioness.

As the malignity of the marchioness is established by her usurpation of the space of the mother and the daughters, so is the wickedness of the marquis identified by his commitment to the structures of primogeniture, the suppression of the mother and daughters, and the valorization of the patrilineal line. Yet, in a typical Radcliffean reversal, the son upon whom the marquis founds his hopes, is from the beginning more closely aligned with his mother, physically and psychologically. His early attempts to reach the source of the maternal groans shows that he, like his sister Julia, is driven by a desire to return to the maternal. Ferdinand's identification with his mother surfaces at his father's deathbed. Hearing his father's deathbed confession concerning his wife's secret imprisonment, Ferdinand lets "go the marquis's hand," exclaiming, "'My mother! … My mother'" (191). Ferdinand's connection to his mother is further consolidated by the discovery that "the dungeon in which Ferdinand had been confined" (195) is connected to his mother's cell. Finally, when Ferdinand is reunited with his mother, his only response to the meeting is "silence" (197); with his maternal need fulfilled, he is plunged back to the pre-linguistic state that precedes the separation between mother and son that is enforced by the law of the father. Ferdinand continues to demonstrate his commitment to the law of the mother. When he takes on his father's role as the man of the family, his chief concern is "promoting the happiness of his family" (199), a counter to the narcissistic selfishness of his father.

In addition to disrupting psychological models, Ferdinand destabilizes legal and economic models of the patriarchy, subverting the lines of patriarchy and primogeniture. At the festival that celebrates "the majority of young Ferdinand" (14), his entrance into the law of the father, Radcliffe tells us twice in two pages, using identical language, that "the gates of the castle were thrown open" (17, 18).[10] This image works to shatter the solid boundaries of private property, the cynosure of primogeniture. This image also prefigures the final destiny of Mazzini castle; in a denouement that revises the conventional Gothic closure of the destroyed castle, "the castle of Mazzini ... was abandoned" (198). Finally, Ferdinand effectively disrupts the system of primogeniture and subverts the male line by failing to regenerate it. In neglecting to marry and to engender a male line, he cedes the role of head of the family to his mother, Louisa, opposing primogeniture with matrilineal inheritance. Louisa sees "*her* race renewed in the children of Hippolitus and Julia" (198; italics added), her daughter. Radcliffe thus reverses primogeniture in rendering the male line invisible and highlighting the female presence, the dispossessed mother, now restored to herself, her property, and her children.

Nor is Radcliffe's disordering of the system of primogeniture, limited to the Mazzini family. Radcliffe creates a web of narrative in which the recurring theme is the disruption of the patriarchal system, frequently through the agency of the good brother. Julia learns that Hippolitus, "desired to resign [to Cornelia, his sister] a part of this estate which had already descended to him in right of his mother" (120), representing thus a double disruption of the patrilineal line. Louisa's biography reveals another instance of maternal transmission; she had been the only heir of her father after her brother and mother were killed in an eruption of Mount Etna. Similarly, Madame de Menon's husband's property is restored to her. The estate was originally usurped because her husband "died without a will, and his brothers refused to give up his estate, unless I could produce a witness of my marriage" (33). The return of her friend Louisa to the world affords Madame de Menon such proof and her property is restored—a subversive, if fantastic, instance of male appropriation of property being countered by the power of the female word. And perhaps, even more than the ghostly tricks, that are, after all, eventually explained, it is the reversal of patriarchal paradigms that marks *A Sicilian Romance* as a romantic fantasy.

The Mother Restored; Gothic Fantasies of Maternal Presence

As indicated above, demystification of the legal and economic structures of oppression through the deployment of literalization, encouraging the reader to see the amplified horror implicit in seemingly mundane systems, is but one method of Gothic subversion. The fantastically imagined reversal of these structures is yet another way in which the Gothic subverts, albeit ludically, the systems of power. Thus, for example, the closure of *A Sicilian Romance* posits a fantastic world in which the structures of patriarchy are reversed through the paradigms of maternal presence and paternal absence.

The persistence of the fantastic response to the real problems of female personal possession is indicated by Anne Brontë's deployment of this strategy in the seemingly realistic *The Tenant of Wildfell Hall* (1848). Like *A Sicilian Romance*, *Wildfell Hall* presents a solution to the problem of female dispossession that denies the social and legal realities of its time by positing the (unrealistic) escape of the female protagonist. Helen, the mother in *Wildfell Hall*, is, in fact, a present and active force during most of the novel. Like other mothers in the Gothic mode, Helen is married to a demonic husband, the dissipated and debauched Arthur Huntington. Huntington is the typical Gothic husband; he locates himself within the actual patriarchal structures of the common law by exerting full possession over his wife and his child. When his son is born, Helen reports that he considers "it" an "acquisition, and hope[s] it will become a fine boy and a worthy heir" (253). To him, the baby is a possession to be utilized in perpetuating the paternal line through primogeniture. Brontë carefully delineates the actual context of the legal trap in which Helen finds herself, by illustrating the pervasiveness of paternal possession of children. When another couple in Huntington's debauched circle separates, the father maintains control of the "two children, both of whom he keeps under his own protection" (354). It is this trap that prevents Helen from leaving even after she becomes disgusted with her husband's decadence. When she asks for permission to leave with her child, Huntington refuses and later accuses her of thinking "to rob me of my son" (372), denoting that the boy is his possession to which she has no legal right. Helen's affections for her child, then, keep her a virtual prisoner of her husband although she is not kept within a locked chamber.

Yet, Brontë imagines an escape from this trap for her protagonist. Like Radcliffe's Louisa, Helen achieves the fantasy of self-possession, economic and social—and in 1848, decades before the passage of the Married

Women's Property Acts of 1870 and 1882, this accomplishment was possible only in the realm of fantasy. On the other hand, by 1848, the Infant Custody Act of 1839, "which provided for a wife's custody of her children in the event of marital separation" (Dolin 4) had become a reality which is most likely why the first line of Brontë's novel is "You must go back with me to the autumn of 1827" (35). In carefully locating her narrative in the time before the passage of the Infant Custody Act, Brontë establishes the full extent of the extra-legal and fantastic nature of Helen's independence. By the time the narrator and the reader of the novel encounter her, Helen has re-established her self-possession and her possession of her child. Responding in kind to paternal appropriation, she robs her husband, absconding with her son. The first words she speaks in the text assert her rights of possession and her maternal presence. Upon seeing Gilbert Markham, the narrator, pick up Arthur, her little boy, she states in "a tone of starling vehemence ... 'Give me the child!'" (47). Brontë's strategy for Helen's financial independence is an appropriate updating of Radcliffe's provision for her self-possessed mother. Whereas Louisa (implausibly) achieves economic stability through inheriting property from her own family and from her husband, Helen evidences the move in her century from inheriting property toward creating capital as a means of accumulating wealth. Helen (implausibly) has a marketable skill and therefore is able to live independently without her husband's money. She sells her paintings to support herself, telling Gilbert, "'I cannot afford to paint for my own amusement'" (69). Gilbert learns the depths of Helen's spirit of economic independence, when she refuses to take a book unless she can pay him for it, "because I don't like to put myself under obligations that I can never repay" (94). That Brontë, like Radcliffe, carefully constructs an accurate picture of the mother's accumulation of wealth exemplifies the balance of fantasy and realism present within each text. Although the economic details are based on actuality, the fact that the person operating within the economic system is a mother is fantasy in Brontë's time as much as it is in Radcliffe's. Indeed Brontë, whose text is ultimately more committed to realism than is Radcliffe's, is unable to sustain her fantasy of female self-possession. Helen ends in marrying Gilbert and relinquishes the maiden name of her mother that she has taken to disguise her identity, thus re-entering the patriarchal order.[11]

As the fantasies of Radcliffe and Brontë suggest, fantasy has its limits in posing resistance to the actual dispossession of women. Surprisingly, there is one path of imaginative (and potentially actual) resistance that the Gothic consistently avoids, a path suggested by an inherent instability within the system of primogeniture, as articulated by Samuel Johnson in 1775: "Consider, of what importance to society the chastity of women is. Upon that all the property in the world depends.... The unchastity of a woman transfers sheep, and farm and all, from the right owner" (recorded in Boswell *The Journal of a Tour to the Hebrides* 282).[12] Thus, the structure is completely dependent upon the integrity of the mother, paradoxically, the person who has the least to gain by perpetuating the system. This is, of course, the reason that the insecure and anxious patriarchy needs to possess the body of the woman so completely.[13]

Yet although Gothic patriarchs consistently suspect their wives of infidelity and fear the consequence of the wife's infidelity, textual instances of illegitimacy as resistance are virtually nonexistent. This limit to the Gothic imagination indicates the strikingly paradoxical Gothic commitment to morality. Even the horrors of Matthew Lewis's *The Monk* and Charlotte Dacre's *Zofloya* conclude with evil (in the form of social disruption) punished, and good (in the form of social conformity) recompensed. *A Sicilian Romance*, for example, ends with the following exhortation: "we perceive a singular and striking instance of moral retribution. Those who do only THAT WHICH IS RIGHT [capitalization Radcliffe's], endure nothing in misfortune but a trial of their virtue" (199). And the reader of *Zofloya*, after being treated to hundreds of thrillingly vile deeds, is told that all is for moral edification: "The progress of vice is gradual and imperceptible, and the arch enemy ever waits to take advantage of the failings of mankind" (268). This staunch commitment to morality, then, forbids the subversion of primogeniture through illegitimacy. Thus, although warning female readers of the dangers of patriarchal systems, and fantasizing about imaginary reversals, the Gothic avoids endorsing any truly revolutionary resistance to these systems.

Castle Rackrent: *A Fantasy of Motherhood Resisted*

A surprising instance of morally acceptable subversion of patriarchal forms may be found in Maria Edgeworth's *Castle Rackrent* (1800), in which the comic subversion of patriarchal possession is so pervasive that the horrifying Gothic subtext of the novel is barely noticeable.[14] Indeed, *Castle Rackrent* is not typically included in the Gothic canon although the forms of its narrative evoke the mode. As in *Otranto* the central action within

Rackrent follows the dissolution of a degenerate dynasty and the final loss of the estate. Most of the essential Gothic elements are present: the disorderly transfer of property, the decay of the appropriating dynasty and the patriarchal suppression of the female characters. All these elements indicate an underlying reason for the title that is, ambiguously, both parodic and quasi-Gothic. Edgeworth's deployment of the motif of the absent mother, however, highlights the parodic subversiveness of her text; in her construction there is no mother because the Rackrent women resist the maternal obligation thrust upon them by the patriarchy. The women themselves reject the role of motherhood and in doing so maintain possession of themselves and of their property.

The patriarchal dynasts of Castle Rackrent attempt to suppress the Rackrent wives in the conventional ways. Sir Murtagh marries his unnamed[15] wife for her money; she spends the rest of her marriage "sparring and jarring" with him in an attempt to maintain control over "her sealing money upon the signing of all the leases" and the money that she takes from the tenants "to speak for them with Sir Murtagh about abatements and renewals" (17). Isabella, the next Rackrent wife, marries after being locked up by her father to prevent her marriage to Sir Condy, who is interested in her mainly for her money. The situation of the wife of Sir Kit, also married for her money, reflects the familiar Gothic paradigm. After a conflict, Sir Kit locks his wife in her room for seven years, mainly because she won't give him her diamonds. Edgeworth's fictional editor thoughtfully provides a footnote detailing the similar although historically actual story of "Lady Cathcart's conjugal imprisonment" (29), validating the very real social context for this particular Gothic motif, and reminding us of the horrors of the law.

Yet in her representation of the fate of the Rackrent women, Edgeworth veers radically from the conventions. Each of the Rackrent wives resists the principles of coverture, sustaining her visible existence by maintaining her wealth and outliving her husband. When Sir Murtagh dies, his wife "had a fine jointure settled on her and took herself off" (18). Isabelle leaves Sir Condy on the eve of his bankruptcy; although injured in a carriage accident, she outlives him and the last the reader hears of her, she is "going to law" (96) about her jointure. Sir Kit's wife is freed upon his death in a duel over a woman; she departs with diamonds intact (36). At the end of each narrative the wife is freed of all legal and economic constraints by the death of her husband. Each wife ends up as a rich widow, the most powerful situation for a women in a patriarchal system, the only way for a woman to be free of both husband and father, the only way for a women

10. Missing Mothers and Suppressed Sisters 119

to be self-possessed and to possess her own property.[16] Thus Edgeworth imagines a world in which every woman achieves a state that was actually experienced only by a lucky few.

But an even more radical subversion by the Rackrent wives is effected as each wife undermines the patriarchal system of primogeniture in failing to provide her husband with the heir he needs to sustain the dynasty. Each of the Rackrent lords dies an untimely death and in each case the conventional system of primogeniture is disrupted due to the lack of a son. After each death, the property is transmitted to a distant heir. When Sir Murtagh dies, Thady, the narrator, tells the reader, "Sir Murtagh, I forgot to notice, had no childer, so the Rackrent estate went to his younger brother" (18), Sir Kit. When Sir Kit dies childless, the property passes to a "remote branch of the family" (39). As the Rackrent dynasty, in typical Gothic fashion, continues to collapse of its own excesses, the property undergoes a fate that violates the limits of the most subversive Gothic text: the Rackrent women fail to produce heirs and the property is gradually lost to the family and to the ruling classes; the ultimate owner of the property is a scion of the peasantry.

The radicalism of this text and the source of its humor is that the eventual recipient of the property is an actual member of the laboring classes, Jason the son of "poor Thady" (8), the narrator of the text. At the closure of the novel, Jason is in full possession of the property. Since the narrative point of view of *Rackrent* is the peasant, the usurpation by the son of the narrator is framed as subversive comedy; from the point of view of the peasant class aristocratic loss of property is high comedy. Moreover, Jason, unlike the conventional Gothic heir, is not a presumed peasant but an actual peasant who has risen in the world not through aristocratic lineage or inheritance, but through his own intellectual labor, thereby redefining himself; Thady tells us that Jason "had made himself attorney Quirk" (72). This divergence from the Gothic masterplot defines *Castle Rackrent* as a comedy of dispossession rather than a tragedy of possession and as a text that ends in the utopian world of misrule. Set within the context of the legal and social realities of property possession, and the Gothic struggle with these realities, *Rackrent* is revealed, despite its fictional editor's claim that it is "a plain unvarnished tale," to be more wildly improbable than "the most highly ornamented narrative" (2) from which the editor tries to distance his text.

Edgeworth thus imagines what Walpole, Reeve and Radcliffe cannot, the reversal of the movement of enclosure, the ultimate restoration of usurped land from the landlord to the peasant—as well as the woman's sustained possession of herself and her property. In this, Edgeworth effectively moves her text from the subversive, but ultimately static world of the Gothic mode—which typically closes in the world of legal realism and restoration, after a central lucid fantasy of disorder—to the truly fantastic world of radical social realism. This is, ultimately, all accomplished in the refusal of women to dispossess themselves through motherhood. In Edgeworth's anti–Gothic world, the woman is visibly present, yet she must renounce maternity in order to resist dispossession. In maintaining their autonomy, through the refusal of motherhood, the Rackrent women actually follow in the tradition of the villainous husbands by abjecting the mother. Ultimately, even Edgeworth's fantasy fails to find a way for women to fully embrace their full potential.

We find, then, that the English Gothic text repeatedly and insistently interrogates the possibilities of personal possession, struggling to counter the structures of power that are constructed to possess the bodies and minds of others. As Foucault indicates, many of these structures emerge in the eighteenth century, the time that also sees the rise of the Gothic. In the Gothic retelling of personal possession and dispossession, a parallel story of *narrative* possession and dispossession emerges. The narrative of the slave Zofloya, whose voice is appropriated as is his body; Collins's story of Marian who is invaded through her journal; Lewis's murdered mother, Elvira, who effects control over her daughter by censoring her Bible; the diary of Helen that is read by Gilbert, albeit with her permission—in each of these narratives, personal possession is accompanied by or effected through possession of the narrative and appropriation of voice.[17] It is not surprising to discover that the English Gothic mode, consistently fascinated by the inheritance and possession of property and of person, demonstrates a related preoccupation with the possession and transmission of narrative, text and voice, the focal point of the next discussion.

Part III

Fragmented Stories; Appropriated Voices

Possession of the Narrative in the English Gothic

11

Gothic Conventions; Narrative Dispossessions

Of the many chilling moments of dispossession in *The Woman in White*, one stands out as particularly horrifying, especially to the reading writer: the invasion of Marian's text, a shocking moment of narrative dispossession. Marian's authoritatively written journal asserts and reflects the certainty of her self-possession, but Marian's narrative control is disrupted when she becomes ill. As her fever unfolds, Marian's loss of self-possession is reflected in her loss of control over her narrative: the well-turned paragraphs of the self-possessed writer are replaced by the brief fragments of the writer who is losing herself to delirium. Marian's dispossession of her text is compounded by the intrusion of other writers into her narrative sanctum. A "Note" inscribed in her diary by Walter, the benevolent fictional compiler of the novel, indicates that "at this place the entry in the Diary ceases to be legible. The two or three lines which follow contain fragments of words only, mingled with blots and scratches of the pen..." (298). Worse is to follow. Walter's note concludes by turning to an additional, less benevolent, layer of invasion:

> "On the next page of the Diary, another entry appears. It is in a man's handwriting, large, bold, and firmly regular.... It contains these lines":
> "Postscript by a Sincere Friend
> The illness of our excellent Miss Halcombe has afforded me the opportunity of enjoying an unexpected intellectual pleasure. I refer to the perusal (which I have just completed) of this interesting Diary" [298].

The "sincere friend" is Fosco and his invasion of Marian's text is threefold: he has read Marian's private diary and taken a suggestively voyeuristic "pleasure" in doing so; he has learned that she has discovered the plot to steal Laura's identity; and he has written in Marian's diary himself, invading the body of her text with the inscription of his pen, dispossessing her of the authority of her authorship.

This single devastating moment of textual dispossession occurs within the larger framework of narrative appropriation within Collins's novel. As Tamar Heller observes, Fosco's "colonization of Marian's voice" (134) is "only a more obvious version of [Walter] Hartright's own strategy for containing Marian's narrative energy" (134). Indeed, Walter too edits and writes in Marian's text, and every narrative in *Woman* falls under Walter's control. He functions as "editor-in chief" of the novel's many narratives; he "has the power to solicit writing ... to arrange the order ... and even to delete what seems extraneous" (115). Thus in Heller's reading, the narrative that develops is single and unified, neatly encompassed by Walter's authority.

And yet, although Walter is editor-in-chief of an unexpectedly monolithic text, he lacks the omnipotence (and omniscience) of the ideal author: the multiple narratives that he weaves into a single narrative do retain a multi-vocality of tone and perspective that resists his authority and apprehension. The last passages of the novel suggests the uncertainty of Walter's narrative possession. In the novel's closure, narrated by Walter, Marian re-introduces him to his own child whose status—and identity—have changed after the death of Mr. Fairlie. In knowing more about his own child than Walter does, Marian assumes a privileged status based on her possession of information. She announces to the unknowing father: "'Are you aware, when I present this august baby to your notice, in whose presence you stand? ... Let me make two eminent personages known to one another: Mr. Walter Hartright—the *Heir of Limmeridge*.'" Marian's statement disempowers Walter (and destabilizes the patriarchy) in that it places the father in an inferior social status in relation to the son. Walter continues in his own voice, but he has been reduced to silence and impotence by Marian's appropriation of his narrative authority and patriarchal status: "So she spoke. In writing those last words, I have written all. The pen falters in my hand.... Marian was the good angel of our lives—let Marian end our Story" (564). This closing passage evidences the typical ambiguity to be found in Gothic denouement. While re-establishing possession of property and identity of the new-born son, Marian's statement paradoxically destabilizes identity and narrative authority of the father, Walter. Marian may have the last words, but they are contained and conveyed within Walter's words and Walter's text. The question of who owns the final word in this narrative remains unanswered.

11. Gothic Conventions; Narrative Dispossessions

The structures and strategies of the English Gothic text reveal an ongoing preoccupation with the proprietorship of narrative and of voice, and a recurring tendency to destabilize both the writer's narrative authority and the reader's hermeneutic and critical control of the text. A number of conventional narrative paradigms reveal the preoccupation of the Gothic with possession of narrative and of voice—and support the subversive Gothic project in undermining the authority of a single narrator, author or reader to fully possess the narrative.

The related tropes of the multiple narrator and the embedded narrative consistently interrogate the ability of any author to possess the multivocal text. A number of early Gothic texts—*The Old English Baron*, *The Monk*, *Frankenstein* (1818) and *Melmoth The Wanderer* (1820)—feature embedded narratives, in which a framing central narrative occasionally cedes the act of story-telling to another author. For example, Lewis's story of Ambrosio, his eponymous monk, recedes when we hear the appropriating narrative of Raymond and the Bleeding Nun. And the male frame narrator of Anne Brontë's *Tenant of Wildfell Hall* cedes narrative authority to the embedded journal of the female protagonist. These embedded narratives present a series of authors rather than any single proprietary authorial voice. This trope continues in the Victorian Gothic, as we saw in the discussion of *The Woman in White* above.

The closure of Yonge's *Chantry House* (1886) provides a variation on this theme.[1] Although the central narrative is unified through the single voice of Edward, he appends to his text a series of "Remarks" in which other family members provide their comments and critiques upon the central narrative, pointing to Edward's narrative omissions: one remarks that "Uncle Edward has not said half enough about his dear old self"; another wonders "what Aunt Anne would have done if Uncle Clarence had not been so forbearing before he went to China"; a third, "what became of Lady Peacock" (II. 226–227). Edward's "Reply" leads to a dialogue in which the characters converse among themselves, displacing Edward entirely from his own text: the concluding paragraphs of the novel record an exchange between Martin and Anne in which Edward does not even take part.[2]

Narrative dispossession takes on political and humorous overtones when the narrative of a dominant character is delayed or interrupted by a subordinate. In *Otranto*, Manfred is driven into a comic frenzy in his attempt to get information about a ghostly sighting from Diego and Jaquez, two servants (30). Their comically inarticulate and subversively meandering narrative is, as Walpole suggests, influenced by "that great master of nature, Shakespeare ... the model I copied," whose tragedies would lose "a considerable share of the spirit and wonderful beauties, if the humor of the gravediggers ... were omitted or vested in heroics" (Preface to the Second Edition 9). Radcliffe's *Udolpho* and *The Italian* also contain passages in which humor is generated by the frustrated attempts of the aristocrat to wring meaning from the winding locutions of the peasant. In *The Italian* the vocal interruptions of the peasant also provide a more pointedly disruptive counternarrative to subvert the conservative marriage and restoration of aristocratic property and identity that dominates the denouement. As the noble couple Ellena and Vivaldi make a final appearance, they are met with a torrent of language from Paulo, the faithful servant. Here Radcliffe explicitly deploys metaphors of power to describe the vocality of the peasant: the words "flew from his lips with the force of an electric shock ... the words passed like lightning from one individual to another" (414) until the two aristocrats are forced to retreat. "Vivaldi and Ellena withdrew amidst a choral shout," leaving the last two pages of the narrative in the possession of the peasants and their shouts of joy. These vocalizations, ostensibly in support of the aristocracy and the restoration of order, are in effect a veiled subversion of social power.

The conclusion of *The Italian* is remarkable in denying the reader the sense of stability typically afforded by a closing narrative frame, in a narrative that provides an opening frame.[3] The beginning frame of *The Italian* takes place in 1764[4] and describes a group of English travelers in Italy who stop at a church belonging to the order of the suitably named Black Penitents. In the frame Radcliffe generates an English Protestant normalizing perspective for the central narrative that is set in a horrifyingly Catholic Italy. The English group is suitably startled to discover "an assassin" given sanctuary in the church. Radcliffe fully deploys her strategy in the dialogue that follows: "An Italian, who was of the party" (2) explains to one of the group that "if we were to shew no mercy to such unfortunate persons, assassinations are so frequent, that our cities would be half depopulated" (3); in response to this irrational logic, the "Englishman could only gravely bow" (3). He need say no more because we readers know that he, like us, is horrified by the culture that produces this rationale. The Italian gentleman[5] offers to send him the manuscript of *The Italian* to shed further light upon Italian culture. The Englishman receives the volume and the last words of the frame are "He read as follows" (4). What follows is Radcliffe's novel. We readers read along, over the Englishman's shoulder as it were, comforted throughout the horror and depravity of Radcliffe's narrative by his solid English presence. We understand that we are reading the story of *The Italian* from the horrified perspective of the unnamed Englishman; this sense of shared perspective lends stability to our response. We are, in fact, fellow readers with the Englishman. There is just one problem: Radcliffe neglects to provide a closing frame. Her text ends within the narrative of Vivaldi and Ellena: the joyous wedding and the shouts of Paulo. The English reader whose presence authorizes and empowers readerly condemnation of Italian practice has completely disappeared (murdered, perhaps?); we readers are left alone stranded and destabilized in Italy among the uncivilized Italians.

❧

Maria Edgeworth pseudo-Gothic novel *Castle Rackrent* (1800) also dispossesses her reader of the security of hermeneutic authority. Whereas *The Italian* destabilizes the reader by erasing the comforting frame reader, Edgeworth deprives her reader of hermeneutic authority by creating an outrageous narrative voice which insists on interpreting horror as commonplace, thereby establishing the irony of her novel. The narrative voice belongs securely to Thady Quirk, the Irish peasant who writes (seemingly) in support of the aristocracy. He is the family servant who has "voluntarily undertaken to publish the Memoirs of the Rackrent Family" (8) and who seems to approve the actions of the Rackrent lords that he narrates. And yet at various moments the power of Thady's conservative perspective falters and the reader is allowed, or forced, to consider alternate subversive meanings for the events that Thady endorses. For example, after the Jewish wife is released from imprisonment by her husband upon his death, Thady tells us "she had taken an unaccountable prejudice against the country" (35–36). Thady's failure to account for her distaste, his obliviousness to the crime of the aristocratic husband, reveals his narrative and hermeneutic inadequacy and leaves a vacuum. This vacuum invites the reader to take hermeneutic possession of the text and to fill the vacuum with the perspective of the silent and imprisoned wife, who, if allowed to speak by her husband and by Thady, in his role of narrator, would certainly come up with a suitable explanation for her annoyance. The unvoiced counter-perspective of the wife, ultimately supplied by the reader, dispossesses Thady of his narrative authority and destabilizes the perspective of the ruling class whose mouthpiece he is.

The destabilizing narrative strategies of Radcliffe and Edgeworth shed some light upon the narrative structure of Reeve's *The Old English Baron* and further validate the reading of Reeve as a conservative writer who promotes centralized stability. Whereas Radcliffe's *The Italian* ends without a closing frame, resulting in a subversive narrative instability, Reeve's narrative lacks an opening frame but concludes with an unanticipated closing frame. At the beginning of the novel, the narrator appears to be impersonal and omniscient: "In the minority of Henry the Sixth, King of England" (7). The narrative unfolds in this manner, yielding to the occasional embedded first person narrative. It is not until the last paragraph, however, that the reader discovers the context of the text that is being read:

> Sir Philip Harclay caused the papers relating to his son's history to be collected together; the first part of it was written under his own eye in Yorkshire, the subsequent parts by Father Oswald at the Castle of Lovel. All of these, when together, furnish a striking lesson to posterity, of the over-ruling hand of Providence, and the certainty of Retribution [153].

The anonymous narrative we have been reading is belatedly revealed as the work of the two benevolent representatives of religious and civil authority: Father Oswald, the good priest of the story, who is following the orders of Sir Philip, the good aristocrat. Thus in Reeve's conservative formulation, the "over-ruling" and consolidating "hand of Providence" is linked to the powerful unifying hands of the priestly author and his aristocratic sponsor. An auditor's judgement of an earlier embedded narrative of Father Oswald—"the whole story is so well connected, that I can see nothing to make us doubt the truth of it" (120)—may be applied to the entire narrative of *Baron*. Multiple meanings and multiple narratives are subsumed within the narrative that is reined in and controlled by the dual powers of State and Church, yielding one certain and conservative meaning. In Reeve's paradigm, the certainty of narrative unity and narrative authority promotes the power of Church and State to create and possess meaning.

As is the case with so many Gothic conventions, an early instance of the deployment of strategies of narrative dispossession may be discovered in the pages of Walpole's ur-text. In the first edition of *Otranto*, Walpole disowns his proprietary rights over the text by inventing an imaginary editor/translator and an imaginary author. The title page of the first edition

11. Gothic Conventions; Narrative Dispossessions

reads: "Translated by William Marshall, Gent. From the Original Italian of Onuphrio Muralto, Canon of the Church of St. Nicholas at Otranto" (xix). In inventing an imaginary English translator/editor, Walpole works to stabilize the authority of his text: like Radcliffe, he provides his insane Italian narrative with a presumably sane English escort—the translator—to accompany the English reader in deciphering the meanings of the text. In the preface written by the imaginary Marshall, the reader is told that the text "was found in the library of an ancient catholic family" (4) and that it is of uncertain date. Marshall speculates that the writer of *Otranto* was "an artful priest." In the preface to the second edition in which he reveals himself as the author of the work—taking responsibility for his previously dispossessed text—Walpole explains this displacement of his own narrative authority. He requests the forgiveness of his readers for "having offered his work to them under the borrowed personage of a translator" and explains that the "diffidence of his own abilities, and the novelty of the attempt, were his sole inducements." Evoking the language of narrative possession, Walpole explains that he did not mean to claim his text and accept authorial responsibility "unless better judges should pronounce that he might own it without a blush" (5).

❧

The convention of the found manuscript that Walpole and many other Gothic writers deploy to relinquish authorial responsibility is linked thematically and logically to a related trope: the fragmented and effaced manuscript. The implausible but consistent internal logic of the Gothic links these tropes in this way: if the manuscript at hand is not the work of the person who presents it, it must have been dislodged from its actual author; the manuscript thus has been lost and is available to the reader only because it has been discovered by someone other than the author. Since long-lost manuscripts may be expected to show signs of wear and tear, the resulting document is often physically effaced and fragmented. Indeed, the trope of the effaced and fragmented recovered manuscript pervades the Gothic canon.

In addition to *Otranto*, many other Gothic texts are purportedly derived from old and fragmented manuscripts. The narrative of *The Old English Baron* is periodically and abruptly interrupted by interlocution like this:

> From this place the characters in the manuscript are effaced by time and damp. Here and there some sentences are legible, but not sufficient to pursue the thread of the story. Mention is made of several actions in which the young men were

engaged.... The following incidents are clear enough to be transcribed; but the beginning of the next succeeding pages is obliterated: However, we may guess at the beginning by what remains [27].

The recovered manuscript that makes up a part of Charles Maturin's *Melmoth the Wanderer* (1820) is "old, tattered, and discoloured" (27) and "mutilated" (28). It is also repeatedly interrupted by interjections like this: "'The stranger, slowly turning round and disclosing a countenance which'—(Here the manuscript was illegible for a few lines), 'said in English'—(A long hiatus followed here, and the next passage that was legible, though it proved to be a continuation of the narrative, was but a fragment)" (31). Maturin indicates the fragmentation with a liberal scattering of asterisks throughout his text. A sub-genre of the effaced manuscript that indicates a particular type of lost meaning is the effaced legal document. In *Chantry House*, for example, the Winslows discover an old will whose intent has been effaced by time. It reads: "'I, Margaret Winslow, being of sound mind, do hereby give and bequeath—'Then came stains that defaced every line, till the extreme end" (II. 171).[6]

As these instances indicate, the fragmented and effaced narrative clearly works to disrupt the reader's hermeneutic possession of the text as meaning falls between the gaps of the fragments. What is less obvious but no less significant is that the trope of the fragmented and effaced narrative paradoxically disrupts the proprietary relationship of the author or the purported editor to the text. For the fragmented text invites the reader to replace the meaning that is effaced from the text; in doing so the reader displaces the author as possessor of meaning. Indeed, the trope of the fragmented text is a literalization of the strategies of dispossession. Whereas the strategies of narrative dispossession take place on the level of the structure of the narrative, deploying particular paradigms to indicate narrative dispossession, the trope of the fragmented narrative operates on the level of the actual physical manuscript, literalizing the act of narrative dispossession.[7]

As Walpole's second preface indicates, the dangers of authorial dispossession posed by the imaginary author are outweighed by the utility of shielding the actual author from criticism, especially useful to the respectable author of the scandalous Gothic. Walpole makes additional use of his imaginary author and editor. In splitting himself into two imaginary authorial figures, the editor and the author, further dispossessing himself of authorial integrity, Walpole creates a space in which he can praise his own work from an apparent critical distance. Hence the imaginary Marshall on the imaginary Muralto: "There is no bombast, no similes, no flowers, digressions, or unnecessary description.... The characters are well drawn ... the mind is kept up in a constant vicissitude of interesting passions" (4). Here we see a great use of the imagined author to dispossess the authority of the reader: Walpole uses his framing editor's excessive comments to pre-empt any critical reading on the part of the reader. Walpole/Marshall further disarms the reader of critical authority by tossing in a few gently negative comments. Proving the objectivity of his critical perspective Marshall claims, "I am not blind to my author's defects" (5) and asserts that Muralto allows his religion to get in the way of his writing: "Here the interest of the monk plainly gets the better of the judgement of the author" (5). In this statement Walpole or Marshall, or whoever it is that is writing, succeeds in completely fragmenting the figure of the writer: the imaginary Muralto is bifurcated into two—the author and the monk—by the imaginary Marshall; all of these personae are, we must remember, the fragments into which Walpole divides himself. Thus in destabilizing the authority of his reader, Walpole also destabilizes the figure of the writer. When we consider that the theme of lost identity is central to *Otranto*, the representation of the writer detached from his unifying identity and thereby dispossessed of his narrative authority is suitable indeed.

12

Contexts of Contested Narratives
Can the Text Be Possessed?

The Rise of Copyright Laws

The representations of the fragmented and attenuated writer and of the anxious and destabilized reader, both dispossessed of the narrative, arise in response to eighteenth-century legal and cultural concerns regarding textual possession. Susan Stewart notes among the many anxiety-provoking revolutions of the eighteenth century:

> the codification of copyright, the linking of the author to a singular and personal intellectual authority, the linking of writing to the author's body, and the legislation of writing as a commodity as well as an act of speech … an advent of "entitlement" that replicates other revolutionary entitlements of the eighteenth century [21–22].[1]

In fact, these transformations culminate in the "question of literary property … the long legal struggle" (Mark Rose 4) regarding the ownership of the text that extended throughout the eighteenth century.

The decline of the patronage system as well as the advent of mass copying and printing marked early disruptions in the stable connection between the writer and the work. The process of multiple copying ensured that the author was dispossessed of the text, although the move from the copyists to print resulted in greater textual stability, a text less susceptible to unauthorized change. Yet, despite the contention of Michael North, that "print stabilizes the relations between a particular writer and a particular text" (1380), only the integrity of the text is stabilized not the relationship of text to author. With the advent of mass printing, the author was further displaced: printing became "the locus of ownership" (Stewart 10). This displacement of authorial authority was accompanied by a displacement of authorial responsibility: printing also became the "the locus of censorship"

(10), the locus of social control upon writing. Indeed Stewart's vivid and horrifying accounts of the physical punishment of printers that accompanied censorship in the seventeenth century recall Foucault's description of torture in *Discipline and Punish*.

The commercial needs of the printers and their successors the booksellers—whose interests were promoted by the consolidation of their proprietorship over the text—resulted in the instatement of the system of copyright in Britain. This move echoes the eighteenth-century attempts to consolidate possession of real estate and person, also exemplifying the shift that Foucault notes in the eighteenth century toward greater consolidation of social and economic power.

The economic needs of the booksellers—more than the destabilization of the relationship between author and text—drove the institution of the copyright laws, although the economic needs of the booksellers were presented under the guise of the proprietary rights of the author.[2] Indeed, the newly-defined figure of the author was not created to promote the rights of the author, for it was not the proprietary right of the author that was the issue at stake. Although it was "the representation of the author as proprietor [that] was elaborated and promulgated" (Rose 5) during the discussion of "the question of literary property," in actuality the question was which of two groups of booksellers would own the texts produced by the authors: the London booksellers who had previously had complete and permanent economic control over the books; or "the booksellers and printers of the provinces who were seeking an independent role for themselves as reprinters of popular titles" (Rose 5). This problem was solved in 1774 in "the great case of *Donaldson v. Becket*" when "the House of Lords ... declared that copyright was limited in term" (5). This meant that the London booksellers could not own a text in perpetuity.

This final ruling disrupted an argument that was central to the case of the booksellers: that the possession of intellectual property is analogous to the possession of real property. This analogy designates the author as proprietor of the work of his hands, entitled to sell the product of his labors to a bookseller in perpetuity: "Though immaterial, this property was no less real and permanent, they argued, than any other kind of estate" (Rose 6). Rose cites a passage from *Gray's-Inn Journal* by Arthur Murphy, a writer and lawyer involved with the legal disputes of copyright, that "is a spectacular example of the attempt to represent literary property as analogous to real estate.... Murphy's fantasy recasts the ubiquitous ancient-modern [writer] distinction into an anatomy of various kinds of land tenure. The production of poetry becomes the production of property" (7–8). Thus, the paradigm of property for Blackstone, as for other eighteenth-century jurists, was land, and it was on the model of the landed estate that the concept of literary property was formulated ... the goal for.... Blackstone, and the other eighteenth-century lawyers engages in the project of stabilizing the concept of literary property ... to establish copyright as an absolute right of property, a freehold [7–8].[3]

Yet the ruling of *Donaldson v. Becket* in 1774 determined that an author could not sell a book in perpetuity, that at some point ownership reverted to the author and thus that text is inalienable property. Thus, the failure of the attempt to anchor the possession of intellectual property to the supposedly more stable model of possession of real estate.

We see then an implicit instability in the system of textual possession that attempts to stabilize the premises of possession of literary property. This instability derives in part from the paradoxical nature of the concept: "in a print culture, the concept of individual authorship allows writers both to sell their works and to retain an inalienable proprietary right over them" (North 1380–1381).

Of course, the instability of possession is the topic that most grips the Gothic imagination. In patterns that recall the Gothic encounter with notions of possession of real estate and person, the Gothic mode, with its inherent instability, provides a hospitable site for the exploration of anxieties that derive from the collision of stable and unstable notions of authorial possession and from legal attempts to fix these notions. As in the anxious meditations upon possession of property and person, the Gothic mode does not destabilize legal realities as much as reveal instabilities inherent within the system, recognizing the futility of legal attempts to contain and to possess. In fact, Rose notes, the effort to contain texts legally "never succeeded" because of the "radical instability of the concept of the autonomous ... author.... The eighteenth-century lawyers sought to fix the notion of literary property, and that project continues today ... all such attempts are ... futile ... because the concept of literary property is itself finally an oxymoron" (8). North concurs and in doing so points to the paradox of property—the convergence of materiality and immateriality—that we have seen before: "literary work thus becomes a peculiar kind of property ... one that is tangible and intangible at the same time, immaterial and yet as real as real estate.... In a sense, then, authorship has never been an unassailable concept" (1381–1382). As we have seen, all property poses this particular paradox. As the history of copyright laws indicates, possession of the literary work is as uncertain as possession of property and self.

The Gothic engagement with the unstable notion of literary property may in fact account for one of the paradoxes of this subversive mode: its surprising commitment to convention and tradition. A number of writers note the economic underpinnings of the newly valorized notion of literary originality that arose in the eighteenth century as the "regime of imitation" (North 1380)[4] was replaced by "eighteenth-century discourse of original genius.... The representation of originality as a central value in cultural production developed ... in precisely the same period as the notion of the author's property right.... By the 1770's the doctrine of originality was orthodox" (Rose 6). As Rose suggests, the doctrine of originality operated as a useful rationale for the commodification of intellectual property. An artifact that is unique, the product of the unique labor of an individual mind, merits particular legal protection and justifies the system of copyright.[5]

Thus, the Gothic tendency to repeatedly copy the same tired conventions is in actuality a paradoxical act of radical subversion, a demystification of the myth of originality. Gothic repetition poses a resistance to Romantic orthodoxy and to the valorization of the individual writer that is paradoxically used to define and contain the writer's relationship to the text. In the recurrence of a set of fixed tropes, the Gothic destabilizes the notion of individual originality and flouts principles that calls for the legalized fixing of possession of intellectual property.

The Dispossessed Reader

Eighteenth-century copyright laws thus attempted to address commercial anxieties of textual possession by creating new anxieties regarding the identity of the author. The establishment of the figure of the author in response to economic imperatives is the development that evokes the notion of authorship articulated by Foucault's "What is an Author."[6] Foucault untangles the idea of the author as a social construct, a metaphor that is useful in certain discourse about texts but one which represses the complex fragmentation of the individual author. Foucault notes the reciprocal proprietary relationship between text and author: the author increases his proprietary control over the text but he also is appropriated by the text, becoming liable to punishment for any transgressiveness of the text, linked to and defined by the contents of the text.[7] Nor is the relationship between the reader and the text stabilized by the new laws.

The reader may actually own a copy of the text. "Printed in book form, a text becomes a separable object offered for sale and thus something that one person can own" (North 1380).

However, the hermeneutic authority of the reader is destabilized in proportion to the instatement of the proprietary rights of the author, an instability that is reflected in the conventions of the Gothic text.

Loren Glass articulates the readerly reaction to the notion of absolute authorial proprietorship in her response to "Against Theory" by Steven Knapp and Walter Benn Michaels: "To say that the text only means what the author intends is another way of saying that the text belongs to the author in some inalienable way, and to assert this proprietary relation as absolute is to affirm a certain cultural way of organizing the relationship between texts and persons" (7). In this Glass suggests that the reader has a counter-proprietary right, the right to appropriate the text and the reading through interpretation. Harold Bloom asserts this right when he says, "Reading ... is a belated and all-but-impossible act, and if strong, is always a misreading" (*A Map of Misreading* 3). That is, the reader has the right to appropriate the text and to revise it by the lights of readerly (mis)interpretation.

And so, the failed economic attempts to consolidate possession of the text—by the booksellers, by the author, by the reader—only highlight the instability of textual possession, an ambiguous situation that invites Gothic intervention.

13

The Theology of Narrative Dispossession in Maturin's *Melmoth the Wanderer*

Dispossessions of Mortal Author and Reader

The resistance of the Gothic text to readerly apprehension, comprehension and appropriation contributes to the sense of oppression and entrapment that envelops the reader of Charles Maturin's *Melmoth the Wanderer* (1820). *Melmoth*, a novel in which the reader is vexed and troubled as much as are the characters, quite successfully earns its place within literary history as the last great novel of the era of the high Gothic: virtually every Gothic trope, including the various tropes of dispossession, is to be found within its many pages and almost countless narratives. The usual scenes of family dysfunction, including near-incest, recur throughout the novel, as does the stock scene of innocence fleeing through labyrinthine corridors pursued by the agents of evil. At least two weddings are horribly interrupted, in addition to numerous thwarted romances. Stanton's manuscript tells of a wedding party in which cries are heard from the "bridal-chamber"; the guests discover "the bride a corse in the arms of her husband" (36). In "The Lover's Tale," John leaves Elinor at the altar after his mother tells him that she is his sister. The recurring theme of the Gothic—the visiting of the sins of the fathers upon the children—is also present in the novel: both Monçada and Immalee, the protagonists of the two major embedded narratives, are betrayed by selfish and cruel parents.

Many of Maturin's characters are subject to moments of personal dispossession like fainting and madness. The threat of the state to personal possession is evoked when Melmoth[1] appears to Stanton in the mad-house and compares his situation to that of the "prisoners in the Bastille" (55). Other anxious moments of personal dispossession result from the diabolic powers of the Catholic Church. After being seduced and abandoned by Melmoth, Isidora/Immalee[2] is imprisoned with her dying baby by the Inquisition: "she was in a prison, a pallet of straw was her bed, a crucifix and a death's head the only furniture of her cell" (20).[3] The dominant form of personal dispossession in *Melmoth* is Satanic possession, including—in an evocation of *Zofloya* and *The Monk*, in which Ambrosio is seduced by a minion of Satan—Satanic possession figured as sexual possession. In a diabolic reworking of the balcony scene in *Romeo and Juliet*, Melmoth woos Isadora/Immalee as she stands at a casement. In language that vividly echoes the language of Satanic possession in *Zofloya*, Melmoth repeatedly asks: "'Isidora! Will you then be mine?'" until she acquiesces, upon which he exults, also repeatedly, "'You are mine!'" (354–355).

In Melmoth's wooing of Isidora/Immalee, Maturin constructs a destabilizing equation between spiritual and material (property) possession, dispossession and transmission. Melmoth promises Isidora, "I will dower you in the most ample territory ever settled on a bride ... your bearded men of law ... your pious mother and proud family ... will never litigate my exclusive title to possession.... Mine heirs must inherit it for ever and ever, if they hold by my tenure." In this speech, Maturin equates the dispossession of the soul with the possession of the territories of hell and all its glories: "The rulers of the earth are there.... There are their riches, and pomp, and power—Oh what a glorious accumulation!" (349).[4]

Maturin's figuring of the appropriation of real estate reflects the concerns of Maturin's time and place: "The first of the Melmoths ... settled in Ireland ... an officer in Cromwell's army who obtained a grant of lands, the confiscated property of an Irish family" (26). Maturin was part of the Protestant minority "which nervously guarded its privileges from the dispossessed Catholic majority in the years between ... 1798 ... [and] 1824" (Baldick xiii). Maturin also recalls other forms of colonial appropriation in the story of Immalee, the "Indian" who inhabits a deserted island and who is visited by Melmoth, the corrupting descendant of the British usurpers of Irish property.

The Fragmented Narrative

Despite his belated arrival upon the Gothic scene, Maturin spectacularly succeeds in refreshing the old familiar forms, effectively deploying the trope of the convoluted, fragmented and effaced narrative to destabilize the reader.[5] The supposedly ancient manuscript presents frequent gaps, empty spaces that reflect the seeming decay of the paper. However, the missing fragments of text do not actually detract from the reader's apprehension of the narrative: in fact, the ellipses provide relief to the hapless reader struggling through the massive text and Maturin always compensates for the fragment so that the reader is never deprived of meaning through this trope. The narrative strategy that does catch the reader in the web of Maturin's narrative—producing an uncomfortable sense of readerly uncertainty, entrapment and oppression—is the structure of embedded narratives that report the wanderings of the title character, from "the mad-house, the jail, or the Inquisition,—the den of famine, the dungeon or crime, or the death-bed of despair" (324). As Melmoth wanders through time and space, so does his narrative with the reader trailing desperately behind. Because a description of the narratives would result only in the confusion that typifies the book, the table below indicates the layers of narration that appear in the novel.

This table is a simplification in that it does not indicate various moments when an interjection from one level appears in another. It also does not indicate when the narratives end: Maturin does provide closure for most of the narratives with the exception of the narrative of Adonijah told by Monçada. We never hear precisely how Monçada escapes from Adonijah's grotto nor precisely what happens to Adonijah. Within this table the numbers apply to the level of narration: seven is the innermost embedded narrative and one is the outer narrative frame of the novel. Given the complexity of Maturin's structure, it is more accurate to present this table as the record of one reader's attempt to grapple with the narrative organization than as the absolute reflection of the structure:

1	2	3	4	5	6	7
1816, Ireland. John Melmoth.						
	1676, England. Stanton's account read by John Melmoth.					

1	2	3	4	5	6	7
		Old woman's account to Stanton.				
	1816, Spain. Monçada's account to John Melmoth.					
		Parricide's story told to Monçada.				
		Adonijah's manuscript. Read by Monçada; told to John Melmoth.				
			1680–1684, Indian Island, Spain. "Tale of the Indian." Story within manuscript. Read by Monçada; told to John Melmoth.			
				Spain. Account of Don Francisco, Isidora's father.		
					16—, Spain. "Tale of Guzman's Family." Told by unknown writer to Francisco.	
					Late 1600s, England. "The Lover's Tale." Told by Melmoth to Francisco.	
						Account of the clergyman: (first) death of Melmoth.

As the table indicates, this is a book that makes many oppressive demands upon the reader: the reader must labor not only to arrive at an interpretation of the text but to discover its simple and literal levels of meaning as well. The reader who is not prepared to engage actively with the text, to provide the sense of organization that Maturin omits, will soon be lost in a meaningless web of words, dispossessed of meaning and of the text. As the table also indicates, various modes of narrative are used to tell this convoluted tale: manuscripts are read; readers relay stories they have read; narrators tell of their own experiences; accounts are heard first-hand or by second-hand report. In each case, though, Maturin delineates a time and place of telling as carefully as a time and place for the unfolding of the events; the result is that this novel becomes a narrative of narration, a tale that relates multiple moments of telling.

Ultimately, the reader is betrayed by the size and structure of Maturin's labyrinthine text: its vast narrative structure yields a text that is as sublimely unknowable and unpossessible as any Gothic castle; the long and convoluted narrative is as difficult to follow as any dark subterranean passage. In this, the structure of *Melmoth*, as well as that of countless other Gothic texts, works as a reflexive manifestation of the Sublime, the defining aesthetic principle of Gothic literature and architecture. The Gothic text, like the Gothic structure, cannot be apprehended at one time by one individual; it invokes the incomprehensible, deferring its meanings, resisting human possession of such meanings.

The Immediate Power of the Spoken Word

The table strikingly indicates the different narrative relationships within Maturin's novel: accounts are read and told in a variety of different situations, reflecting the eighteenth and early-nineteenth century preoccupations with the changing modes of transmission of text and narrative, as the more intimate forms of person-to-person storytelling gave way to the more distanced and mass-produced communications of commercial publishing. Whereas some narrative situations involve a one-to-one telling (Monçada's telling of his adventures to John Melmoth, for example), some instances of storytelling feature narrators far removed from and unaware of the audience (for example, the old woman whose account of Melmoth is transcribed by Stanton in the seventeenth century and read by John Melmoth in the early nineteenth century).

As Susan Stewart notes in *Crimes of Writing*, the revised form of distanced narrative resulted in a renewed interest in the older forms of immediate storytelling: "folkloric or oral forms as a model for immediacy, organicism, and tradition" (5). Stewart elaborates, "Emerging literary modes such as ... the fragment ... all emphasize the secondary ... quality of literary discourse" (22).[6] Thus in the "Lover's Tale," located in seventeenth-century England (the only narrative in *Melmoth* that is set in England), Maturin or Melmoth, the narrator of the tale, pointedly valorizes immediate traditional oral narrative: "how much superior are the touches on one who paints from the light and the heart, and the senses,—to those of one who dips his pen in his inkstand, and casts his eye on a heap of musty parchments, to glean his facts of his feeling from them!" (453). Maturin reinforces the power of the spoken word (although not the power of the narrator, as we shall see) in the other narrative that is told to Don Francisco, Isidora's father, "The Tale of Guzman's Family." In this story, the spoken word has the power to kill. Ines, the good wife, seems to die upon hearing her husband's plan to sell his soul to Melmoth in order to save his starving family: "'a word then has killed her'" (429).

The Power of the Written Word

Yet "The Tale of Guzman's Family" demonstrates the respect *Melmoth* holds for the power of the written word as well. In this story, the written word—in the form of the discovered will, that familiar Gothic emblem of rediscovered signification—restores both life and possessions to the dispossessed. By the time the will has been discovered not only is the wife presumed dead, the children of the family too have been seemingly killed by their father to spare them future misery. And yet in a sort of Gothic-comic ending the members of the family return from the dead as a result of the will that restores their appropriated wealth. Upon hearing the good news, the wife is "restored to sudden and perfect consciousness"; her daughters too recover "from their death-like swoon" (433). We already know that little Maurice has only feigned his death, having "the cunning to counterfeit death" and thereby fool his father (430). In "The Lovers Tale," Maturin again promotes the existential power of the written word in the form of a will. The patriarch of the family, who is left without sons, bequeaths "his immense estates to his grand-daughter Margaret." The will thus has the effect of reducing the patriarch's daughter to a dispossessed ghost: "she hovered around the walls of the Castle like a departed spirit groaning for its re-admission to the place from which it had been driven and feeling and giving no peace till its restoration was accomplished" (470).

The transcendent power of the written word—and the association of Melmoth with this power—is further consolidated in the "Tale of the Indian," the narrative that encompasses the two narratives told by Melmoth. In the Indian's tale, the "Indian" Immalee says to Melmoth—the supernatural demon who is slowly taking possession of her—"you possess the happy art of writing thought" (318). To the illiterate Immalee, Melmoth's possession of the power of literacy, the power to make thought visible, is one of his many supernatural abilities. Indeed, the construction of Melmoth as Satan, or as a close associate of Satan, allows us to see the theological aspect of verbal power in *Melmoth*; for the power of the word that is ascribed to God in the Christian tradition—"In the beginning was the Word, and the Word was with God, and the Word was God" (John 1:1)—is also located within his double, Satan who (like Zofloya) requires only the verbal commitment of the intended victim, in this case Immalee, to advance his demonic project and take possession of the soul.

Dispossession of the Human Author

Yet, although Melmoth, the Satanic protagonist, is empowered as narrator, his human framing author is not. In fact, there is a moment when the figure of the writer is indicted and killed for appropriating the diabolic tale. The first tale told to Isidora's father, "The Tale of the Guzman Family," a tale that reveals the diabolic workings of Melmoth, is told to Don Francisco by a stranger, a fellow-traveler in an inn. Later that night, Melmoth reveals to Don Francisco "the fate of those whose curiosity or presumption breaks on the secrets of that mysterious being, and dares to touch the folds of the veil in which his destiny has been enshrouded by eternity"—meaning himself (438). Entering the room of the usurping story-teller, Don Franciso recognizes "the figure of the being who had been conversing with him the preceding part of that very evening," now "a corse!" (438). His crime, Melmoth informs Don Franciso, is that he sought to appropriate a narrative not his own: "He sought possession of a desperate secret—he obtained it, but he paid for it the dreadful price that can be paid but once by mortals. So perish those whose presumption exceeds their power!" (439). The moral of this story appears to be that he who is "only a writer, a man of no importance in public or private life" (439) should not dare to appropriate and retell the stories of those supernatural forces who rule the world.

Thus, although *Melmoth* works to valorize the power of the word, Maturin, who was an Anglican priest, discounts the authority of the human author to appropriate the word. In Maturin's formulation, the right to possess the word belongs only to divine or diabolic authors. Indeed, Maturin works explicitly to displace his own authorial control. In a telling footnote to one of Melmoth's rants to Immalee, Maturin, in his own guise as author, writes:

> As by a mode of criticism equally false and unjust, the worst sentiments of my worst characters ... have been represented as *my own*, I must here trespass so far on the patience of the reader as to assure him, that the sentiments ascribed to the stranger are diametrically opposite to mine, and that I have purposely put them into the mouth of an agent of the enemy of mankind [303].

Maturin thus disavows his own words and dispossesses himself of the meaning of his text, ceding authorial control to supernatural textual authority, revealing the "bankruptcy of language" (298) when employed in human enterprise. In an emblem of the erasure of human speech (in the tale of Monçada) the Spanish monk tells of receiving a letter from his brother and "*swallowing it* [italics Maturin's] immediately after perusal" (177). In this revised re-enactment of the Catholic Communion in which the act of swallowing perpetuates divine meaning, the meaning of the letter, the product of a human hand, is effaced by being swallowed.

❧

In his litany of dispossessed human authors, Maturin includes one episode that recalls a familiar pattern of authorial usurpation: narrative dispossession of the female writer. In a long episode within "The Tale of the Indian," Fra Jose, the evil priest, effects control over the writing of Isidora's mother. Her letters are the result of "his dictation," because as the overpowered mother writes, "he in a manner holds my pen" (379). Isidora's mother represents yet another version of the missing mother, missing because her writing is obliterated. Indeed Maturin sets the effacement of the mother's writing within a larger pattern of effaced female texts. The scene of effaced writing is preceded by a scene in which we discover the mother obliterating her own grandmother's narrative textile: "*overcasting* a piece of tapestry wrought by her grandmother, representing the meeting of king Solomon and the queen of Sheba. The new work, instead of repairing, made fearful havock among the old" (377). Maturin emphasizes the connection between the effacement of the tapestry and the effacement of the written text: "As little trace of her original epistle did Donna Clara's present one bear, as did her elaborate overcasting to the original and painful labours of her grandmother." Maturin also explicitly condemns the overly zealous Catholic mother for the "inextinguishable and remorseless assiduity" (378) with which she approaches both tasks of obliteration. Through this doubled image of the effaced tapestry and the effaced letter emerges the image of the palimpsest, in which later texts are superimposed upon earlier ones, effacing the original meaning. In Maturin's extended metaphor, the image of the palimpsest suggests the frailty of that ephemeral medium, writing; the narrative is always susceptible to being covered by another usurping narrative, especially when distanced from the caring control of the primary author, a reminder of the authorly anxiety of Maturin's time.

Dispossession of the Supernatural Author

In the pattern of usurped and displaced narrative authority developed by Maturin, even God and the diabolic Melmoth are not completely exempt from moments of dispossession of narrative authority. In "The Lover's Tale," Melmoth tells of a moment when the word of God is effaced: "the Bibles ... [were] flung into the flames," together with the bodies of their readers (445). Melmoth himself is also subject to narrative dispossession; in his telling of "The Lover's Tale" to Don Francisco, he catches himself in a linguistic slip that is not noticed by Don Francisco. Maturin writes, "'It was at this period,' said the stranger [Melmoth] to Aliaga [Don Francisco], 'I first became acquainted with—I mean—at this time a stranger ...was seen to watch the two figures'" (496). Thus Melmoth inadvertently lets slip that he is the stranger who appears to the lovers within the story. Not surprisingly, even Melmoth cannot keep a tight rein on this complicated and overwrought narrative—it is only surprising that he does not slip more frequently. And despite these brief moments of slippage, the tendency of *Melmoth* is to valorize the possession of the narrative by transcendent supernatural powers and to subvert narrative possession by the human author.

Dispossessions of the (Catholic) Human Reader

The power of the human reader to apprehend the text is also undermined by the complicated strategies of Maturin's novel. There is a spectacular moment of reading in "The Lover's Tale" in which a reader sits with a book "on her knee, on which she fixed her eyes intently—the light that came through the casement chequering its dark lettered pages with hues of such glorious and fantastic colouring, that they resembled the leaves of some splendidly-illuminated missal, with all its pomp of gold, and azure, and vermilion" (452). This is a splendidly wrought image, yet when we think through the visual impact, we realize that to the reader, the colored light would have the effect of obliterating the dark letters on the dark pages. This image exemplifies the model of readerly distance and displacement that is articulated by the good wife in "The Tale of Guzman's Family." When she recollects the comfortable past of the family during which time they would read of the tribulations of saints, she says, "How we deceived ourselves, in believing that we indeed participated in the feelings of those holy men, while we were so far removed from the text by which they were proved! We read of imprisonments, of tortures, and of flames!—We closed the book, and partook of a comfortable meal" (428). In this speech Ines identifies the incapacity of the reader to truly apprehend the meaning of the text; in her formulation, true understanding only comes through the actual experience of suffering. Maturin points to other moments of textual misapprehension on the part of readers. He tells of the Catholic celebration of "the martyrdom of St. Ursula and her eleven thousand virgins" as exemplifying a moment of Catholic misinterpretation. Upon being correctly "interpreted," the record of the original event reveals "the martyrdom of a single female named *Undecimilla*, which the Catholic legends read *Undecim Mille*" (293). Even a text as powerful as the Bible is, in Melmoth's telling, subject to misinterpretation. "Even in the pure pages of that book ... [a flawed reader may find] "a right to hate, plunder, and murder" (307). In this, Maturin explicitly locates the loss of hermeneutic apprehension firmly in the humanly flawed reader: "The book contains nothing but what is good, and evil must be the minds, and hard the labour of those evil minds, to extort a tinge from it to colour their pretensions withal.... They all agree that the language of the book is, 'Love one another,' while they all translate that language, 'Hate one another'" (307).

The Unified Text

This statement clarifies the debt of Maturin's narrative theory to Protestant theology: God is the only authorized author although his text is countered by that of the devil, an equally powerful narrator. God's text, the Bible (and presumably his larger text, the world) is perfect, as it is, with no need for human (Catholic) extension or extrapolation. If human perceptions of the Word and the world are imperfect, it is due to the fallibility of the human reader who ruins the text by failing to read it correctly. Within

Maturin's paradigm, interpretation is figured as sin; his novel, as he indicates in his preface, is a warning to the sinful auditor who has "departed from the Lord, disobeyed his will, and disregarded his word" (5), as the Catholic reader has departed from a close reading of Scriptures. Not only are Maturin's fictional readers and auditors implicated in this sin of confusion. For the actual reader of Maturin's text—the reader who reads over John Melmoth's shoulder from the other side of the outside frame of the novel— is the most confused of all and is thus most guilty of the sin of "disregarding the word." However, the fault is within our reading and not within the narrative. For Maturin's narrative is, like God's, fully informed by immanent meaning; even the various devices that seem to fragment the narrative do not disable the meaning of the text. The crumbling manuscript, for example, does not disable meaning; the details that are effaced never impair the flow of the narrative. Nor does the elaborate narrative structure impair the meaning in any way, "the story is seen to pass unimpaired through these several layers of report and recall ... this novel is secretly as much about transmission as it is about transgression" (Chris Baldick xi–xii). As Baldick also notes, "[the] distinctive narrative voices are in fact tonally continuous, so that the reader will often forget ... just who is speaking at any given point" (xii); this secretly unified text is spoken in a voice that is actually uniform, evocative of the unifying effect of God's word. What we really have is a narrative whose varied surface confuses the erring reader, a narrative in which the immanent meaning is available only to the dedicated and faithful reader who sees the single underlying meaning beneath the variegated narrative.

An example of the immanent unity of Maturin's narrative occurs during "The Tale of the Indian" that is told to John Melmoth by Monçada, who has read the tale in Adonijah's narrative. As Monçada tells of the activities of Melmoth when he is away from Immalee's island, he says: "Absent from her, he returned to the world to torture and to tempt in the mad-house where the Englishman Stanton was tossing on his straw—" (298). As John Melmoth who is Monçada's auditor and the reader realize, this is the same Stanton we have already met; we know of his encounters with Melmoth from John Melmoth's earlier reading of his manuscript. Thus these two disjointed and seemingly unrelated texts converge to form a single story: the activities of Melmoth as he moves from Stanton to Immalee in the seventeenth century. We readers and John Melmoth have to work to discover this unified meaning. The careless or lazy reader, indeed the sinful reader, is at fault if the immanent meaning that represents the all-encompassing word of God fails to appear in the reading of the seemingly disjointed and confusing narrative.

The Final Dispossession of Human Author and Reader

And yet Maturin—mirroring the diabolic project of his title character—does create a text that tempts us into the sin of careless reading. Baldick notes that the reader of *Melmoth* is deprived of the "reassuring presence of a pious and rational omniscient narrator" (Baldick x); this absence, like the absence of the closing frame of the Englishman in Radcliffe's *The Italian*, leaves the reader without a stable perspective upon which to ground the reading. In fact, the conclusion of Maturin's novel recalls Radcliffe's denouement: the concluding sections of Maturin's text also lack the symmetry of closure for each narrative. Upon closing Isidora's tale, "The Indian's Tale," with her death, Maturin makes a great narrative leap. Monçada's promised conclusion would return to and simultaneously close all the embedded levels of narration—revealing to John Melmoth "the fates of the other victims, whose skeletons were preserved in the vault of the Jew Adonijah in Madrid ... the circumstance of his residence in the house of the Jew, his escape from it, and the reasons of his subsequent arrival in Ireland" (535). But the conclusion is interrupted by the appearance of Melmoth to John Melmoth and to Monçada in the outer frame. The human narrator, Monçada, is dispossessed of his narrative by the diabolic Melmoth who deprives Monçada's auditors, John Melmoth and the reader, of the comforts of closure.

Thus the final narrative moment in *Melmoth* represents the dispossession of both human narrator and human reader by supernatural and diabolical force; Maturin confirms the inutility of human possession of the narrative by dispossessing the reader of the meaning to be found in the closure of the text. In this Maturin confronts two certainties of narrative possession of his time: the commercial notion that the text may be securely possessed legally and the Enlightenment notion that the narrative of human life may be apprehended by the rational mind. The ultimate dispossession of reader and author in Maturin's text undermines the security of commercial possession of the text; even the reader who holds in-hand the book that has been purchased with hard-earned capital finds the meanings of the book evading capture. Similarly, Maturin's novel constantly reminds the reader of the inadequacies of human reason in apprehending meaning. Yet Maturin uses the flexible Gothic text to resist the certainties of the Enlightenment while simultaneously illustrating its effect. For the world of *Melmoth* is ultimately a post–Enlightenment world from which the authorial voice of God is absent; this absence is emblematized by the absence of a stable narrative voice in Maturin's text. As Melmoth indicates, in the post–Enlightenment world even the divine author is distanced from his text. Thus, although God's text, the Bible, is visible, God is absent; indeed, only the voice of the agent of the devil, Melmoth, is audible in Maturin's text. Inhabiting this textually fallen world, it is impossible for the reader to correctly understand the text; we, like the innocent Immalee, are enticed and betrayed by the diabolic voice of *Melmoth*.

14

Dispossessed and Dispossessing

The Wandering Jew's Possession of Voice and Narrative

In addition to Satan, there is another diabolic figure lurking within the dark figure of Melmoth the Wanderer. Wending through time and space, refusing to die, Melmoth evokes yet another supernatural threat, the Wandering Jew.[1] The story of the Wandering Jew originated in medieval Christian mythology; "first mentioned in 1228 by a monk" (McEvoy *The Monk* 450, note 177).[2] He is a Jewish cobbler who, from the liminal space of his lintel, witnesses Jesus stumbling under his cross on the way to Golgotha. When the Jew casts off the collapsing messiah, Jesus curses him with eternal life and exile.[3] During the course of his journeys the Wandering Jew, dispossessed of his own space (like the ghost), occasionally stumbles into the Gothic mode; like the figure of Satan, he is a convenient code for the utterly alien, inhuman evil that bedevils the Gothic text.[4]

Du Maurier's Victorian Wandering Jew

The wending figure of the Wandering Jew leads the reader from *Melmoth* to the text of a later era, George Du Maurier's *Trilby* (1894). Although Du Maurier never directly labels his villain Svengali as the Wandering Jew, his novel constructs a nineteenth-century version of this dark icon to address concerns regarding possession of the narrative, of the voice and of art.[5] Like Frankenstein's monster and like Dracula, the figure of Svengali demonstrates his potency by escaping the boundaries of the text that confines him, stalking his way into the popular imagination where he is known, although his novel long-forgotten.[6] Many of the essentials of Svengali's persona—his dark foreignness, his quasi-supernatural mesmerizing powers, deployed to possess a young impressionable female performer—still append to the popular conception of this mysterious figure. However, one essential trait of Du Maurier's Svengali has been lost in the translation from text to mythic figure: the essence of Du Maurier's monstrous Svengali is that he is a Jew. This fact of racial and cultural identity is an essential element of Du Maurier's Svengali, his primary identifying feature, the sole source of his malevolence. Svengali is the diabolic Wandering Jew reinvented for his time.[7] His entrance into Du Maurier's text is a gesture to the Gothic influence as well as a response to the popularity of the mid-nineteenth-century publication of the translation of Eugene Sue's *Wandering Jew* (1844–1845) and the subsequent stage adaptations that revived this supernaturally immortal figure.

When Svengali intrudes upon the text, heretofore populated by proper British types, Du Maurier immediately confirms the association of his ethnicity and his diabolism: he is "a tall bony individual of any age between thirty and forty-five, of Jewish aspect, well-featured but sinister" (11). Nor does Du Maurier allow his reader (or the characters of the novel) to forget the identifying feature of his villainous "Oriental Israelite Hebrew Jew" (234) whose "real name is Adler" (165). Svengali displays the physical attributes stereotypically associated with the Jew: he is possessed of a "long shapely Hebrew nose" (230),[8] "thick, heavy, languid, lusterless black hair ... bold brilliant black eyes, with long heavy lids, a thin, sallow face, and a beard of burnt-up black, which grew almost from under his eyelids; and over it his moustache, a shade lighter, fell in two long spiral twists" (11). Additionally, "he was both tawdry and dirty in his person ... greasily, mattedly unkempt" (39). Nor does Svengali's behavior temper his offensively Jewish exterior. His manners, too, are those of the stereotypically obtrusive Jew: "He would either fawn or bully, and could be grossly impertinent. He had a kind of cynical humour, which was more offensive than amusing and always laughed at the wrong thing, at the wrong time, in the wrong place ... his egotism and conceit were not to be borne" (39).

Du Maurier is very careful to distinguish this physically and morally offensive foreigner from the Englishmen who are the heroes of his novel. Before Svengali sullies the novel with his entrance, Du Maurier works to establish in the persons of "three well-fed, well-contented Englishmen" (4) the various types of the "normal Englishman" (11) against whom Svengali is clearly opposed: Taffy, the Yorkshireman, "big ... [and] fair, with kind but choleric blue eyes, and the muscles of his brawny arm were strong as iron bands" (4); Sandy, the Scotsman, "with a face ... blithe and merry and well pleased" (6); and Little Billee, the small, delicate and sensitive artist "with large dark blue eyes, delicate, regular features ... he was also very graceful and well built, with very small hands and feet" (6).

The slippage in Du Maurier's scheme for distinguishing between the British human and the demonic foreigner occurs in his description of little Billee. Recalling Gothic contestation of attempts to create and contain categories,[9] Du Maurier's description informs the reader that the "winning and handsome" Englishman displays in his face:

> just a faint suggestion of some possible very remote Jewish ancestor—just a tinge of that strong, sturdy, irrepressible, indomitable, indelible blood which is of such priceless value in diluted homeopathic doses, like the dry white Spanish wine called montijo, which is not meant to be taken pure ... or like the famous bulldog strain, which is not beautiful in itself, and yet just for lacking a little of the same no greyhound can ever hope to be a champion. So, at least, I have been told by wine merchants and dog-fanciers.... Fortunately for the world, and especially for ourselves, most of us have in our veins at least a minim of that precious fluid, whether we know it or show it or not [6–7].

After the initial shock of reading this egregious passage, structured upon race prejudice and twisted eugenics, the modern reader may take comfort in noting the discomfort of the writer; his far-flung evocation of the models of wine-making and dog-breeding suggests that Du Maurier, or his narrator, senses that he is on shaky ground. Even more vexing is the problem this passage poses to the project of the text. This racist passage discloses a serious flaw in Du Maurier's separatist paradigm: the vexing, repulsive, and transgressive Jew, whose blood eludes the barriers of racial containment,[10] is also the source of great art. Indeed it is Billee and not the other racially pure English types who succeeds in becoming a great artist just as it is Svengali who "had been the best pianist of his time at the Conservatory in Leipsic" (39). To complete the stereotype, Du Maurier later tells us that Billee benefits in more practical ways from his healthy dose of Jewish blood; upon achieving financial success he becomes "an excellent man of business. That infinitesimal dose of the good old Oriental blood kept him straight.... He loved to make as much money as he could, that he might spend it royally in pretty gifts to his mother and sister" (151).

In fact Little Billee's invisible, albeit beneficial, absorption of Jewish qualities points to the anxiety that supports Du Maurier's racist project. With the advent of Jewish Emancipation and assimilation, the Jew became less visible distinct. The possibility of invisible Jewish infiltration into British society and the British gene pool created a need for clear and visible distinctions between the English self and the newly invisible Jewish Other. Du Maurier invokes Gothic tropes and strategies to make the invisible

Other spectacularly obvious, thus comfortably diminishing the threat of invisible infiltration of the British self, that is, to avoid dispossession of the English self by the horrifying Jewish Other.[11]

Du Maurier attempts to solve the problem of the dangerously invisible Jew by creating the spectacularly and inhumanly repulsive Jew, the foreigner equipped with quasi-supernatural powers. Whereas Billie is a troubling figure, disrupting the distinct categories that buttress Du Maurier's theories of racial and cultural separation, Svengali's otherness is comfortably visible, obviously not English in appearance or in behavior. Every time he speaks he announces his foreign and transgressive nature, mangling the English language with his "Hebrew-German accent" (88). His voice, in fact, clearly establishes that Svengali is not only non-English but non-human as well. He speaks with a "throaty rook's caw, his big yellow teeth baring themselves in a mongrel canine snarl" (88).[12] His depiction in animal terms thus further consolidates the separate categories that Du Maurier works to construct. In fact, the animalizing metaphor, which conflates two species of creatures, moves through the category of the non-human toward the monstrous. Svengali is not only rook-like or dog-like, he is an unnatural combination of the two. Thus, in attempting to establish Svengali's animalistic tendencies, Du Maurier collides against Svengali's monstrous trangressiveness.

Not only is Svengali the inhuman and monstrous Other, Svengali is also established in the novel as the Satanic Other. Like Satan, Svengali is a fallen angel—glorious in heaven, a source of evil upon falling to earth: "Svengali playing Chopin on the pianoforte ... was as one of the heavenly host.... Svengali walking up and down the earth seeking whom he might cheat, betray, exploit, borrow money from, make brutal fun of, bully if he dared, cringe to if he must—man , woman, child, or dog—was about as bad as they make 'em" (40). Du Maurier deploys his talent as a graphic artist to reinforce this theme. In the illustrations that accompany the text, Svengali is figured as the iconic devil with a dark and pointed beard (17, 43) and pointed (Pan-like) ears (249) wielding his tool of power: in this case, the baton (202). The long hair "so offensive to the normal Englishman" (11) that associates him with the image of the disreputable artist-Jew also references devil iconography; his "beard of burnt-up black" (11) announces that he hails from realms of fire.[13]

Possession by the Dispossessed

Du Maurier adds an additional facet of demonic iconography long used to link the Devil and the Jew that is most relevant to *Trilby*. As Robert

S. Wistrich notes, "Jews, like the Devil, were also identified with the sin of unbridled lechery" (4). For it is Svengali's physical and spiritual possession of the beautiful and innocent Christian girl, Trilby, that links him most explicitly to the figure of Satan. From the first their interchanges are tainted by a troubling sexual subtext. In his flirtations with Trilby, Svengali's "playfulness [is] like that of a cat with a mouse—a weird ungainly cat, and most unclean; a sticky, haunting, long, lean, uncanny, black spider-cat, if there is such an animal outside a bad dream" (70). In this description Du Maurier moves from describing Svengali as animalistically and realistically lecherous toward aligning Svengali with the sexual potency of the dark supernatural, with the stuff of bad dreams. From Trilby's perspective, "he seemed to her a dread powerful demon, who ... oppressed and weighed on her like an incubus" (88): Jew as demon; Jew as lecher.

Du Maurier amplifies Svengali's identity as the diabolically lecherous Jew, unnaturally focused upon Trilby's body in a number of his interchanges with her. His examination of Trilby's singing apparatus is conducted in language that at once decomposes and fetishizes Trilby's body (a tendency Svengali shares with all the men who idolize Trilby in the novel), objectifying and sexualizing her singing organs:

> "The roof of your mouth is like the dome of the Panthéon; there is room in it for 'toutes les gloires de la France'.... The entrance to your throat is like the middle porch of St. Sulpice when the doors are open for the faithful ... and not one tooth is missing—thirty-two British teeth as white as milk and as big as knuckle bones: and your little tongue is scooped out like the leaf of a pink peony, and the bridge of your nose is like the belly of a Stradivarius ... and inside your beautiful big chest the lungs are made of leather! ...and you have a quick, soft, susceptible heart" [48].

When Svengali is angered by Trilby's rejection of his attentions, he again fetishizes and sexualizes her body, although in a more openly hostile way. He warns her that she will end up in the city morgue: "One fine day you shall lie asleep on one of those slabs ... the cold water shall trickle, trickle, trickle all the way down your beautiful white body to your beautiful white feet until they turn green.... And people of all sorts, strangers, will stare at you through the big plate-glass window" (72).[14] Svengali includes himself in the host of gazers upon Trilby's body. After Trilby voluntarily leaves Billee and his friends because Billee's family deems her an unsuitable match (thereby consolidating her signification as the symbol of goodness and innocence), her body is completely taken over by Svengali who makes her his mistress.

Svengali further manifests his demonism in taking spiritual or psychological possession of Trilby, though his powers of "mesmerism" (50). When Trilby is overcome with "neuralgia in her eyes" (46), Svengali's cure consolidates his powerful control over her: "Trilby was spellbound, and could not move," until "'I will now set her free,' said Svengali" (47). He reminds her of his power, encouraging her to return to him for future cures, telling her, "'*You shall see nothing, hear nothing, think of nothing but Svengali, Svengali, Svengali!*'" (50). Once Trilby becomes the singer "La Svengali"—her identity subsumed by his—the intermittent demonic possession becomes constant. The ventriloquistic nature of Svengali's possession of Trilby also defines him as the Devil; as he sings though her, she becomes the conventional possessed body, speaking (singing) with the voice of the Devil. Du Maurier further develops the Satanic trope in Svengali's possession of Trilby by gesturing to a number of other Devil narratives in addition to that of the diabolic Wandering Jew. Svengali is Satan tempting Eve in Paradise: "One jarring figure in her little fool's paradise, a baleful and most ominous figure that constantly crossed her path, and came between her and the sun, and threw its shadow over her, and that was Svengali" (70). Svengali is also the Devil seducing Trilby with a Faustian bargain: her body and soul in exchange for her musical success. In hearing Trilby sing as "La Svengali" the narrator recounts, "It was Faust! It was the most terrible and pathetic of all possible human tragedies" (205).[15] The dispossessed Satanic Wandering Jew thus takes possession not only of the mind and body of the Christian woman, but of her voice and art as well.

Not surprisingly, Du Maurier calls on the trope of the double to figure Trilby's dispossession of self under Svengali's control. This possession is figured as the construction of an *other* Trilby, a (musical) instrument of Svengali who looks like Trilby but sounds like Svengali. Trilby's thoughts: "When I am the singer.... I am *Svengali*" (205). It is this doubling of Trilby—the independent "real" Trilby and the Trilby possessed by Svengali—that accounts for the confusion of her friends as to whether La Svengali is actually Trilby. After La Svengali, who looks like Trilby, ignores Billie, the Laird says, "It's not Trilby—I swear! She could *never have done that* —- it's not *in* her! And it's another face altogether" (225). As the friends suspect, the Trilby they see as La Svengali is not Trilby, "in fact, our Trilby was *dead*" (289). As Gecko, Svengali's assistant, explains:

> *There were two Trilbys.* There was the Trilby you knew, who could not sing one single note in tune ... with a word—Svengali could turn her into the other Trilby, *his* Trilby—and make her do whatever he liked ... she suddenly became an unconscious Trilby of marble who could produce wonderful sounds ... and think his thoughts and wish his wishes ... that was the Trilby he taught how to sing....

That Trilby was just a singing-machine—an organ to play upon—an instrument of music ... a voice, and nothing more—just the unconscious voice that Svengali sang with [288].

Gecko's statement is particularly telling because it recalls the myth of Galatea, the ivory statue made by Pygmalion who becomes a real woman through his love of her. The Pygmalion story too broaches questions of artistic possession and personal possession; Du Maurier's evocation suggests that his story is a reversal of the myth. Whereas in the myth the artist relinquishes control of the object of art, allowing Galatea to become a subjective human being, Svengali appropriates a human being and transforms her into an instrument of art. He is far more Satanic possessor than artistic mentor.

The Realistic Story of the Diabolic Jew

Yet despite the supernatural aura of his villain, the commitment of Du Maurier's novel to realism, the dominant literary mode of his time, is evident. With the exception of Svengali, his characters are all realistically drawn. Du Maurier takes great care in locating his particular characters within a precise place and time. Paris and London are described with great visual particularity and Du Maurier, or his narrator, is quite insistent on locating the narrative within a particular time, the time of the recent past that is still retrievable through memory. The reader is told repeatedly that the first episodes of the book occur in "the fifties" (68, 86). At one point the narrator explicitly addresses the need of the reader to keep the chronology of the narrative in mind: "The fin de siècle reader ... must remember that it happened in the fifties" (114). As this instruction indicates, Du Maurier is also careful to locate his reader in time. He also takes care in indicating the time of the writing; describing a picture painted during the 1850s episode in Paris, the narrator writes, "Last year ... (more that thirty-six years after it was painted)" (139). The chronology of the narrative is thus carefully framed between the late 1850s and late 1890s. And within the narrative, Du Maurier is careful to sprinkle various markers that indicate the exact placement of his narrative in historical time: his favorite "'cinq ans après,'" is "in emulation of the good Dumas" (185), a famous proponent of realistic writing. The sense of Du Maurier's great obligation to the imperatives of realism is best revealed in a statement of the narrator. Contemplating the closure of his narrative, he articulates the subordination of his own wishes to the demands of truth and realism: "It is a great temptation ... to enrich [the] hero beyond the dreams of avarice and provide him with a title and a castle and park!"—by killing off the many relatives who stand between him and his fortune—in "a Shakespearean holocaust.... But truth is inexorable" (278).

Like other realist writers who dwell on the surface appearance of things, Svengali sets his narrative among artists concerned with issues of visual art. Set in the art world of Paris,[16] *Trilby* is suffused with images of the pictorial arts. The eponymous character is a sometime model, "she surpassed all other models ... and was equally unconscious of self with her clothes on or without!" (64). Du Maurier's proper English heroes are all visual artists—and all realist artists as well. Du Maurier faithfully represents their art: Sandy's "lifelike little picture of a Spanish toreador" (5); Taffy's "realisms (for Taffy was a realist)" (9); Billee's "funny little pen-and-ink sketches ... so lifelike, so real, that you could almost hear the beautiful things they said" (9).

In its focus on the graphic arts *Trilby* follows a pattern similar to that noted by Alison Byerly who observes that in George Eliot's novels "the association of individual characters with specific arts produces a moral hierarchy in which visual art is exposed as a detached and static simplification of reality, theatrical art is linked with a dangerous deception of self and others, and music alone is capable of representing truth" (10–11). Like Eliot,[17] Du Maurier creates a moral hierarchy of the arts, differing from Eliot, however, in his ranking of the art forms: Du Maurier valorizes the visual arts. In *Trilby,* the "good" characters are associated with the visual arts. Evil and decadence typify the musical arts and their most visible practitioners in the book: Svengali and his assistant, Gecko. Alison Byerly's reading helps to define Du Maurier's connection of music to moral turpitude by noting the contemporary association of music with the loss of self-possession: "The mesmeric control that Svengali has over Trilby's music in Du Maurier's novel is a late manifestation of the nineteenth-century cultural preoccupation with the idea of music as a kind of sexual hypnotism. The popular movements of mesmerism and spiritualism were both tangentially associated with music" (139).[18] Another way to account for Du Maurier's hierarchy is to contextualize it within the anti–Semitism that suffuses the novel. From the earliest times of the emancipation and assimilation of the Jews into European culture, Jewish contributions to the arts were more prominent in the musical world.[19] Du Maurier's elevation of the visual arts, the arts most distant from Jews, over the musical arts, the forms associated with the Jews,[20] and his moralization of this hierarchy is one of the strategies he deploys in discrediting his Jewish villain.

Artistic Possession and Dispossession

The thematic representation of art and artists in *Trilby* highlights issues of artistic possession and dispossession. Du Maurier emphasizes that Svengali's possession of Trilby's mind and her body is secondary to his possession of her singing voice and of her art. When we first hear Trilby sing, her performance is "grotesque" and "funny.... It was as though she could never once have deviated into tune, never once have hit upon a true note" (18). Upon becoming "La Svengali," Trilby's singing is the toast of Europe. That this transformation is the result of demonic power rather than effective voice tutoring is made eminently clear. As Gecko, Svengali's closest comrade, reveals in responding to Taffy's comment that Trilby was an artist, "'Yes! But all that was Svengali, you know. Svengali was the greatest artist I ever met! Monsieur, Svengali was a demon, a magician!'" (284). Possessed, Trilby is reduced to being a singing-machine—an instrument upon which Svengali plays, "the unconscious voice that Svengali sang with" (288).

Trilby is also rendered an object of possession through the graphic arts. Svengali is not the only character to decompose and fetishize Trilby's body in the name of art. Early in the novel little Billee, displaying his own (or Du Maurier's) fetishizing displacement of Trilby's sexuality, makes a drawing of one of Trilby's "astonishingly beautiful feet" (15), feet so perfect that "the shape of those lovely slender feet ... facsimiled in dusty plaster of Paris, survives on the shelves and walls of many a studio throughout the world" (15). Billee reveals his talent for realism in the rendering of Trilby's foot:

> In five minutes or so, with the point of an old compass, he scratched in white on the dark red wall a three-quarter profile outline of Trilby's left foot, which was perhaps the more perfect poem of the two. Slight as it was, this little piece of impromptu etching, in its sense of beauty, in its quick seizing of a peculiar individuality, its subtle rendering of a strongly received impression, was already the work of a master. It was Trilby's foot and nobody else's ... and nobody else but Little Billee could have drawn it in just that inspired way [20].

The drawing of Trilby's foot is a complex image, working at cross-purposes: it simultaneously represents the objectification of the woman and particularly the female model in art; however, it is also a symbol of resistance to the commodification of art.

The notion of art as commodity, as possession, dominates the discourse of art in this novel. The goal of the young struggling artists whom we first meet in Paris is the commercial success that Little Billee does finally achieve with his work:

> [The] famous canvas "The Pitcher Goes to the Well"... was sold three times over on the morning of the private view, the third time for a thousand pounds—just five times what he got for it himself.... I am well aware that such a vulgar test is no criterion, whatever of a picture's real merit. But this picture is well known to all the world by this time, and sold only last year at Christy's ... for three thousand pounds [139].

In the disclaimer of the narrator, we see a brief moment of authorial dispossession: although he wishes to project a higher set of values, it is clear that his valuation of Billee's work is determined by those thousands of pounds. This commodification—the process that dictates the removal of the art from its contexts and from the artist—is refused by Billie's drawing of Trilby's foot, the work of art that is defined by the individuality of the artist, the subject and the medium. The drawing cannot be commodified because it is drawn upon a wall and therefore cannot be sold and bought. It can only be appreciated *in situ*, that is, it cannot be deprived of what Walter Benjamin identifies as an essential element of the "authenticity" that distinguishes a work of art from a reproduction: "its presence in time and space, its unique existence at the place where it happens to be" (220). And so when the artists are "reunited in Paris...'cinq ans après'" the original events (184), they find "under a square of plate-glass that had been fixed on the wall by means of an oak frame, Little Billee's old black-and-white- and red-chalk sketch of Trilby's left foot, as fresh as if it had been done only yesterday! Over it was written: 'souvenir de la Grande Trilby, par W. B. (Litrebili)'" (192). This work of art, resistant to commodification and dispossession remains defined by context, artist (Litrebili is the French rendering of Little Billee) and subject. Yet Du Maurier shows his bias toward commodifiable art in the ultimate fate of the drawing: when the friends return to Paris once last time "vingt ans après" (275), the drawing has disappeared, a victim of progress: "Trilby's foot, and the poem, and the sheet of plate-glass have been improved away" (279). Du Maurier seems to suggest that unpossessible art—art that has no commercial value but only intrinsic artistic and emotional value—is not destined to endure.

Indeed Du Maurier provides a counter-image to the drawing of Trilby's foot that confirms the enduring power of commodifiable art: the commercially successful photograph of Trilby, produced at the height of the success of La Svengali. This photograph, like Billee's drawing, features Trilby's left foot:

> her photograph is in the shop-windows.... One of the photographs represents her in classical dress, with her left foot on a little stool, in something of the attitude of the Venus of Milo, except that her hands are clasped behind her back; and the foot is bare but for a Greek sandal, and so smooth and delicate and charm-

ing, and with so rhythmical a set and curl of the five slender toes (the big one slightly tip-tilted and well apart from its longer and slighter and more aquiline neighbour), that this presentment of her sells quicker than all the rest [233].

What is telling about the two images of Trilby's left foot is that the drawing, the individual work of art, resists commodification while the mechanically reproduced art, the image of Trilby's foot, welcomes commercial commodification and possession by the consumer. Whereas the drawing of Trilby's foot is inextricably connected to its creator, the photograph, whose dispossessed creator is unidentified and unknown, is most closely connected to the consumer. And whereas the unique and unsellable drawing disappears, the reproducible photograph endures.

※

Indeed the most powerful visual image in this novel of art and artists is a photograph of Svengali that mysteriously appears from beyond the grave. After the death of Svengali, as Trilby lingers on her deathbed, depleted by the sudden withdrawal of his artistic and psychic energies, she receives a mysterious package containing "a large photograph, framed and glazed of Svengali ... looking straight out of the picture, straight at you ... his big black eyes were full of stern command" (271).[21] The shock of the "you" is the first indication of the power of this photograph; until now, the reader has been politely addressed in the third person, as "the reader." Yet here not only is Trilby implicated in the glance of her mentor—and of course, Svengali's power in life has been located in the power of his gaze—so too, is the reader.

In this photograph we see the vexing and supernatural uncanniness of Svengali as well as his power. The identity of the photographer, who has captured Svengali's image, is unknown, and irrelevant. Instead, the photograph effaces the distinction between reality and artistic representation. The photograph is ultimately not a representation of Svengali, created by some unknown artist, but is Svengali himself, the undead Wandering Jew. Like Svengali, the photograph is of dubious Eastern origins and has wandered through Europe before arriving at its destination. "From the postmarks on the case, [the photograph] seems to have traveled all over Europe to London, out of some remote province in eastern Russia—out of the mysterious East! The poisonous East—birthplace and home of an ill wind that blows nobody good" (271). The photograph also erases its representational status by enacting Svengali's actual power over Trilby. Trilby speaks to the photograph, responding to it as if it were addressing her. As in life, the photograph of Svengali—as seen by Trilby although not by the narrator or the reader—commands her to sing. Addressing the mute photograph, Trilby asks it, "Encore une fois?" and responds, "Bon! Je veux bien! Avec la voix blanche alors," continuing in this vein, seemingly repeating the musical instructions that Svengali in his photographic form is conveying to her through his photographed yet still-powerful eyes.

The intrinsic power of the representation of Svengali is proved when Trilby begins to sing, not in her own feeble voice, but with the powerful voice that originates with Svengali: "there was enough of it to fill the room—to fill the house—to drown her small audience in holy, heavenly sweetness" (272). After her uncanny solo, Trilby speaks her last words before dying, again addressed to Svengali: "Et maintenant, mon ami, *je suis fatiguée—bon soir!*" and a final *"Svengali.... Svengali.... Svengali..."* (272), echoing, ventriloquistically, Svengali's early incantation (50). In her dying repetition of the spell that Svengali first uses in enacting his mesmeric powers over her, Trilby dies as she has lived, the empty vessel of Svengali's possessing voice. It is Svengali's troubling power that endures, mysteriously and supernaturally located in the photograph, the image that *should* operate as the containing icon of realism, that should reduce Svengali to an impotent object.

Roland Barthes suggests that the photograph is always troubling to a commercial culture, like the one Du Maurier endorses, because it disrupts the notion of ownership. "'Photography,' he says in *Camera Lucida*, is a 'disturbance (to civilization)'.... The disturbance is ultimately one of ownership" (Barthes cited by Michael North 1379).[22] The nature of photographic reproduction troubles the attribution of individual authorship that, as we have seen, is inherent in the notion of artistic possession of art: "In short, photography confronts authorship with autography ... the subject, in other words, inscribes itself on the film" (North 1379).[23]

This does seem to be the case in Svengali's photograph—although dead, he is the only visible agent of his powerful image. Indeed, the language that Barthes deploys to describe the experience of viewing photography is emblematized by the image of Svengali's photograph. Barthes writes "about being seized by photography. In his early essays he identifies a 'penetrating trait' in the photograph and associates this with the picture's 'obtuse meaning'" (North 1379). In this Barthes suggests the troubling inversion that occurs in the episode of Svengali's photograph. The picture, which should be the possessed and commodified object, becomes the subject, effecting possession upon its viewers—not only upon Trilby but upon the reader as well.

Realism and Photography

Nancy Armstrong's study *Fiction in the Age of Photography* works to account for the pervasiveness of realism—with its valorization of objective visual representation—during the late nineteenth century, as exemplified by the primacy of the visual arts in *Trilby*, and also helps to explain the power of Svengali's photograph. Armstrong connects the nineteenth-century move toward literary realism with "the sudden ubiquity of photographic images in the culture at large" (6).[24] The rise of photography during the period of Victorian fiction, she suggests, changed the terms of meaning from the word to the image: "'the image'—or more accurately, a differential system thereof—supplanted writing as the grounding of fiction" (3). Literary realism prevailed, within Armstrong's paradigm, because it "referenced a world of objects that either had been or could be photographed ... [supplying readers] ... with [the] kinds of visual information" (7) for which they had developed a desire by virtue of the dominance of the visual image in popular culture. Hence the move to realism: a "fiction [that] equated seeing with knowing and made visual information the basis for the intelligibility of a verbal narrative" (7).

The uncanny power of Svengali's photograph lies in its violation of the realist equation of seeing with knowing; it violates the terms of possession of art, commercially and epistemologically. Svengali's final appearance, re-incarnated as the photograph that exerts his now-explicitly uncanny power, reveals the coalescing of new fears anchored by old anxieties. We see the new fear engendered by the new medium of reproduction, the photograph, evidencing a concern that this new technology might be used to replicate evil beyond death. And yet, this new set of concerns is encoded in a traditional topic, the Wandering Jew, whose evil evades death. Du Maurier presents the fear of his times that the photographic image is a ghost of sorts that—like more archaic ghosts—threatens to extend their haunting possession of the living.

In the image of the photograph Du Maurier deploys the transgressive figure of the uncanny Jew—the figure that already vexes the problem of genre and category—to complicate questions regarding the relationship between representation and reality that haunt the realist tradition and that are amplified by photography. How can representation capture and reenact reality without losing its privileged status as art? How can a literary mode that valorizes the actual exist as a literary mode at all unless it creates, through convention and artifice, some separation from reality? As a consequence of these questions, the realist text is always a little unstable, a little inconsistent, struggling to maintain its own status as art. Additionally, realism must maintain its own generic identity by fending off the excesses of its predecessor, Romantic literature, keeping at bay the messy complications—structural, tonal and topical—of the Gothic.[25] The realistic project of the late-nineteenth century is also complicated by the imperatives of a competing form: the sensation novel, a more direct descendant of the Gothic.[26] As a result, the late Victorian realist writer struggles to accomplish generic definition and containment, resulting in a focus upon boundaries—generic and otherwise—that is paradoxically opposed to the realistic project. Thus realism, although claiming an unmediated encounter with reality, needs to embrace the boundaries of art, turning to the limits of art like plot and closure to reflect a reality that lacks the form and order of art.[27]

The self-imposed order of realism, then, forces the realist writer to exclude some realities from the text including all transcendent and extranatural planes that are deemed "unrealistic" by post–Enlightenment imperatives including the divine and the supernatural. As we see from the attempt of the author and the characters to abject Svengali from *Trilby*, not only is God exiled from the realist text, the Devil too—that favorite Gothic character—is dispossessed from the man-made Paradise in which there is no place for transcendent good or evil. And yet, though the realistic text can only account for human evil, the repressed notion of transcendent morality insists on emerging, even more startlingly transgressive against the realistic background. Thus Du Maurier attempts a naturalizing displacement with the figure of Svengali: he introduces transcendent evil into the text in the figure of the Satanic Jew while at the same time containing this evil within the bounds of realism.

Political Realism: The Naturalized Uncanny Jew

Even the presence of the supernaturally villainous Jew is not as big a threat to the realism of novel as it might initially seem, for the uncanny figure of the evil Jew was already naturalized within political and cultural discourse of Du Maurier's time. Due to the process of assimilation the Jew was no longer visibly identifiable as the Other. The process of Emancipation allowed the Jew to invisibly infiltrate realms previously open only to Christians, posing a dangerous threat of social invasion. The figure of the Satanic Jew was the ideal solution to this particular Jewish Problem. Framed as Satan, the quintessential identifiable Other, the Jew was less able to secretly infiltrate and disrupt categories. The figure of Satan endures thus as a post-theological means to identify and thereby contain that elusive Jewish Other, the people who are "*inclassable*, outside the natural hierarchy of races, beyond the human pale. Not even a race strictly speaking (since they were 'unnatural'), perverse, demonic, the intrinsically evil 'other'—in a word, the Jews [who] were the Devil incarnate in human form" (Wistrich 3). Thus, the figure of the Jew as Satan became a practical utilitarian solution to a political and social problem. In the actual world inhabited by George Du Maurier, there was nothing at all unnatural in figuring the Jew as Satan. This trope informed contemporary political discourse and action including the rhetoric and graphic images associated with the Dreyfus Affair that rocked France, beginning in the same year (1894) as *Trilby* was published. The basis of this scandal was the false accusations of treason lodged against Captain Alfred Dreyfus, a young French artillery officer of Jewish descent.[28] Although Dreyfus was eventually cleared, his defenders had to oppose the cultural assumptions that dehumanized the Jew, refusing to accept him as a human being who could be fully integrated into French society. In the unfolding of the Dreyfus Affair it is possible to see the political use of the trope of the Satanic Jew. Wistrich notes, "the myth of the all-powerful Jew ... acquired a new lease on life: so did the medieval fantasies of the Jew as Antichrist, agent of Satan and corruptor of morals. The traitor Dreyfus [was construed] as a reincarnation of Judas" (9). The mechanics of the Dreyfus Affair demonstrate the naturalization of the demonization of the Jew in nineteenth-century Europe, the translation of millennia of theological and literary tropology into quasi-normative political discourse.

It is this construct that Du Maurier references when he creates a monstrously diabolic Jew to inhabit his realistic novel. In the figure of Svengali, Du Maurier creates a seemingly realistic reflection of the political and social sensibilities of his time and place. In constructing the Jew as demonic Other, Du Maurier relies less on artifice than on convention, less on creation than on mimesis. Because the Devil had been neutralized by the Enlightenment and because the trope of Jew as Devil had been naturalized by long use in the theological, political and social worlds, the presence of Svengali, the Satanic Jew, does not immediately seem to vex the realism of the text that frames him; Du Maurier appears to accomplish a neat balancing act, managing to adhere to the imperatives of realism while simultaneously injecting his text with a whiff of the sensational and always entertaining "uncanny" (201, Du Maurier's word). Just as the British types or stereotypes convey a realistic portrait of expatriate artists in the Paris of *la vie bohème*, so does Du Maurier's portrait of Svengali draw upon the accepted tropology of the Jew, invoking the strategies of realism and the contexts of history to naturalize and encode the figure of supernatural, transcendent evil—to create a realistic representation of the Jewish Devil, the figure of the Other contained by realism, and by the realistic text.

Dispossession by the Repressed

Yet, the model of absolute supernatural evil—and the character who emblematizes it—ultimately dislocates *Trilby* from the realist tradition and relocates it into the Gothic tradition, where the essential struggle is often between human good and supernatural evil.[29] Although Du Maurier arranges for a public and realistic death for Svengali—sitting in his box at the theater while Trilby performs—Svengali returns, as the wandering photograph, but also as a character who simply refuses to die.

A final irony of *Trilby*, a text that considers issues of personal and artistic possession and dispossession is that it reflexively enacts the authorial dispossession of its writer. The figure of Svengali ultimately destabilizes the realism of Du Maurier's text thereby dispossessing the authority of its author to generically determine his own novel. Although Du Maurier relies on history and tradition to naturalize his representation of the Satanic Jew, rendering it safely and acceptably realistic, the very process of demonization relocates his text to the realm of darkness and horror. The supernatural power of the demonized Jew, allows Svengali to wrest control of the narrative from the author; the novel veers off the realist path, into the Gothic tradition, and thence, into near-oblivion.[30]

The seemingly realistic Jewish musician, who is actually the emblem of supernatural evil, also wanders away from the possession of his creator. As the memory of *Trilby* fades from the popular imagination, so does the connection of Svengali to his creator: Svengali now exists floating freely in the popular culture. Loosed of all bonds to his originating text, Du Maurier's Satanic Jew seems an "autograph," a character who has created himself, as he seems to have created his own photograph.

The Haunting Gothic Text

The consistently transgressive English Gothic mode, the mode that resists readerly containment and apprehension, thus resists writerly possession as well.[31] We can certainly say that the texts of *Trilby* and *Melmoth*—and their authors—are possessed by the ghosts of the Gothic,[32] as are the many other narratives that revisit Gothic methods and concerns.

In fact, the Gothic dispossession of texts encourages us to recognize that all narrative is haunted, possessed by the voices of the dead. Dickens spooks us with a reminder of our haunted readerly state in "A Christmas Carol" when he narrates: "Scrooge ... found himself face to face with the unearthly visitor [the ghost] who drew them [the bed curtains]: as close to it as I am now to you, and I am standing in the spirit at your elbow" (27)[33]—try reading that passage at night in a lonely house. As Dickens suggests, we readers are all haunted, conjuring up and possessed by the voices of disembodied writers.[34]

PART IV

Beyond the End

Dispossessing Closure

15

"It is only the theory I want"

Repossessing Fiction in Sarah Waters's Affinity

It is January 1875. Margaret, the protagonist of a Victorian Gothic novel is alone in her room, contemplating suicide. We know that she has no other option as she has been dispossessed of everything: money and clothes, identity, the plot she has carved out for her future happiness; her diary has been invaded by the gaze of another. Like Du Maurier's *Trilby*, she has been displaced through the power of mesmerism. In fact, we encounter all that we might expect in a Victorian novel, except that this novel is Sarah Waters's neo-Victorian *Affinity*, published more than one hundred years after *Trilby*, in 1999.

The preoccupation of the English Gothic with issues of possession endures through the twentieth century and into the twenty-first, as may be confirmed with a glance through the *oeuvre* of Sarah Waters, whose recent Gothic novels, including the neo-Victorian *Affinity* (1999) and *Fingersmith* (2002), present a panoply of moments of Gothic possession and dispossession. The origins of the neo-Victorian novel[1] can be identified in the 1960s with the publication of Jean Rhys's *Wide Sargasso Sea* (1960) and John Fowles's *The French Lieutenant's Woman* (1969); a more recent example is Michel Faber's *The Crimson Petal and the White* (2002). Featuring a re-enactment of the Victorian novel, often with allusions to specific nineteenth-century texts, the neo-Victorian mode adds layers of post-modern consciousness and self-consciousness and offers a rich new stage for the Gothic tradition, suggesting yet again the transformative power of the English Gothic that allows it to endure through the centuries.[2]

Like other Gothic texts, from the inception of the mode, the neo-

Victorian locates itself in a distant benighted past—as the Victorian surely appears from our brightly-lit vantage point—using the past to examine concerns, often concerns surrounding issues of possession, that are actually contemporary to the writer and primary readers of the text.[3] *Fingersmith*, Waters's breath-taking revision of Wilkie Collins's *The Woman in White*, revisits issues of possession of self as well as possession of property and the narrative.[4] But in *Affinity* Waters outdoes herself. This novel, which traces the ultimate and complete dispossession of Margaret, a bookish Victorian spinster, almost obligingly illustrates the familiar Gothic preoccupation with possessions of property, self and narrative.

(Dis)Possession of Property

In keeping with its Victorian setting, the property that is purloined in *Affinity* is not real estate, although as we shall see, the novel does feature a big haunted pile. In fact, Waters's Gothic reflects the typically acute awareness of the situation of property and the female property owner in its world. The material property accurately takes the form of commodities and capital, and Waters, in proper Gothic fashion, takes the time to establish the legal status of the property in question, especially toward the end of the book, when Margaret is unknowingly being divested of her material possessions. Thinking that she is plotting an escape with Selina, an incarcerated spiritualist with whom she is in love, Margaret works to liquidate her assets. For a woman centered in the spirit world, Selina displays a surprising awareness of the economic foundation of things. The moment the women begin to hatch their apparent elopement, Selina says to Margaret: "You must have money of your own. There must be things that you might sell" (274). Selina's plan to be spirited from a prison cell to Margaret's bedroom is based in some inchoate way upon Margaret's desire—"You need only want me, and I will come" (287). Yet Selina recognizes that to get to Italy, they will "need tickets ... for the train and the boat. We shall need passport papers" (286). Selina tells Margaret that she should "visit my bank and draw from it as much money as I can" (298), ensuring an accumulation of capital that Selina can then steal when she absconds with Ruth Vigers, her actual lover, leaving Margaret behind in possession only of the books that are of no value to Selina or Ruth. Selina and Ruth thus reflect (except in gender) all the old Gothic villains, the Montonis, the Foscos, who come to the Gothic text buttressed by the legal knowledge and power that will ensure the successful dispossession of their victim. Once again we see the

Gothic conflation of the world of the impossible with the world of the practical.

Like her Gothic predecessors, Margaret is attractive to her seducers, sadly, not because of her personal charms but because of her economic assets. Waters precisely delineates the economic situation of her character; Margaret turns to her brother-in-law, "'I should like you to explain to me the business of Mother's money and of mine ... the income I should have" (289). She discovers that—like most desirable women in the Gothic—there is an economic basis for her desirability: "You too, Margaret, are wealthy, quite in your own right" (290). Waters takes the time to provide the practical and economic details. Margaret goes to the bank and gets her own money, although, as a woman, she lacks the spirit of capitalist entitlement: "*thirteen hundred pounds....* It is my own money, and yet I felt like a thief" (302). She goes "to Waterloo, to purchase tickets for the tidal train; and then I went to Victoria, to the Traveller's Office" (303) for passports. Waters carefully reflects the legal reality of Victorian England in 1874, which we know is the time of Margaret's attempted escape, from her numerous diary entries. Margaret learns that she has money left to her by her father "that is securely mine.—'Unless, of course ... you marry'" (291). Waters thus reminds us that until the passage of the Married Women's Property Act of 1882, a woman like Margaret would have forfeited her property to her husband under the system of coverture.

And sadly, Margaret, though still unmarried, is divested of her material goods by the two schemers. At the end, Margaret discovers that "She had taken everything, except the books" (339): Margaret's own "gowns and coat, and hats and boots and gloves and brooches ... and, of course, the clothes I bought Selina. And she has the money, and the tickets, and the passports marked *Margaret Prior* and *Marian Earle*" (340). This theft, more than any other aspect of the betrayal, drives Margaret's thinking and action when she first discovers the plot. "*I have been robbed*, I thought, *by my own servant!*" (342). Decomposed she runs to a policeman, "I said I had been robbed ... two women, with my clothes on them!" (343), growing silent only when she realizes that she herself is deeply implicated in the plot to help a prisoner escape from jail. Margaret's reaction suggests the power of material possessions and the dislocating nature of dispossession that robs her of the things that define her: her clothes, her jewels, her papers. And so it is not entirely surprising to see that at this moment of profound loss and betrayal, the moment at which the foundation of Margaret's life and her future has been stolen, she is fixated upon the *things* that are the least of her losses.

Possession of Self

Waters reminds us that identity is inextricably bound up with material possessions; as we have seen in so many Gothic texts, who we are determines what we own and *vice versa*. In stealing her papers and her clothes, Ruth Vigers clearly plans to steal Margaret's identity, travelling under her name, with her tickets, and also taking Margaret's anticipated place in Selina's bed and life. Yet, Ruth is also re-appropriating her ownership of her own self, of which she was dispossessed by the Victorian class system—as indicated in Margaret's notion of Ruth being her "*own servant*" (342). Ruth's dispossession of Margaret inverts the relationship and quite compellingly proves to Margaret that Ruth, although a servant is not a possessed object.

Indeed, *Affinity* is suffused by moments and images that reflect and dispute the possibilities of self-possession and of the possession of others: body, mind, or spirit. The dominant image of physical possession, confinement, links the novel most directly to the Gothic tradition, which Waters updates to reflect the time and place of her novel. Millbank Prison, "so solid and so antique" (7) that it seems eternal to Margaret, directly evokes the old confining structures of the Gothic tradition. In the past it featured a dry trench like "the moat of a castle, with a drawbridge" (60). The prison contains its own Gothic dungeon. A punishment room lies "below the level of the Thames itself … [through] several antique wooden doors" (179). Each wall "hung with iron-with rings and chains and fetters" (180). It is "a ghastly chamber" (180), "our chain-room, where we keep our shackles, jackets and the like," to which Margaret responds with appropriately old-fashioned "horror" (179). Like a Gothic convent the prison contains a "cloister-like passage, that held the cells" (18); each cell is as "bare" as a nun's, containing little more than "a Bible and a religious book: *The Prisoner's Companion*" (19). It is, recalling its older name, a "penitentiary" (60), in which confinement and solitude are to yield to penance. And yet, Millbank is closer to the dungeon than to the convent in its present philosophy. As a matron says to Margaret: "We are not here to help them, ma'am. We are here to punish them" (207). As in the case of its Gothic predecessors, those hoary representations of social power whose destruction is imagined in the closure of the typical Gothic text, the demise of Millbank Prison is also prophesized. The old Porter predicts, "She'll come down one day, I am certain of it, and take the lot of us with her! Or else, this wicked earth that they have set her in will give one great swaller, and we'll all go down like that" (313).

In typical Gothic tradition, the central structure of the text reflects the power of its times. Unlike the pre-modern Castle and Church of the earlier Gothic, that represent the powers of State or Church run amok, Waters's structure reflects the reasoned law and order of Victorian times; it is a prison, used to punish behavior that breaches the social norm, murder and theft, yes, but also behaviors like attempted suicide and abortion that are also criminalized by Margaret's well-regulated Victorian world, "your poisoners, your vitriol-throwers, your child-murderers ... the thieves and prostitutes and counterfeiters" (15).[5] This confining structure "is not charming. Its scale is vast, and its lines and angles ... seem only wrong or perverse." To Margaret, the prison seems designed by "a man in the grip of a nightmare or madness—or had been made expressly to *drive* its inmates mad" (8).

Nor is Millbank Prison the only confining space in Waters's novel. In typical Gothic fashion, the theme of physical confinement—of loss of possession of the body by the prisoner—is doubled by the situation of Margaret, confined to the space of her room, her "own dark cell" (274), in which she, a proper woman is imprisoned by the domestic space of her home. Like prisoners of Millbank, Margaret is also the cynosure of the confining gaze. She knows that her mother is observing her closely, as the matrons watch their prisoners: "she has been watching me, as Miss Ridley watches, and Miss Haxby" (223).[6] Like Selina, the prisoner of Millbank, confined to her enclosed space, Margaret dreams of escape from her warden, her mother, who entraps her in the role of the proper Victorian woman.

Questions of possession of the body also arise in *Affinity* through Waters's incorporation of the practices of nineteenth spiritualism into her plot.[7] The crimes for which Selina has been imprisoned—the assault of one lady, and the death of another—are tied to her claims that she connects to the spiritual realm with the assistance of her familiar, a spirit named Peter Quick. Waters destabilizes certainties of self-possession through the theme of spiritualism in a number of ways. As a spiritualist, Selina loses her self-possession to the spirits, who speak to her clients through her— "Usually a spirit would speak through me" (144)—that is the spirit would possess her. In fact Mrs. Brink's desire for Selina to bring her the spirit of her mother would entail a full renunciation by Selina of herself: "She required me to give up my own flesh, for the spirit-world to use it for itself" (164).

Eventually, the reality begins to dawn upon the reader, if not upon Selina's clients, or even the lawyers who prosecute her case, as Waters explicitly conflates spiritual and sexual possession. What Selina presents as spiritual help is actually quite physical, and indeed, sexual. At the trial,

Madeleine's mother testifies: "I had hopes that Miss Dawes might be able to assist in restoring my daughter to a proper state of health.... Miss Dawes persuaded me that the condition had its origins as a spiritual ailment, rather than a physical one" (137). Miss Dawes's statements notwithstanding, it becomes clear that Selina, and Peter, help the hysterical young girls who compose their client base by offering them sexual release. After the episode which leads to Selina's incarceration, she reports in her diary: "Madeleine had marks upon her & when the doctor saw those his voice grew quiet & he said this was queerer business than he thought" (3).[8] And Selina reports to Madeleine's mother that "my daughter had been roughly handed by a male spirit" (139). Margaret reads in testimony from Selina's trial: "Some ladies found this influence beneficial in the alleviation of certain indispositions and complaints.... Symptoms such as ... weakness, nervousness, and aches" (145). The treatment involved "laying on of hands.... Rubbing and shampooing ... for which ... visitors were required to remove certain articles of clothing" (145).

And yet, the knowing Selina is possessed no less than the innocent Madeleine. And Selina's possession by Peter is clearly also sexual as well as spiritual. We initially meet Peter Quick as Selina's possessing "guardian, her familiar-spirit ... her *control*" (166). Selina tells Margaret, "He came for me.... I was his" (166). Selina's description of Peter's possession makes clear to the reader, though not to the innocent Margaret, the sexual nature of this spiritual relationship. When Margaret asks, "What was it like, when he came to you?" Selina responds, "It was like losing her self, like having her own self pulled from her" (166). At some point, when the reader figures out that Peter Quick is actually Ruth, the reader comes to understand that what Selina is really talking about is being sexually possessed by Ruth.

As Selina suggests the tragedy of being physically and sexually possessed by another, Margaret demonstrates the mirrored tragedy of being dispossessed of oneself; as she moves through the novel she is divested not only of her property, and her identity, but of her reason and sanity, and ultimately her hold upon her own life. The very title of Waters's novel, *Affinity*, taps into the trope of the double which so often correlates to the destabilizing of the integrity of individual identity. When Margaret hears of Selina's seeming isolation, her lack of a "pal" in prison, she thinks: "*you are like me*" (82). Selina manipulates Margaret's sense of her own isolation, of her singlehood, and offers the possibility of affinity to Margaret, a Victorian spinster who has previously yearned for another woman. Selina offers Margaret the possibility of spiritual love, transcending the limiting binary of physical sexuality that has been so painful for Margaret. When it comes to gender, "'the spirits are neither, and both'" (210). Nor is true spiritual love dependent upon the gendered body: "'Did you think there must be here, a man with whiskers, and over here, a lady in a gown?'" (210). Selina proposes a non-sexual, non-physical "affinity" (210) of one soul for another. What Selina is offering to Margaret, in what is ultimately a seduction, is the possibility of Margaret following her lesbian tendencies and coming to love Selina herself. Indeed, as Margaret's identity and sanity unravel, with the help of the doses of laudanum and chloral hydrate she consumes, she does lose sight of the boundary between herself and Selina. On discovering Selina's "curling rope of yellow hair" on her pillow, at first she "thought I saw *my own head* there, above the sheet" (258).

The notion of affinity provides Selina, the spiritualist, with her seductive power in more than one instance. Mrs. Brink, yearning for her long-dead mother, is drawn by "the likeness between her mother" and Selina; Selina identifies "a—a sympathy" (165) between them.[9] In Selina's loving words to her, "'What's the matter, Aurora?'" Margaret hears an echo of "the voice of Helen," (187) her first love, who first "gave me" (114) the name. Of course, Margaret's use of the name Aurora, from the heroine of Elizabeth Barrett Browning is another doubling, or halving, that chips away at her own personal integrity, moving toward the eventual loss of her self.

Narrative Dispossession

In keeping with the always allusive and repetitive Gothic tradition, Waters's novel contests the boundaries of textual integrity that keep one text from bleeding into another; *Affinity* displays the obsessive textual doubling, references to other texts, that makes the Gothic canon appear like a house of mirrors to the reader who enters. Waters's protagonist, bookish woman that she is, has a tendency to see herself within the context of literary characters.[10] Perhaps hoping for a bit of adventure in a very flat life, she wonders if like the villains in "Mr Le Fanu's novel about the heiress who is made to seem mad Mother is in league with Mr. Shillitoe, and he means to keep me on the [prison] wards, bewildered" (29) Margaret chooses the pet name by which both Helen and Selina call her, Aurora, from Barrett Browning's *Aurora Leigh*. The name Margaret chooses as Selina's escape alias is "Marian Earle," from the same poem. Similarly, romantic Margaret chooses the "twentieth of January, St. Agnes' Eve" (299) as the night of her escape with Selina. In a moment that is perhaps a warning of the inability of Selina to respond truly to Margaret, Selina displays a complete ignorance of Keats and everything that he might mean. Margaret, blind to all except that within a book, represses her "dismay" and "fear," asking herself: "Who was there ever, to teach her things like that?" (300).

Not all the allusions emanate from the book-drenched depths of Margaret's mind. Some allusions are less visible, as Waters directly plants some them in the narrative, to be discovered by the reader. When Margaret visits the prison kitchen, she learns that the food for the women inmates comes from the men's prison. Margaret hears the men and has "a sudden vision then of the men as *goblin* men with snouts and tails and whiskers," evoking the goblin men of Christina Rossetti's *Goblin Market* (1869) who provided their toxic food to the heroines of the poem. Or, should we conjecture whether Margaret (writing in 1874) is thinking of the Rossetti poem, and is this another moment where we see Margaret's tendency to repress eros? Dickens's *Bleak House* also seems to haunt Waters's novel. Margaret—"I … feel myself a ghost at Cheyne Walk" (307)—seems to recollect the Ghost Walk at Dickens's Chesney Wold, and the ghost whose return signals bad fortune to the family. As Ann Heilman points out in "The Haunting of Henry James: Jealous Ghosts, Affinities and *The Others*," *Affinity* also evokes that modern ghost story, Henry James's *The Turn of the Screw*. The most visible link between the two texts is the name of Selina's destructive spirit, Peter Quick, which points to the villainous ghost of *Turn*, Peter Quint. Heilmann notes Peter Quint's "deviant libidinousness in a novel about an hysteric lesbian awakening and in her own twists of the screw" (112). Certainly both texts feature erotic triangulation and shift back and forth between a world in which the supernatural is possible, and a reality in which madness and illusion prevail.[11]

There is at least one more textual haunting of *Affinity* that seems inescapable to the reader of *The Woman in White*, which is certainly an urtext for *Fingersmith*: the shocking invasion of the diary of Marian in Collins's novel by the evil Fosco is doubled in *Affinity* by the equally shocking invasion of Margaret's diary, by the apparently equally evil and servile Vigers, household servant of Margaret and her mother. Waters makes it clear that Margaret's journal is an essential component of her identity. That book, she tells Selina, "was like my dearest friend. I told it all my closest thoughts, and it kept them secret" (111). It is clear that Margaret's book offers her an intimacy and autonomy denied her by her family and society. When Margaret's mother interrupts a conversation—"'You mustn't let Margaret tell you prison stories, Helen'"— Margaret turns to her journal: "If I many not talk of my visit, then I can certainly sit and write about it, in my own book." Yet, as the reader and Margaret find out, the diary will betray her, just as Selina does. Margaret's book as her place of sanctuary renders Vigers's invasion all the more intrusive.

Margaret's journal begins on September 24, 1874, synchronized with the beginning of her visits to Millbank: "the story I have embarked upon to-day" (8). The last dated entry is for January 21, 1875 (322) and traces Margaret's discovery that Selina will not be coming to her from the prison. A last undated entry, presumably from the same day—"I cannot say what time it is" (349)—tells of the burning of the journal: "All my book is burned now … and when this sheet is filled with staggering lines it shall be added to the others" (348). Margaret adds: "How queer, to write for chimney smoke!" (348), and yet her compulsion to write the last page seems accounted for in her sense of invasion. "I thought of this book, where I wrote all my secrets—all my passion, all my love" (339), all read by Ruth. She thinks of "the smears of Vigers' gaze upon the pages, sticky and white" (348). Only the final page will be free of Vigers's gaze; it represents Margaret's pathetic attempt to maintain some autonomy. In fact, Margaret's journal is doubled. As she explains to Selina, she keeps two records. She keeps a note-book with her, and takes it "with me wherever I go … what I wrote in it I sometimes later put into another book, that was my diary" (111). It is into this note-book that Selina writes her name with Margaret's acquiescence, another moment of textual intimacy: Selina trembles as she holds the pen; "a glistening bead of ink welled at its nib" (113). Of course, Selina is already betraying Margaret, as the next thing she writes, a note for Margaret to read later, alludes to a locket that the spirits have presumably taken, but which has, in fact, been stolen by Vigers.

Margaret's doubled diary is additionally doubled by Selina's journal, which presents a parallel narrative. Selina's diary provides the opening and closing frames of the novel, which begins confusingly with an entry dated August 3, 1873. In it Selina retails the events of her downfall with Mrs. Brink and Madeleine that led to her incarceration, although to the reader this hectic narrative is almost meaningless at this early moment. After this entry, Selina's diary recommences with an entry dated September 2, 1872. Selina's entries then take us up until August 1, 1873, right before things fall apart for her and her spiritualist schemes, with the inadvertent death of Mrs. Brink, and the seeming assault of Madeleine. Waters sets up the two diaries of Selina and Margaret to demonstrate a curious textual permeability, illustrating, perhaps, the affinity that Selina promotes, as well as textual instability. Thus, when Margaret's diary ends with her conjectures upon just meeting Selina—"I wonder what her name is?" (30)— Selina's diary picks up on the very next page with her practice inscriptions: "Selina Dawes

/ Selina Ann Dawes / Miss S. A. Dawes" (31), all directly answering Margaret's privately written question.

Waters's disputation of the integrity of the text makes a strong case for the dispossession of the authority of the writer of the text, enlarging upon the systematic interrogation of the possibilities of any possession in the English Gothic text. In fact *Affinity* accommodates itself to an array of critical approaches beyond the focus of this discussion of possession and dispossession. Most notably, Waters sets up her novel to illustrate two major critical paradigms: Michel Foucault's notion of the panopticon and Terry Castle's notion of the "apparitional lesbian." Making full use of the strategies of fiction, Waters fleshes out these two scholarly images to create a spectacular novel of ideas.

Sarah Waters's Panopticon

As Margaret follows the matron down into the "lower, drearier wards" of Millbank, scholar that she is, she feels "like Dante, following Virgil into Hell" (28). But even at this early point of the novel, the contemporary scholar will be tending toward another point of reference, Foucault's panopticon. It is clear that Waters imagines her prison as an example of that humanly demonic structure. Millbank prison, made up of a series of pentagons surrounding a "hexagon-shaped building at the prison's middle" (8), derives its power from panopticonism. The inmates are trapped by their constant visibility; Miss Haxby is the "argus of the gaol" (11). On Margaret's first visit, she climbs a "spiral staircase that wound upwards through a tower ... set at the centre of the pentagon yards" (10). From the office at the top of the tower, she is shown "the three earth yards, each separated from its neighbor by a high brick wall that ran, like the spoke on a cart-wheel, from the governess's tower" (13). From this all-encompassing vantage point, Margaret can see the women prisoners: "They spilled in the yards and formed three great elliptical loops" (14), bodies controlled ocularly machine-like in space. Inside their cells, too, the prisoners are pinned by visibility. Each cell features "a vertical iron flap which can be opened at any time ... and the prisoner viewed ... the women term it *the eye*" (23). This new form of Foucauldian dungeon, the penitentiary, thus encloses and invades, trapping the body within the focal point of the gaze, ensuring that the body is subject to the control of the state, punishing the subject for transgressing the laws of the state.

Those of us who have read Foucault's *Discipline and Punish* (1975) might be startled by the *uncanny* resemblance of Water's structure to Foucault's panopticon, or to be more accurate, the panopticon of Jeremy Bentham, the nineteenth-century utilitarian philosopher whose structure inspired Foucault's notion of panopticism. Foucault's description of the structure could serve as a model for Millbank Prison, its double: "At the centre, a tower; this tower is pierced with wide windows that open onto the inner side of the ring; the peripheric building is divided into cells.... By the effect of backlighting, once can observe from the tower ... the small captive shadows in the cells of the periphery.... In short, it reversed the principle of the dungeon.... Visibility is a trap" (Foucault 200).

A number of critics readily accept Waters's overt offer to explore the panopticon of Millbank. Rebecca Pohl connects the structure of the panopticon with the labyrinth, an evocative way to represent any Gothic structure and narrative. In "Victorian Panopticon: Confined Spaces and Imprisonment in Chosen Neo-Victorian Novels," Barbara Braid notes the replication of the space of the panopticon in the domestic space of the novel: "The house as a domestic space seems to be also a place of restriction" (77)—perhaps no longer the most original insight regarding the Gothic novel. Kym Brindle takes a more original tack, noting that Margaret is also subject to surveillance in her prison-home: "Vigers operates from the central tower of the panoptic mechanism that fixes Margaret so completely (71); Vigers is "the ghost in the panoptic machine" (76).

The Appearance of the Apparitional Lesbian

Even more scholars are drawn to Waters's limning out of the figure identified by Terry Castle in *The Apparitional Lesbian: Female Homosexuality and Modern Culture* (1993). In her extraordinarily original and influential work Castle argues that traditionally any character that suggested lesbian tendencies was repositioned as a ghostly figure, not of the material world, not fully human. Castle presents the example of Olive in James's *The Bostonians* who "undergoes there a strange bodily and psychic etiolation, becoming paler and paler, weaker and weaker, until on the last page she seems to disappear altogether" (7). Castle outlines the logic of this process: "Once the lesbian has been defined as ghostly ... she can be exorcized.... The spectral lesbian is ultimately expelled from the 'real' world of the fiction" (6–7). Yet, as Castle recognizes, the writer can also make use of the convention of supernatural spectralization to revive the figure, a method unavailable to a material, realistic form: "The dead are indeed brought to life; the absent loved one returns" (46). Ultimately Castle turns to psychoanalytic theory to identify the Freudian underpinnings of all Gothic returns: "One might think of lesbianism as the 'repressed idea' at the heart of patriarchal culture.... One might go so far as to argue ... that patriarchal ideology necessarily depends on the 'compulsory' suppression of love between women" (61–62). Indeed, the patriarchy does depend on the propagation of the dynasty through heterosexuality. From this perspective, homosexuality aligns itself closely with the Gothic project of dispossession, destabilizing the certainties of power and ownership. Castle identifies the influence of the apparitional lesbian on twentieth-century literature:

> The haunted nature of modern lesbian writing attests directly, I think, to the process by which lesbianism itself has entered into the imaginative life of the West over the past two centuries.... Twentieth-century lesbian writers have been able for the most part to ignore the negative backdrop against which she has traditionally (de)materialized. By calling her back to passionate, imbricated life ... they have succeeded in transforming her ... to an affirming presence [64–66].

It is difficult, perhaps, *not* to see *Affinity* as a fictional response to Castle's theory. Castle presents her book on the apparitional lesbian as a kind of séance calling up the ghost, making visible the invisible, calling back a "worldly being" (16), the human lesbian. Waters responds with a novel about spiritualists and séances and lesbians who are humanized and lesbians who are spectralized. And what better fictional space for the resurrection of an apparition than a Gothic novel? For the English Gothic novel, marginalized and subversive, has had a long affinity for queerness, both lesbian and gay, from the moment the closeted Horace Walpole began the tradition with a story of dark secrets revealed. In *Queering the Gothic*, William Hughes and Andrew Smith, who trace the queer subtext of the Gothic from its inception in the eighteenth century, assert in their introduction, "Gothic has, in a sense, always been 'queer'" (1) meaning unstable, non-normative, transgressive and a source of anxiety to the patriarchy, with its dependence on certainty, fixity and possession.

Margaret the repressed, silent, spinster, amply fills the role of Castle's spectralized lesbian. Speaking to Helen, who has denied their old relationship and move to a heterosexual marriage, Margaret says, "Don't go too near the bed! Don't you know it's haunted, by our old kisses" (204). Margaret does indeed follow the trajectory noted by Castle in nineteenth-century literature as she moves through repression toward spectralization and presumable suicide at the end of the novel. Conversely, Selina and Ruth follow the pattern of the twentieth-century literary lesbian anticipated by Castle; each is metaphorically revived from the dead. Selina—in a re-enactment of the old Gothic standby, release from premature burial—escapes from prison. Ruth, the practically anonymous servant woman, also escapes from a prison, the prison of servitude. This connection is enhanced when Margaret visits Ruth's room at the end of the novel: "a room that held *nothing*, like the cells at Millbank" (341). Indeed, Selina is being uncharacteristically honest when she says to Margaret, "Peter is in as dark a place as I am ... only waiting—quite like me—to serve his term out and move on" (85). Ruth has been waiting to complete her term of employment as Selina waits to complete her prison term. As they escape together, Ruth is reborn into her fully realized identity: the strong, dominant, lover of Selina, sweeping her off to a lifetime of love in Italy.

Nor is Waters's fulfillment of Castle's theoretical paradigm lost on the critical community. In fact, scholarly writing on the lesbian in *Affinity* is haunted by the apparition of Terry Castle. Mark Llewellyn, Paulina Palmer, Lucie Armitt, Sarah Gamble, Demelza Hall, Kym Brindle, Rachel Carroll, Sarah Parker and Ann Heilmann—all turn to the apparitional lesbian in their accounting of Margaret. As the outpouring of critical literature indicates, as Waters follows Foucault to the letter, replicating Foucault's image in her novel, so she quite closely follows Castle, setting the figure of the apparitional lesbian against a fictional backdrop, and providing her with a story.

In fact, Waters seems to adhere so closely to theory when filling out the images of her novel, that she appears to leave no real space for other scholars to say much that is original about her text. To note that Millbank is a panopticon, or to note that Waters materializes the apparitional lesbian is simply to re-state the obvious. That Waters writes with an acute awareness of theoretical constructs is not at all surprising since she came to fiction by way of the academy. Jerome de Groot tells us, "Waters wrote a PhD thesis on historical fiction that was passed in 1995" (58).[12] And so, perhaps, we can argue that Waters is herself a doubled writer, able to play the roles of writer and critic simultaneously, displacing in a unique way the hermeneutic role of the scholar.

The Invisible Subaltern

Affinity does offer an additional, unobserved theoretical figure, waiting to be observed by the reader who resists the distraction of the specters of Foucault and of Castle. For while the gullible critic gazes upon the materialization of the panopticon and the apparitional lesbian, Waters, adopting the strategies of the spiritualists who are her subjects, slips an unseen theoretical figure into the picture: the silent and invisible subaltern who is the focus of Gayatri Chakravorty Spivak's "Can the Subaltern Speak" (1983). That is, the marginal, silent, indeed invisible Ruth Vigers, whose subordinate position renders her invisible to the eye of Margaret whose perspective dominates the novel, and to the reader limited by Margaret's point of view. Ruth partakes of a reality hardly recorded by the narrative, a non-normative reality very different from that of the experience of Margaret, a member of the dominant class. To borrow Spivak's terms, Ruth plays the role of "the desiring subject as Other" (68) in Water's novel. In fact Ruth's desire—for Selina, for freedom—drives the novel. But her silence and invisibility as a servant obfuscates the narrative until the very end, when we do finally recognize Ruth. As Spivak indicates, Ruth's desire and the plot she unfolds to achieve it, are invisible in the novel, because she is invisible. In fact, Waters's Ruth is an exemplar of the ghostly Other, dehumanized through difference, seeming to lack a substance, and thereby subjectivity and desire. As Spivak suggests, Ruth's invisibility is overdetermined: "Clearly if you are poor, black and female you get it in three ways" (90). Ruth is poor, female, lesbian and plain—rendering her invisible to the reader, as well as to most of the other characters in the novel. Because she does not fulfill our heroic definition of a heroine—or, of a villain—Ruth unfolds her plots under our eyes without raising any suspicion.

In "Not at Home: Servants, Scholars, and the Uncanny," Brian McCuskey provides a historical context for Ruth's deployment of the powers of the spiritualist to promote her own ends. He notes "one unannounced principal of nineteenth-century spiritualism is the frequent extension of the séance circle to include the household staff" (422). Whereas the servant was typically figured as the invading outsider, to be repressed and ignored, spiritualism provided a uniquely permeable interface to servants, providing them with the opportunity to mingle with their employers, and to advance themselves socially and economically. Although the Priors do not knowingly welcome the spiritualist into their midst, Ruth and Selina certainly act upon the invasive possibilities of spiritualism to insinuate themselves into the household. McCuskey also provides a psycho-social explanation for the linkage between the subaltern and the supernatural. Noting that the servant represented the stranger from the outside, even the invader in the home, and drawing upon Freud's notion of the uncanny, McCuskey observes that "Freud's search for the uncanny [leads] him repeatedly to the figure of the servant, begin with the etymology of the *unheimlich*" (425). Certainly Ruth is the uncanny servant, the resident stranger who renders the home a strange and unrecognizable place.

The true apparition of *Affinity*, the apparitional subaltern Ruth Vigers, is the character veiled by Waters and ignored by the characters and readers of the novel. Ruth, as well as the prison matrons including Mrs. Jelf, are invisibly interchangeable—the reader cannot readily distinguish between Ruth and Ellis, another servant in the house, and the various matrons tend to meld together into a single homogenous whole.[13] Compared to them, the lesbian characters are quite visible and uniquely particularized in this novel. We hear of the special relationships between women in the prison. We know of the past relationship between Helen and Margaret, and of Selina and Ruth. We watch as the relationship between Selina and Margaret unfolds. These are not Castle's apparitions; they are fully developed human beings, visibly acting out their desires.

Waters reminds us that certainly in Margaret's time and place invisibility was expected of the serving class, who did not fully count as human presences. During Selina's trial, Mrs. Silvester reports that her daughter was "quite alone. She was accompanied only by her maid, and of course by our driver" (138). When Mrs. Prior plans to leave Margaret at home, she frets about Margaret being home alone, "'with no-one here to nurse you'" (296), although as she fully knows and as Margaret reminds her, a cook and a servant would also be in the house. Ruth's invisibility to Margaret is demonstrated when Margaret views a "pencil-drawing [that] shows a bust of Peter Quick." Looking at "his" dark eyes, Margaret thinks: "they seem *familiar* to me, as if I might have gazed at them already—perhaps, in my dreams" (154)—in fact, they are the eyes of her own servant, whom she does not recognize. Indeed, the physical intimacy experienced by Margaret and Ruth as mistress and servant renders the invisibility of Ruth's body that much more startling. When Margaret sees a wax cast of the hand of Peter Quick at the spiritualist museum, she is oblivious to its familiarity. This is the hand that ministers to her; later in the novel, in fact, Vigers puts her hand to Margaret's head in what to Margaret "seemed the kindest gesture ... that anyone had ever shown me" (254). Yet Margaret does not recognize this hand. She reports seeing an alien limb: "the hand of a man ... yet hardly a hand ... five bloated fingers and a swollen, vein-ridged wrist" (130). Only in the wisdom that comes with hindsight, does Margaret recollect the reality of Ruth's hands, "I think of her dressing me, brushing my hair.... When I remember her fingers I see them bulging, yellow at the joints" (349).

Even after Margaret realizes the importance of Ruth, she dismisses her as a ghost, a cipher: "*Vigers*. What was she, to me? I could not even recall the details of her face, her look, her manners" (340). Indeed, Waters offers a moment of supreme irony when Mrs. Prior overhears Margaret's dinner discussion, "Mother—who had been directing Vigers," and returns dismissively to the conversation, "'Who are you talking of? Not ghosts, still'" (102). What the dinner companions ignore is that there is a real ghost among them, Ruth, who certainly gains much useful insight into Margaret's vulnerabilities from the dinner conversation that follows touching on the previously planned visit to Italy of "Helen and me" and that Helen "was always a great guest of ours" (102). A final irony occurs when Margaret liquidating her funds in (unknowing) preparation of being robbed by Ruth, turns to Vigers to validate her sanity: "Vigers, will you tell Mr Prior how well I am?" (293).

Appropriately, Ruth is invisible because her full name, her identity, is suppressed.[14] In Selina's diary she is Ruth, in Margaret's diary she is Vigers. This duality suggests that in each case she is, as a servant, only half a human being, with only half a name. When her full name is invoked, like that of a spirit at a séance, Ruth Vigers ceases to be a spectral presence and truly appears to the reader as the human explanation for the mysteries of the novel. As Margaret is speaking to Mrs. Jelf, unravelling the plot in which Selina has caught her, Miss Jelf mentions "the other lady" who lives at Margaret's house. To the shock of Margaret, and the reader, Mrs. Jelf explains that the other lady is "Selina's main, Ruth Vigers" (336). Suddenly Margaret and the reader put together the two halves into a single whole, visible human being: "*Vigers my servant, Selina's maid*" (336).

Not only is Ruth invisible to most of the characters though most of the book; she is also mostly silent. Silence, of course, also suits a good servant and a good apparition. Even Selina partakes of this class prejudice; at Mrs. Brink's house she is startled to see an uncanny "woman standing looking at me! ... But it was only Mrs. Brink's maid, Ruth. She had come quietly ... like a real lady's maid, like a ghost" (119). Margaret also approves of Vigers's silence, reporting that Vigers keeps her secrets from her mother: "Vigers, good girl, has never told" (285). To invoke the Lacanian model of language and desire, the former coming into being to express the latter, the enforced silence of the subaltern demonstrates the repression of the subaltern's subjectivity and desire. With no apparent desire to articulate, she has no need for language. As Waters leads us to recognize, Ruth actually manages to use her silence and invisibility to her advantage to unfold her plot; for her, silence is power. Because she is invisible and unheard, Ruth can glide around rooms, overhearing conversations, reading diaries, penetrating spaces, moving objects through space, in ways that seem supernatural to those who cannot see the live human being in front of them.

The backdrop of Ruth's deferential silence heightens the shock when she does articulate her subjectivity and her desire, at the end of Part Two of the book, mid-way through the novel, and then again at the end of the novel. The first time we hear the voice of the subjective Ruth is after the arrival of Peter Quick, Selina's control; we later learn that Peter is the spiritual persona of Ruth, who uses the control to express and fulfill her desires, taking sexual liberties with the young ladies who come to Selina for healing. Although none of this is yet entirely clear to Selina nor to the reader, Part Two ends with a new and important shift of power. As Selina moves out of the room to cater to the spiritual needs of Mrs. Brink, her patroness, "Ruth looked at me once & nodded. 'Good girl,' she said" (195). Suddenly, startled as we are to hear Ruth's voice and her dominant tone, we see the true balance of power in this book. Selina, who controls Mrs. Brink and Margaret, is herself controlled by Ruth. The hierarchy of power and possession in the novel is flipped as the practically invisible subaltern is discovered behind the curtains manipulating the entire plot. This notion of Ruth is confirmed and clarified by the end of the novel. Ruth, who has unfolded the plot that completely dispossesses and displaces Margaret, speaks again to articulate her desire and her right of possession over Selina, in the final words of the novel. As in the earlier speech, Ruth amplifies her dominance, and infantilizes Selina, reducing her to a "girl": "'Remember,' Ruth is saying, 'whose girl you are'" (352). Finally we readers have come to understand that Ruth's seeming powerlessness and invisibility are actually the source of her power; she uses her marginality and invisibility to enact her will, undetected and undeterred.

The Invisible Transgressive Woman

Ruth's name signals yet another specter, the eponymous disruptive character of Elizabeth Gaskell's Victorian novel *Ruth* (1853).[15] The inspiration for Gaskell's novel is relevant to this discussion. Hilary Shor indicates, "in 1849, while visiting prisoners in a Manchester jail, Elizabeth Gaskell met a sixteen-year-old prostitute named Pasley who had been incarcerated for theft" (158). Gaskell's Ruth (like her biblical namesake the Moabite) is another destabilizing outsider, invisible to her culture, marginalized because she is a "fallen woman," impregnated and abandoned. Like Waters's character who is known as either Ruth or Vigers, depending upon context, Gaskell's character has two personae, the fallen Ruth, the respectable Mrs. Denbigh.

Perhaps the most important connection is that both Ruths articulate the class *ressentiment* that Audrey Jaffe identifies in Gaskell's character who, she argues, invisibly infiltrates the Victorian home, and infects others with anti-patriarchal impulses. Shor notes that like Waters, "Gaskell is playing off readers' expectations" (158), in this case readers' ideas of the narrative of the fallen woman.[16] While Gaskell, writing in the nineteenth century, has little choice but to kill off her subversive Ruth, Waters's neo-Victorian Ruth is the sole character who is unambiguously triumphant and in full possession—of Selina and of Margaret's identity and goods—by the end of the novel.

Waters's Explained Supernatural

Waters deploys the figure of the invisible Ruth, the apparitional subaltern, to develop an updated version of Ann Radcliffe's explained supernatural, in which the closure of the novel explains away all the seemingly supernatural events, the events for which Margaret and the twentieth-century reader could find no rational explanation. Towards the end of the novel, rational, educated Margaret has become fully convinced of the supernatural realm; she is convinced, "'It was the spirits ... that took her,'" Selina, from the prison (331). And the reader is not far behind in being close to suspending all disbelief, the web that Selina/Ruth/Waters have woven is so tight. But as Margaret finally discovers, "there had been no spirit-help—there had been only the matrons" (332), the invisible women who spirited objects, and finally Selina herself through the walls of Millbank. And of course there had also been Ruth: "It was her [Vigers] hand that had placed it [Selina's hair] upon my pillow—'And all the time, Selina said the spirits brought it'" (338). And so, finally, Margaret—and the reader—realizes that Selina has been playing the same kind of spiritualist tricks upon her that had gotten her into jail in the first place.

The duping of rational Margaret and the rational reader indicates the masterful and psychologically adept manipulation of each. Waters and Selina provide every opening for modern doubt. We know that Selina has made a career of manipulating young women for money. We know that Peter Quick's appearances begin after a curtain is placed before an alcove with a door. Waters reminds us that the spiritual tricks have their explanations. In Selina's diary we encounter recipes "To keep a flower from fading" and "To make an object luminous" (74). Selina even is daring enough to demonstrate her "spirit-tricks" (166) to Margaret: taking some salt and a knitting needle, she—ironically—inscribes the word "Truth" into her arm. But like any good spiritualist, Waters provides the reader with just enough inexplicable information to encourage the reader to suspend disbelief. For example, Mrs. Brink is, indeed, brought to Selina by means other than rational: she dreams of Selina's "face & my name & the address" (94). Similarly in her diary Selina records an encounter with a bereaved mother. Within her spiritual state, she sees a necklace with the "shining faces" of the dead babies, but kindly neglects to tell the mother that "there was room on the thread for 2 more jewels" (55). How to account for this rationally? Waters doesn't seem to say. And so, it becomes harder and harder to distinguish the tricks from the "real" supernatural. We readers are as Brindle notes suspended in a particularly Todorovian situation of reading, caught between the twentieth-century skepticism which imbues us, and Waters's very compelling presentation of events that remain inexplicable, or at least unexplained.

Waters astutely takes advantage of the vulnerability that leads to the success of the spiritualist: like any good dupe, like Margaret, the reader wants to believe. Poor Margaret, alone and abandoned is primed to accept all that Selina tells her; when drawing the net tighter, Selina says, "'You want me near.... Or—why do you have my name upon the pages of your journal? Why do you have my flowers? *Why, Aurora, do you have my hair?*'" (271). With Vigers invisible, there is no available reasonable explanation; this is all too much for Margaret, the rational scholar who desires love. And it is really too much for the rational reader, the reader who may be skeptical about the romantic possibilities of heterosexual love after all these years of Gothic disappointment, but who might nurture hopes for the possibility of lesbian love. We come close to believing in the possibilities of love and of the supernatural because we want to, because the possibility of happiness in lesbian love is, in this novel, inextricably entwined with the possibility of the supernatural.

Dispossessing the Scholar

Waters amplifies the extent of Margaret's loss of herself to spiritualist frauds by emphasizing that Margaret is a rational scholar, the kind of thinker who would typically discount the possibility of the supernatural. To say that Margaret is a bookish woman is an understatement. Many of the literary allusions present in the novel are supplied by Margaret who draws from her history of reading to make meaning of her life. Margaret is a scholar who has studied with her father, a gender alliance that suggests an affinity for male rationalism rather than female superstition. She is the kind of person whose response when she stumbles upon the world of the supernatural is to go to the library, the *"British National Association of Spiritualists—Meeting-Room, Reading-Room and Library"* (127), to do research. Here is a woman who, in preparing to elope with her lover and upend her life, packs a trunk full of books, "I had put them all into a trunk" (314).

Perhaps Margaret is drawn to Selina's notion of affinity, because it so closely echoes the picture of human love developed in Plato's *Symposium*. Selina tells her: "We are the same, you and I. We have been cut, two halves from the same piece of shining matter" (275). Margaret is that special kind of young woman, who can be seduced by the thrill of Plato. Indeed an interchange with Stephen, Margaret's brother-in-law, leaves no doubt of her nature. Asking about her finances she says, "'It is only the theory of the thing that I want.' His knowing reply: 'I wanted the theory, he said, of everything, and always had" (290).

And yet despite her love of knowledge, and of theory, Margaret is enticed from the path of reason into a complete belief in the spiritual which destroys her. As many critics note, the late stages of Margaret's obsession with Selina, even before she is betrayed, finds her reduced to a ghost: "I am becoming my own ghost! ... I think I will haunt this room, when I have started my new life" (289). Indeed, Margaret moves from the world of reasonable male scholarship to the irrational Gothic world of the supernatural, madness and drugs, as she takes even higher and higher doses of the chloral hydrate and laudanum used to pacify Victorian women, moving further and further into madness and hallucination. Finally Margaret loses all, possessions, identity, writing, as they are stolen from her by Ruth and Selina. As Selina says to Margaret, referring to her suicide attempt (and before the chilling meaning is fully clear): "'You were careless with your life ... but now I have it'" (322).[17]

Displacing the Critic: Repossessing Fiction

But Margaret is not the only one dispossessed by the plots of *Affinity*. Waters clearly works to set up empathy between Margaret and the reader of the novel. The reader is drawn into Margaret's perspective as Margaret's journal composes most of the book. And her situation as an independent, intelligent, educated woman who cannot find a place for herself in her own Victorian world is calculated to evince sympathy on the part of her twentieth-first-century counterpart. Many readers of the novel are subject to the sense of readerly dispossession evoked by the surprisingly unexpected ending of the novel; we are lost in the twists of the labyrinthine plots of Selina and Ruth, and of Waters, that we were not able to forsee.[18]

In *Queering the Gothic*, Hughes and Smith note the power of the Gothic to "mock, surprise and shock" (3). Ultimately, this is the source of Waters's power as a writer. For despite the tendency of critics to focus on her sexual politics, the romantic relationships she presents are fairly conventional, except in their less-than-shocking homosexuality. The shock value of her material lies not in its sexual nature, but in the tendency of her stories (*Fingersmith* and *The Little Stranger*, for example, in addition to *Affinity*) to totally confound the expectations of the reader, dislocating their confidence in their own powers of apprehension. As Sarah Gamble notes in discussing *Fingersmith*, Waters's novels are meant to be re-read, as the reader cannot really pick up on the significance of much of the text until reaching the closure of the novel. As Gamble asserts, in Waters's fiction, "Reading is not a reliable means of attaining authentic knowledge" (52). "Knowledge is attained not by reading, but through desire" (53). This does seem to be the humbling message that Waters conveys to her readers. And so it is not surprising to see the reader dispossessed by the text of *Affinity*.

Moreover, Waters sets up a special affinity between the scholarly Margaret—who loves books and theory—and the scholarly reader of the novel, the reader who can trace the literary allusions of the book and discern the theoretical apparitions in the text, the reader who knows Keats and Barrett Browning, Foucault and Castle. Waters knows these readers and their affinities because (as she remarks on spinsters and ghosts, types that recognize their own) she was an academic before she was a novelist. In an interview with Kaye Mitchell, Waters reports, "I had done my academic work in the 1990's and was very much in the post–Foucauldian/Jeffrey Weeds tradition of thinking about heterosexuality and homosexuality" (128).

By invoking the very contexts that so compel her scholarly readers, Waters sets them up for special disappointment and dispossession, as Selina disappoints Margaret by offering and then withdrawing that which she so desperately desires. Ultimately the allusions to novels and to theory are like the magically appearing flowers and other tricks that distract us from what's really going on—we are being dispossessed of our powers of reading and interpreting. Rachel Carroll notes that the novel also disappoints readers who come to the novel with ideological expectations: "*Affinity* confounds the very desires which it seems to evoke; that is, the way in which it refuses to satisfy the desire of the contemporary reader for the retrospective materialisation into late Victorian existence of lesbian identity" (1).

And yet, dispossessed as we scholarly readers are, we are not like Margaret left bereft. We are perhaps deprived of the cold comfort of our theoretical constructs, but what remains is the delicious reward long supplied by Gothic fiction, the sublime pleasure identified by Burke of fear and loss experienced at a remove. We have undergone experiences that would have been dreadful had we actually been there, but that is actually satisfying because it was contained within the confines of Gothic fiction. Perhaps it is not unfair to speculate that Sarah Waters is also deploying the ludic possibilities of the Gothic to poke fun at her earnest readers, hurting at most our egos, reminding us that while she used to be one of us, she has now joined ranks with the Ruths of the world, the invisible spinners of impenetrable Gothic plots of dispossession, running off to Italy with our money, if not our lovers, while we stay at home and read.

16

The Political Fantastic

> "A strange mixture of matter and spirit"
> [James "The Ghostly Rental"[1] 69]

The comparative reading of the various manifestations of the English Gothic that unfolds in the previous chapters reveals the transforming and transformative capabilities of the mode. As the material and cultural contexts of possession and its attendant anxieties change over time, the countless Gothic conventional motifs evolve as well. This reading reveals that despite an obvious commitment to convention, the Gothic is a fluid and flexible mode; its conventions evolve in response to the specific historical and cultural contexts in which they are produced. This flexibility accounts for the sometimes-mystifying endurance of the popular power of the Gothic. Indeed, the ongoing preoccupation of the Gothic with possession accounts for its long endurance and continuing resonance in the popular and critical imagination; it is the human condition to desire and to suffer loss. Human life and human history are defined by the cycle of possession and dispossession that haunts the Gothic imagination and that anchors a vast array of tropes and texts.

The careening of the Gothic from moments of possession to moments of dispossession illustrates the kind of instability that engenders critical debate as to whether the Gothic is a conservative mode, confirming dominant ideologies, or a subversive mode, demystifying dominant ideologies.[2] To translate this debate into my terms: does the Gothic ultimately promote the restoration of possessions to their legal owners, thereby consolidating existing social structures—rendering it a conservative mode; or does the Gothic posit unstable states of dispossession—rendering it a subversive mode?[3] Critics who read the Gothic as a conservative mode—critics like Stephen Bernstein, who sees the Gothic as reinforcing ideologies of marriage, property and class; Cora Ann Howells, who sees the Gothic narrative as moving toward normalization; and Tilottama Rajan who, in contextualizing Wollstonecraft's *The Wrongs of Woman* within the Gothic tradition, indicts the Gothic for "its complicity in the attitudes of patriarchy"(178)—tend to focus on the conventional Gothic closure in which hegemony, order and normalcy are safely restored, along with property and identity. Rajan, for example, talks of the need to read "beyond the ending" (171) to discover the political strategies of the Gothic (and any) text. However, these critics repress the ambiguous instability of the typical Gothic closure—the instability that results when the restored property is rendered uninhabitable and unpossessible beginning with the Castle of Otranto that collapses when restored to the legitimate heir. The instability of the Gothic closure and the fantastic disruption within the central narrative of disordered possession attracts the attention of critics like Marilyn Butler and Susan Wolstenholme, who discover subversive tendencies in the Gothic.

The critical stance in this debate seems to depend on whether the critic privileges the center of the text or the dénouement, and thus says more about the perspective of the critic than of the text which, like the elephant in the tale of the blind men, simultaneously displays all of the elements whose synthetic power is missed when each element is perceived in isolation. The argument for privileging the closure of the text is supplied by D.A. Miller's *Narrative and Its Discontents*, a study that examines the tensions manifested by the discordance between the center and the closure of texts. Miller argues that the closure of the text represents the state endorsed by the author. And yet the enduring ludic power of the central Gothic narrative of disruption and dispossession appears to disrupt this theory, as does the reluctance of the Gothic narrative to let go of the central moment (evidenced in the deferred ending) and the unstable resolution. As Maggie Kilgour observes the "unsatisfactory" ending of the Gothic novel "compared to the delicious experience of the middle of the text, might in itself suggest a radical, antiteleological, model for reading in which closure, which necessarily involves some restabilisation of categories, is deprivileged" (8). Indeed, the obsessive return of the Gothic text (both intertextually through motifs like the deferred ending and intratextually in the recurrent Gothic paradigm) to the central moment of subversive dispossession indicates that the central moment of disruption is the one to which the Gothic writer (and reader) longs to return. Moreover, the uncertainty of the Gothic closure also undermines D.A. Miller's contention that the closure indicates the stable state endorsed by the author. For rather than denoting a clear promotion of the certainties of legal possession, the unstable Gothic ending conveys an insecure and uncertain meaning. Thus the reluctant and uncertain decline of the Gothic text into the world of practical realism and legally defined possession indicates not so much the desire of the text and of the writer as a sense of obligation to realism.

※

The forced and reluctant return of the Gothic to the world of realism, the literary world that reflects the structures of the actual world in which legal and economic possession is valorized, invites a further line of inquiry: why does the Gothic demonstrate a compulsion to return to the world of realism; why not remain in the utopian world of freedom and dispossession? This question is somewhat casually dismissed by Kilgour in the aside quoted above regarding the necessary "restabilisation of categories"; yet it does merit some attention. E.J. Clery moves toward one explanation of the tendency to realism in her discussion of Radcliffe, suggesting that Radcliffe's insecurity as a female writer disables her enactment of a full rebellion against the literary norms of realism and the philosophical norms of the Enlightenment. Clery's reading of Radcliffe's return to realism certainly works to explain the tendency to realism in other writers of the female Gothic, a tendency also noted by Terry Castle (*Masquerade and Civilization*) and Butler ("The Woman at the Window"), who consider the subversive tendencies of fantastic fiction by eighteenth-century English women and examine ways in which the utopian fantasy is curtailed by a return to realism. Indeed, the gendered accounting—that traces the return to realism to the insecurities of the writer—might work as an overarching explanation for the generalized tendency toward realism in the Gothic closure, as this is a mode that is dominated and influenced by women and other writers who have cause to be insecure because they are marginalized and dispossessed.

A related pattern that also invites further consideration is that the Gothic generally shies away from any explicit endorsement of radical and subversive activity. Social and economic transformations are typically contained within the central fantastic narrative and are generally represented in the destruction of existing structures rather than through the construction of alternate structures. So while the Gothic does critique the actual world, by providing a fantastic alternate or by exaggerating the horrors of oppressive structures, it provides few solutions that may be translated into praxis in the actual world. Even Lewis, whose text falls far from the umbrella of the "female Gothic" with its attendant constraints, closes his revolutionary text, *The Monk*, with an indictment of revolution in the form of the murderous mob.

Real Gothic Danger: The Leakage of the Rhetoric of Demonization into Political Discourse

Perhaps English Gothic writers feel constrained to end their texts in the world of realism because they are aware of the dangers of Gothic rhetoric uncontained by the closing frame of the novel. As the earlier discussion of the figure of Svengali and the imagery of the Dreyfus[4] case suggests, whereas the Gothic exaggerations of repressive structures reveal ludic subversion when confined to texts, the leakage of Gothic tropology and rhetoric into the political world usually results in actualized terror rather than liberation, what Max Horkheimer and Theodor Adorno call "the reversion of enlightened civilization to barbarism in reality" (Preface *Dialectic of Enlightenment* xiv). As the figure of the Satanic Jew destabilizes and dispossess literature, so does demonized figuring of Others destabilize and dispossess civilized discourse.

The danger of uncontained and dispossessed Gothic tropology, the Gothic that leaks out of the containing boundaries of literary discourse, is that it provides a cultural frame of reference to naturalize the demonization process that buttresses racism and other forms of group hatred, to encode the human who is the unknown Other, as fearful and evil. A corollary of this argument is that fear and hatred of any human difference is always horrifyingly evocative of the Gothic, always relying on the trope of the dehumanized Other and always wrenching the narratives of literature and culture from the realm of realism's "what is" to the realm of the Gothic: "what should not be."[5] When confined to the world of Gothic fiction, Gothic tropes provide the pleasures and recognitions that Edmund Burke discovers in his work on the sublime, the pleasures of pain and fear contained by art, rendered pleasurable because the reader knows that ultimately the dangers are imaginary and impotent. Unleashed from the realm of fiction to the world of political and cultural discourse, the dangers of the Gothic cease to be imaginary. Indeed the trope of the demonized dehumanized Other applied to cultural discourse is an early and foundational step in the relentless drift of modern history toward Gothic horror.[6]

Perhaps one of the many paradoxes of the Gothic is the appearance of its strategies in the political world lead directly to a recognition of the need for Enlightenment rationality and containment, as Horkheimer and Adorno suggest in their essay "Elements of Anti-Semitism: Limits of Enlightenment." Writing during the 1940s when "the dialectic of enlightenment is culminating objectively in madness" (169), Horkheimer and Adorno argue for the power of Enlightenment thinking to keep Gothic excess at bay, to keep the forces of unreason from transforming "the world into the hell they have always taken it to be" (165).

The Politically Fantastic Gothic Text

Safely contained within the text, the English Gothic narrative moves reluctantly through the subversive disorder that dominates the core of the narrative toward the conservative but uncertain restoration of order, stability and possession that marks the closure. Indeed, the failure of the Gothic narrative to sustain the moment of ludic disruption, the final failure of the utopian vision of disorder and dispossession, is a defining moment of the Gothic mode. For the restoration of the social order ensures that the patterns of oppression will begin again both in the world and within the Gothic canon that endlessly replays the cycles of revolution and restoration. It is the inability of the Gothic to sustain the central fantasy that, in fact, accounts for the characteristic lugubriousness of the mode.

The image of the unstable Gothic, eternally vacillating between the subversive central narrative and the conservative closure—the closure that is itself ultimately unsure of its commitment to restoration—accounts for the difficulty of identifying the political ideology of the Gothic with any certainty. This unstable model is consistent with the Gothic project of resisting essentialist apprehension, of resisting boundaries that contain and define meaning. And so, perhaps the only way to describe the politics of the Gothic is to draw on the dynamic and tense model of Todorov's fantastic,[7] an ambiguous state in constant tension between the supernatural and the rational, between "reality and imagination" (167). In Todorov's formulation, the fantastic text resists resolution on either the rational plane or on the supernatural plane. Thus Todorov's definition of the fantastic is ultimately anti-essentialist. The fantastic is defined not by what it is but by what it avoids: the supernatural on the one side and the rational on the other. In avoiding both categories, in sustaining irresolution, as Todorov indicates, the fantastic interrogates the construction of the distinct categories: "by the hesitation it engenders, the fantastic questions precisely the existence of an irreducible opposition between real and unreal" (167).

The English Gothic totters ambiguously between the poles of the supernatural and the real, and between the codes of the imagination and of the law. When viewed as a whole with equal attention given to center and to unstable closure, the text reveals a constant tension between the conservative and the subversive. The Gothic text suggests rebellion or restraint depending upon which section is observed and depending on how much importance in placed upon the unstable subtext of the closure. When the text and the canon, with its insistent intratextual return to dispossession and to containment, is considered as a whole, it reveals itself as the political fantastic wavering ambiguously and irresolutely between two ideological poles.

Thus the politics of the English Gothic is in alignment with its poetics. In looking simultaneously at the subversive center and the unstable closure of the Gothic text we see that the text, consistently transgressive, straddles the boundaries between the real world, as reflected in the representation of legal structures of possession, and the world of the imagination, which allows for ludic dispossession effected through supernatural and otherwise unrealistic means. In its realistic moments, the Gothic tends toward conservatism, reflecting and solidifying the structures of society; in its imaginative moments, the Gothic tends toward subversion, envisioning impossible worlds of freedom. But most Gothic texts contain both kinds of moments, both approaches: "the strange mixture of matter and spirit" that James's narrator locates in his story. Indeed, it is the synthetic paradigm that accounts for the power of the Gothic.

The transgressive and inclusive English Gothic that counters the modern movement toward boundaries and divisions offers the possibility of the organic world for which modern philosophies yearn. The Gothic, approaching the serious business of actual legal possession with the tools of the imagination and fantasy, erases the bounds between law and fiction by showing them both to be artificial fictions. In this the Gothic (and the Romantic) motif of the lifted veil takes on added resonance. Not only does the Gothic lift the veil constructed by society to obscure the real horrors of social systems, it also lifts the veil that lies between the realms of the material and the immaterial, the real and the supernatural. In conflating the seemingly opposing worlds of rational law and irrational fiction, the Gothic re-presents legal and economic concepts of possession as unstable fictions, and warns its readers to be wary of the dangers of both planes.

Conclusion

Toward a Transatlantic Investigation

Possession and Dispossession in American Gothic Literature

> Puerile superstition and exploded manners; Gothic castles and chimeras, are the materials usually employed.... The incidents of Indian hostility, and the perils of the western wilderness are far more suitable [Brockden Brown *Edgar Huntly* 3].

The previous chapters argue for the centrality of the concept of possession in the English Gothic text, asserting that anxieties of possession and dispossession inform the text and organize the mode. Indeed, the linguistic fluidity of the word "possession"—available to supernatural, psychological and legal applications—allows for the possibility of using this concept as a kind of anchor for the English Gothic, with the understanding that a long and winding chain allows each text to float as it will from the center.

This assertion has been founded upon many moments in which we see the English Gothic text focus upon issues of possession and dispossession: property lost and stolen; people physically detained or dispossessed of their mental faculties; tales, written and oral, dislocated from their narrative source. We have seen these moments of possession and dispossession effected through methods that ranged from the properly legal to the irrationally supernatural. Yet, given the nature of the Gothic text and Gothic studies, the very seeming solidity of this paradigm suggests an underlying instability.

In fact, as this text nears its conclusion, as the final brick appears ready to be set into the defining wall, a crack appears, and upon closer inspection widens into a gigantic gap in the form of an unaddressed question: what about the American Gothic text?

As Bridget M. Marshall and others have recently noticed, the boundary-breaking Gothic mode does not readily lend itself to the binding category of national literature. Even when the boundary is as vast as the Atlantic Ocean, the separation between the English Gothic and the American Gothic is readily transcended. In fact, there are numerous "connections and continuities between the British and American versions of the Gothic.... Establishing a stark line between British and American Gothic seems specious" (Marshall, *Translatlantic Gothic Novel* 2–3).[1] Yet, as Marshall notes, transatlantic examinations of the Gothic are still relatively rare: "Most scholars of the Gothic are clearly rooted in either the British or American tradition; little scholarship exists addressing the transatlantic nature of the genre" (2).

Gothic Literature: American Transformations

American literature is, even more than English literature, informed by the Gothic tradition.[2] From its first centuries, American literature is dominated by the dark, haunted and haunting texts of writers such as Brockden Brown, Washington Irving, Poe, Hawthorne, Melville. As American literature continues to expand and grow into the twenty-first century the Gothic mode continues to flourish, mutating into the Southern Gothic, the "Frontier Gothic" (Mogen). The Gothic mode is much favored by contemporary African American writers—Toni Morrison, Gloria Naylor—and by the writers of other cultural traditions, many of whom draw upon the fantastic traditions of their culture of origin to write "ethnic" Gothic texts (Brogan). The tradition of the Female Gothic also continues to flourish in America: the dark underbelly of Louisa May Alcott's *Little Women*, surfacing in her sensational short stories; Charlotte Perkins Gilman's widely-read "The Yellow Wallpaper"; the domestic horror of Shirley Jackson's *We Have Always Lived in the Castle*. These writers, like their English counterparts, turn to the Gothic text, to work out the place of the dispossessed woman, who haunts the house of the American Dream, as her English double haunts the English castle. And the enormous success of Stephenie Meyer's *Twilight* vampire romance series confirms that the Female Gothic is alive and well in twenty-first-century America.

As these American varieties of Gothic literature attest, the Gothic mode, like the dandelion brought over as an ornamental from England, transforms and takes on new meanings as it takes root and flourishes in American soil, as asserted by Brockden Brown in the passage from *Edgar Huntly* that provides the epigram of this chapter. Brown's narrator promises his reader something new; he will deploy "means hitherto unemployed by preceding authors" (3), transforming and Americanizing the old "materials," long familiar as Gothic conventions. In his work, "Gothic castles" will be replaced by the new site of the American Gothic, "the Western wilderness" and the old haunting figures, the frightening "chimeras" will be replaced by the equally frightening, and in Brockden Brown, equally inhuman perpetuators of "incidents of Indian hostility." In describing Brown's use of the wilderness setting, Siân Silyn Roberts observes, "Far from eschewing British forms, Brown adopts them to describe a space that obeys the same epistemological principles as the castle or dungeon" (23), that is a space removed from the realm of the norm, in which the unnatural, or supernatural, may occur.

In tracing these connections, Roberts—who provides a useful review of the recent critical literature of American Gothic studies—sets herself apart from "the majority of critics [who] tend to agree that the Gothic's transmission across the Atlantic ... resulted in altogether new incarnation of the form, with wholly 'American' preoccupations ... chiefly race, frontier expansion and revolution" (22). In fact, an application of the lens of possession to the American Gothic tradition, will reveal dominant preoccupations that are similar indeed to those of the precursor English tradition. For while the terms and contexts of possession change and transform in America, and the American Gothic transforms to reflect these new situations, the central anxiety of possession and dispossession continues to vex the American Gothic text, as it does its English precursor.

American Anxieties of Possession and Dispossession

Even a cursory examination of the American Gothic canon reveals a corresponding preoccupation with issues of possession of property, person and narrative. Certainly American history and culture afford rich possibilities for anxiety regarding possession and dispossession. America was founded upon the dispossessions of the Native American, from whom the land was stolen, and the African American, from whom the body was stolen. The independence of the country came about through the revolutionary appropriation by the American people of the political power of the

English crown and the colonial property of the English people. Thus, like the typical English Gothic text, the American story begins after the great moment of usurpation and dispossession—revolution, the unraveling of the peoplehood of Native Americans and the enslavement of the African Americans. Nor were the English, Native Americans and African Americans the only groups who were dispossessed in the new young country. As far as married women went, the liberating revolution never happened; restrictions of English Common Law continued to be applied to American women, who were no more free than their English counterparts.

From its earliest moments then, the American psyche harbors dark and unpleasant realities. Yet, the preferred image of a bright new country free of the shadows of a dark past dictates the repression of these realities. In the Preface to *The Marble Faun*, Nathaniel Hawthorne reveals the extent of this repression. Writing in 1859, Hawthorne claims the need to set his Gothic tale in Italy rather than in America because his "native land" provides "no shadow, no antiquity, no mystery, no picturesque and gloomy wrong, nor anyting but a commonplace prosperity, in broad and simple daylight" (vi). In proper Freudian fashion, however, the repressed realities of American culture re-emerge to haunt the American imagination in the form of dark Gothic literature. Critics, including Leslie Fiedler, D.H. Lawrence and Toni Morrison, provide variations of the Freudian explanation, responding to readers who might depend upon views typified by Hawthorne and consider the prevalence of the dark literature of the early American centuries to be a puzzling paradox. In *Love and Death in the American Novel* (1960), Leslie Fiedler argues that repressions of sexual and racial anxieties lie at the core of the American novel. D.H. Lawrence identifies the figure of the dispossessed Native American lurking within the shadows of American literature in *Studies in Classic American Literature* (1923), as Toni Morrison discerns the abjected figure of the possessed African American in "Romancing the Shadow" (1993). Lawrence expands on the notion that the suppressed guilty fears of the possessor in consequence of dispossessing others lies at the foundation of the American Gothic. He argues that for the possessing, unmastered American, the free white male, freedom was actually a source of anxiety, the fear of being alone, in control, in Lawrence's words, of being "masterless."

Perhaps the anxiety of possession that is most amplified in American culture is the anxiety of possession of voice and narrative, possession of the authority of authorship. The early American was placed in the strange situation of having to discover a new self, like Washington Irving's Rip van Winkle who goes to sleep a subject of George III and mysteriously awakes to find himself an independent American. The new American writing subject had to work through this dilemma: how to write as an American within a background and tradition of English literature? Indeed, like Rip van Winkle the American writer awakes into an uncanny situation, haunted by the past, and possessed by his old, English, doubled self, he arrives belatedly to his own tradition, stuggling with what Robert Weisbuch characterizes as "the burden of Britain" (ix).

We find American writers turning to the tradition of the Gothic with its preexisting preoccupation with possession to consider the new varieties of anxieties of possession that they encounter upon American soil. Brockden Brown obsessively retells stories of the appropriation and loss of capital and real estate, including Native American land. His delirous and sleepwalking characters re-enact the dispossession of the American self. His dislocated voices re-enact the situation of the dispossessed American narrative. In Washington Irving's "Legend of Sleepy Hollow," Ichabod Crane's encounter with a particularly American version of the supernatural forces him to reconsider how he will possess property, and forces the American reader to consider the sources and owners of American narrative. Edgar Allan Poe's mad narrators and characters dispute the powers of apprehension of the American Enlightenment, as his quasi-European aristocrats dispute the potency of American democracy, a system that is also destabilized by Hawthorne's dark grasping American aristocrats, whose House of the Seven Gables, the narrator anxiously stresses, is *not* like a "gray feudal castle" (10). Nor are the concerns and strategies of the English Gothic tradition limited to the works of the writers of American fictions. Writers of slave narratives like Frederick Douglass and Harriet Jacobs also draw on the tropes of the Gothic to tell their horrifying stories of dispossession. As we move more closely to our own times, we note Toni Morrison's use of the forms of the ghost story to tell the story of dispossessed slaves in *Beloved*, or the Gothic strategies deployed by Louise Erdrich in *Tracks*, a story of the appropriation of the land of Native Americans.

These writers and many more turn to the traditions of the English Gothic and its preoccupation with issues of possession to consider the anxieties generated by moments of possession and dispossession in American history and culture. Repeatedly they provide the variations to the theme that is set by the English Gothic. Certainly these variations merit further developed scrutiny.

And so, like the typical Gothic novel, the present volume ends—if not in chaos, confusion, and despair—then in a moment of critical instability, a moment that moves from the confident contemplation of the carefully constructed paradigm that places anxieties of possession at the center of the English Gothic tradition, to an uneasy awareness of the unanswered questions raised by the looming and irrepressible presence of the American Gothic text.

Poised at the doorway of a gloomy room we gaze upon the space of the American Gothic tradition. Or, to draw upon more fitting imagery, we stand at the mouth of a gloomy cave or at the edge of a trackless forest, peering into the shadows that lie ahead. To venture forth might be unsettling, but like the journey of the Gothic subject into the dark unknown, the American expedition might lead to an encounter with knowledge and understanding.

Chapter Notes

Introduction

1. To borrow Kate Ferguson Ellis's term.
2. From the Latin root "sedere" meaning to sit, indicating the association between the physical act of appropriation and conceptual possession.
3. The OED traces the development of "obsession" from sixteenth century meanings of "besiegement" through the seventeenth century concept of being besieged by demonic forces and hence by overwhelming ideas.
4. David Punter paves the way for the present study; in *Gothic Pathologies* (1998) he discusses the transgressive relationship of the Gothic to legal structures as I do in the chapters that follow. Punter, who frames the struggle as a war of "the rival regimes ... of surveillance and the imaginary" (3), anticipates the assertions of this study regarding the power of the ludic in noting "the Gothic is able, because of its freedom from the law, to play; and when play happens (anywhere, and at any age) then powerful feelings are mobilized" (12). Punter continues, "Gothic is therefore all about supersession, about the will to transcend, and about the fate of the body as we strive for a fantasy of total control, or better, total exemption — from the rule of law" (17). Punter also anticipates my argument in asserting that "the Gothic is ... extra-legal" (200) and the Gothic is a "terrain of loss" (203). Yet the argument of this study diverges from that of Punter in a significant way. Although Punter's definition of the Gothic as a terrain of loss presupposes the question of possession, he never focuses on this complex of concepts in his discussion. Moreover, to Punter, the representation of loss in the Gothic is negative and tragic; the Gothic is a mode "in mourning" (203). As I shall argue, the representation of loss in the Gothic is the emblem of subversion and represents the ludic moment of triumph over legal structures; it is the failure to sustain dispossession that accounts for the somber tone of the mode.
5. We know that in literature and culture little is produced *ex nihilo*. A fascinating discussion of an earlier literary response to cultural contexts of possession may be found in *Enclosure Acts*, a collection of essays edited by Richard Burt and John Michael Archer that examines "discourse of enclosure, closure, and containment in ... the sixteenth and seventeenth centuries ... essays on the enclosure and consolidation of land ... and on the redefinition and enclosure of sexuality and the body within the symbolic order" (1). Essays in the collection deal "variously with bodily enclosure and the enclosure of property" (2), thus tracing an earlier association of the cultural context and the metaphor that is discussed in the present study. Burt and Archer share a theoretical approach with this study as well; they too evoke a "containment model [that] can be traced back to Michel Foucault's critique of the traditional definition of power as repression, a force that comes from above to threaten the individual with rules and prohibitions" (2).

Another collection of essays that also presents an interesting point of contact with the present study is *Literary Fat Ladies: Rhetoric, Gender, and Property*, edited by Patricia Parker. Not coincidentally, many of the essays draw on Foucault's formulations in considering "walls or partitions ... rhetorical partitions, a division of the subject into parts" (8).

6. Indeed, as Harold Perkin notes, the eigh-

teenth century was the time of "the birth of class" (176) as a social category: "The most profound and far-reaching consequences of the Industrial Revolution was the birth of a new class society ... characterized by ... the existence of vertical antagonism between a small number of horizontal groups, each based on a common source of income" (176).

7. In writing of Foucault, Mark Edmundson quite helpfully works to align Foucault's thinking with the vocabulary of this study: "His haunting agency, which is everywhere and nowhere as evanescent and insistent as a resourceful spook, is called Power.... Power generates sets of terms, vocabularies, that lock us all into inert roles.... Power [is] a *preternatural* force. It's something more potent that mere humanity. And it possesses us, haunts us (41–42).

8. G.W.F. Hegel explicates the connection between possession and power: "To have power over a thing *ab extra* constitutes possession" ("Property" 45, p. 42).

9. A wonderfully explicit example of the opposition of literature to the forces of hegemony is to be found in Dickens's Christmas book *The Chimes* (1844). In this book, the protagonist Trotty has internalized the message that the poor must be depraved to behave as they do. Reading the account (based on fact) of a starving young woman who drowns herself and her child, Trotty acknowledges the condemnation of the poor by the rich: "It's too true, all I've heard to-day; too just, too full of proof. We're [the poor] Bad!" (133). The rest of the narrative is devoted to unfolding to Trotty the injustice of his words as he learns from the Chimes that "Who turns his back upon the fallen and disfigured of his kind ... does wrong to Heaven and Man, to Time and to Eternity" (142). Dickens thus teaches his poor protagonist to resist the subtle dissemination of power that Foucault argues is irrestible.

10. The reading of Sarah Waters's *Affinity* in Chapter 15 uncovers a similar critique.

11. In this my reading is diametrically opposed to critics like George Haggerty who argues that the Gothic is defined and informed by its forms –its formal effects—and that these forms are the source of the enduring power of Gothic fiction.

Chapter 1

1. *Otranto* is not the *first* Gothic novel. Anne Williams calls the idea that *Otranto* "sprang fully armed from Horace Walpole's dreaming brow in 1764" (13) a Gothic myth of origins (8). The engendering of this myth is demonstrated by Walpole's letter to William Cole dated 9 March 1765 in which Walpole describes waking "from a dream, of which all I could recover was, that I had thought myself in an ancient castle (a very natural dream for a head filled like mine with Gothic story) and that on the uppermost bannister of a great staircase I saw a gigantic hand in armour" (Mowl 182–183). But Walpole was influenced by non-supernatural forces as well. Mowl notes that Thomas Leland published *Longsword* (1762) two years before *Otranto* and that the French had earlier invented and developed the Gothic tradition (187). *Otranto* is, however, the most influential precursor of the genre in English.

2. First published in 1777, as a response to *Otranto*, under the title *The Champion of Virtue*.

3. Douglas Hay, writing of the eighteenth century, argues that during that time property was reified and "deified" (19) and that the heightened desire to protect property led to an increased discipline through law; behaviors that had previously been merely marginal were redefined as crimes, subject to punishment. "The criminal law ... was critically important in maintaining obedience and deference, in legitimizing the *status quo*, in constantly recreating the structure of authority which arose from property and in turn protected its interests" (27). Thus, for example, since the "largest possession" of the English ruling class was land, which could only be appropriated through forgery, "forgery was punished with unmitigated severity throughout the century, by death" (60).

4. Building, of course, on the work of earlier writers. In *Two Treatises of Government* (1689), Locke proposes that a chief justification for the structures of government is that they work to defend the property rights of the subjects of the state, rights that are, Locke argues, inalienable, and free of moral or political controls.

5. The design of which was probably influenced by Trinity College, Cambridge, and Walpole's own folly, Strawberry Hill (W. S. Lewis xi).

6. As Peter Buse and Andrew Stott note, "where we find ghosts, there are bound to be anxieties about property.... Whether property is a Gothic ancestral home ... [or a] Romantic heroine's inheritance ... it is never free of ghostly vicissitudes, contrary to all rhetoric of propriety and possession which would exorcise past struggles over it" (9).

7. As Adorno concedes in his critique,

"Theses Against Occultism," ghosts "inveigh against materialism" (243).

8. A number of essays exploring the convergence of ghostly possession and the questions of property and possession may be found in *Ghosts: Deconstruction, Psychoanalysis, History*, edited by Buse and Scott.

9. Raymond Williams discovers another instance of the representation of the English landowner as invading Goth: citing Goldsmith's view that rural England before enclosure was like Italy before its conquest by Theodoric the Ostrogoth, Williams points to "the persistent image" of enclosers as "invading barbarians" (*Country and City* Chapter 13). Samuel Kliger also resorts to this set of tropes when describing a particular approach to English law that he calls "Gothicism," a belief that "England had once been free in its tribal assemblies, and [that] the freedom of Parliament therefore should be retrieved" (112).

10. Kayman defines property as "a deliberate and self-conscious fabrication, which is recognized as such by everyone and hence cannot be challenged for veracity in court" (380). The concept of property ownership is, as E.P. Thompson recognizes, a "fallacy" that "in our waking hours, we know very well to be untrue" (328). It is, in fact, the "tenure," the idea of owning the land, which is owned; in Offer's formulation property is "a bundle of rights, enforcible by law" (5). Property is an abstraction rather than an actual piece of land. The nightmare of the Gothic anticipates the awakening of "twentieth-century jurisprudence" in discovering "that property, like God, was dead ... that the unity, tangibility and objectivity that were property's very essence were illusions—property was a mere phantom. Property was not a single identifiable thing but an aggregate of parts, an arbitrary collection of legal rights" (Schroeder 1).

Chapter 2

1. "Enclosure had been proceeding for centuries before the eighteenth century but we are convinced that it was much more rapid in the eighteenth century following the new form of enclosure by private Act of Parliament. Parliamentary enclosure has been adequately traced and 1750–60 was the beginning of a rapid increase in its rate" (Allan Thompson 50). Turner argues that there were two distinctive periods of Parliamentary Enclosure, during which 40 percent of Parliamentary Enclosure was enacted. The first period was from the 1760s to the 1770s, the second from 1793 to 1815 (153).

2. The origins of the Gothic also coincide with the era in which England turned its full attention to colonial expansion, an equally rewarding opportunity to seize land from others. In *The Gothic Family Romance*, Margot Gayle Backus argues, for example, that the horrifying tropes of the Gothic in English and Irish Gothic literature reflect the destructive effects of imperialism on the Irish.

3. Roger Londsdale's note on Oliver Goldsmith's "The Deserted Village" (1768–1770) suggests that literary modes other than the Gothic were responding to contemporary changes in the landscape: "during Goldsmith's childhood, [Genl. Robert Napier] purchased the estates round the village and began to enclose an area 'of nine miles in circumference,' causing hundreds to move to other parts of the country, or to emigrate to America" (670). Indeed, Goldsmith's poem describes the virtual ghost town that results from the depopulation enforced by "the tyrant's hand" where "one only master grasps the whole domain."

4. Williams notes the particular expansion of the construction of great houses in the eighteenth century, an expansion that coincided with the birth of the Gothic mode. Indeed, Walpole's home, Strawberry Hill, was the architectural counterpart of his imagined castle; its labyrinths were likely the model for the labyrinths in the Castle of Otranto. Williams quotes Matthew Arnold ("Culture and Anarchy") who sees the great house of England as "a great fortified post of the Barbarians." Williams elaborates: "it was in the eighteenth century, most visibly, that these strong points of a class spread in a close network over so much of Britain. Some of them [the great houses] had been there for centuries visible triumph over the ruin and labour of others. But the extraordinary phase of extension, rebuilding and enlarging, which occurred in the eighteenth century, represents a spectacular increase in the rate of exploitation: a good deal of it, of course, the profit of trade and of colonial exploitation" (105–106).

5. Keith B. Poole provides intriguing evidence for the impact of the enclosure movement upon the Walpole family. "When building Houghton Hall, Sir Robert Walpole... discovered that the village of Houghton 'did not improve his view.' With an arrogance unequalled by few, even in that age, he had the whole village removed to another spot nearby out of sight. It was the abandoned, original village which inspired Oliver Goldsmith to write his poem, *The Deserted Village*" (20). Although fascinating, this statement is admittedly somewhat suspect, appearing as it does in *Britain's*

Haunted Heritage, a text that proports to document myriad instances of ghostly manifestations in Britain.

6. Edmund, later reveals a key that he uses to unlock the chamber in which his murdered father is buried: a literalization of the skeleton in the closet.

7. To use the terminology of J.G.A. Pocock.

8. Ronald Paulsen points out that other instances of political unrest and violence in the late eighteenth century included "the Gordon Riots of 1780...as well as the crowd of 150,000 that gathered at the meeting of the London Corresponding Society in Copenhagen Fields in 1795...the riots of 1794–95 with their death toll, and the naval mutinies at Spithead and the Nore in 1797" (216).

9. The account, a satirical telling of the discovery of a race of Patagonian giants reminiscent of Rousseau's noble savages, is told in the form of a letter written by a supporter of the project of colonialism who is subverted by the excesses of the language of his report. Thus, the letter-writer blithely reports that "as soon as they are properly civilized, that is enslaved ... [the] giants shall be subject to the parliament of Great-Britain" (97) by Captain Byron who seeks to "take possession of the country for the crown of England" (97). One form that this enslavement will take is that the Americans "shall not wear a sheep's skin that is not legally stamped" (97)—a thinly veiled reference to English taxation of the colonies. Walpole's opposition to the centers of power is best evidenced in his anticipation of post-colonial rhetoric. Here are his ironic words: "Whoever finds a country, though nobody has lost it, is from that instant entitled to take possession of it for himself or his sovereign" (100). The satirical tone of the letter makes it clear that even in 1766 Walpole recognizes that in actuality no land is lost and unpossessed—all land is known to and possessed by its native peoples, a fact repressed by the project of empire.

10. Joan Thirsk's discussion of the various debates surrounding primogeniture provides a useful context for the Gothic interrogation of primogeniture. Thirsk notes that the "growing strength of primogeniture" (182) in the early sixteenth century and the resultant harm that ensued to younger sons resulted in "rumblings of a controversy against its harsh consequences" (183). Thirsk traces the controversial discussion of primogeniture that began in the sixteenth and seventeenth centuries and continued into the eighteenth and nineteenth centuries; as the practice of primogeniture filtered down to the middle classes in those centuries, the controversy expanded as well.

11. James Thompson also notes the tensions within families that developed during the late seventeenth and eighteenth centuries. He reads Congreve's "protonovel," *Incognita: or, Love and Duty Reconcil'd* (1692), as an attempt to reconcile tensions: seeking to uphold "both the child's individual claim to desire and the paternal claim to familiar authority" (19).

12. Walpole's figuring of the soul possessed by melancholy indicates the Gothic concern with the limits of self-possession that will be the focus of the following chapter.

Chapter 3

1. The economist Joan Robinson notes Adam Smith's evocation of an "idyllic past" in which the laborer got back the full value of his labor without landlord or factory owner to taint moral relationships" (quoted in Webb 30).

2. Francis Wheen's biography of Marx also evokes the Gothic as a code for the fantastic, unrealistic and unmanageable text when describing Marx's writing. He proposes reading *Capital* (1867–1893) as "a work of imagination: a Victorian melodrama, or a vast Gothic novel whose heroes are enslaved and consumed by the monster they created" and cites Marx's description of "'Capital which comes into the world soiled with mire from top to toe and oozing blood from every pore'" to prove that when reading *Capital* "we are entering a world of spectres and apparitions" (Wheen 305). Another accounting of Marx's Gothic affinity is provided by Jacques Derrida whose *Specters of Marx* argues that Marx (like the Gothic mode) is haunted by the presence of Shakespeare, particularly by the presence of Hamlet's ghost. In reading the famous first line of the Manifesto, Derrida hears a Shakespearean echo: "As in Hamlet, the Prince of a rotten State, everything begins by the apparition of a specter" (4). And like the ghost of the Gothic, Hamlet's ghost is about time, the disjointed time of the present, in contrast to the idyllic time of the lost past, the time that preceded the moment of usurpation and disruption: "the dis-joining of time, but also of history and of the world, the disjoining of things as they are nowadays, the disadjustment of our time" (18).

3. In their respective prefaces, both Walpole and Reeve express the goals of their narratives. Unsurprisingly, Reeve's stated intention is the more conservative of the two. The project of her narrative is to engage the attention of the reader in order to "direct it to some useful, or at least innocent, end" (4). In

Reeve's formulation this end is disrupted by the excesses of Walpole's fiction, characterized by a "sword so large as to require a hundred men to lift it ... a helmet that by its own weight forces a passage through a court yard into an arched vault ... a picture that walks out of its frame ... a skeleton ghost in a hermit's cowl" (Reeve 4–5). All these, Reeve argues, strain the "limits of credibility" (4), ultimately resulting in a narrative that, instead of working to "engage the heart" of the reader, manages instead to "excite laughter." Walpole, on the other hand, reveals a desire to entertain as well as to instruct. Writing as William Marshall, the purported translator of the First Edition, Walpole nods weakly to the possible moral applications of his narrative: "I could wish he [the purported unknown author of the work] had grounded his plan on a more useful moral than this; that the sins of fathers are visited on their children to the third and fourth generation" (5, this Biblical injunction surfaces in a surprising number of Gothic texts). Yet the enthusiasm of Walpole's two prefaces rests in the possibilities of his narrative to entertain: "his work can only be laid before the public at present as a matter of entertainment" (Preface to the First Edition 4); he is "desirous of leaving the powers of fancy at liberty to expatiate through the boundless realms of invention, and thence of creating more interesting situations" (Preface to the Second Edition 7).

4. Other critics have also noticed the implicit radicalism of Radcliffe's texts. In "The Woman at the Window," Marilyn Butler argues that it is the fantastic nature of the Gothic, the detachment from realism and the real world which frees Radcliffe to explore the very real issues of female sexuality and the female unconscious. Robert Miles (*Ann Radcliffe*) argues for a reading of the radical subtexts of Radcliffe's apparently conservative texts. "Her texts engage critically with her culture" (4), including her promotion of romantic, as opposed to dynastic, marriage.

5. The presence of DuPont is itself an example of the deferred ending. Emily and the reader expect that Emily's rescuer will prove to be her lover, Valancourt, and that her rescue will result in the closure of the text. This closure is deferred by Radcliffe's insertion of the character of DuPont, her deferral of the final reunion of Emily and Valancourt.

6. Radcliffe's novel traces the entire arch of usurpation and restoration; unlike the others, belatedly opening after the fall, *Udolpho* begins at the idyllic moment of perfect harmony and ends in the same situation and place, La Vallée, Emily's childhood home.

Chapter 4

1. The difference between Manfred and Heathcliff highlights the transformation of the threatening male from the wholly evil villain of the eighteenth century to the multi-dimensional hero-villain of the nineteenth century, exemplified by Heathcliff and by Charlotte Brontë's Mr. Rochester.

2. Sturrock notes Yonge's strong religious convictions, that derived from her association with the Oxford Movement and her "quasi-filial relationship with John Keble who was vicar of Otterbourne" (21).

3. Her immensely popular novel, *The Heir of Redclyffe* (1855), reveals a debt to the Gothic tradition, although it is ostensibly a novel of middle-class domestic life, the story of a noble, Christ-like character and his influence on a Victorian family. Among the Gothic motifs to be found in *Redclyffe* are the massive ancestral home, the ancestral curse, contested property, questions of inheritance, suspicions of ghosts, and the conflation of marriage and death. Yonge's novel also declares its allegiance to the Gothic tradition in the invocation of the lines that might well be the mantra of the Gothic (cited by both Walpole and Hawthorne in the prefaces to their Gothic texts, *The Castle of Otranto* and *The House of the Seven Gables* (1851) and cited, too, in Collins's *The Woman in White* (1860): "the sins of the fathers shall be visited on the children" (71).

4. Georgina Battiscombe notes: "In *Chantry House*, a story of rural England in the days of George IV, she recaptured for a moment the atmosphere of that lotus-eating time before steam-engines ruined the peace of the country-side or *The Tracts for the Times* blew a blast loud enough to wake even the Church of England from slumber" (154).

5. Yonge's episode recalls the scene in *Wuthering Heights* in which Heathcliff orders the sexton to dig up the earth covering Catherine's coffin—"I opened it.... I saw her face again"—and shuts the coffin when the sexton says, "It would change, if the air blew on it" (218). The episode echoes even more closely the events of *The Old English Baron*, in which Edmund discovers the literal skeletons in his family's closet, that is the bones of his father, buried away in a subterranean room, "the fatal closet" (131). *Baron*, too, concludes with the reburial of the bones (145).

6. The nineteenth century provided new occasions for concerns over the stability of property rights. Offer observes the consequences of redistribution of property between individuals and groups: "the attenuation and

emergence of property rights in the nineteenth century was not highly visible, but it was a central mode of internal change and continued to affect British society" (Offer 3). Offer adds that due to the onset of agrarian depression in Britain and Ireland in the late 1870s, the "land question" came to preoccupy the political nation (36).

7. Yet another disruption in transmission occurs as the property passes "through two heiresses" the last of whom, Margaret Fordyce, dies "childless, leaving the estate to her stepson, Philip Winslow, our ancestor" (1.65).

8. That is, the law of 1707 when Margaret Fordyce writes her will and the law of the 1830s when the action of *Chantry House* occurs. By the time of the writing of *Chantry House*, the Married Woman's Property Act, which "secured to a woman ... as her separate property 'all real and personal property which shall belong to her at the time of the marriage...'" had been enacted—in 1882 (Joan Perkin 305).

9. There is also a biographical explanation for Yonge's preference for female property transmission: Yonge's family inherited her beloved childhood home Otterbourne from her maternal grandmother; Yonge herself was displaced from the line of inheritance because of her gender.

10. The Winslows struggle with this question from the time of the discovery of the misappropriation. When Clarence Winslow, thinking on the legal plane, declares that Margaret's newly discovered will "will hardly invalidate our possession after a hundred and thirty years," Emily, his sister, rebuts the law with the moral view.

Chapter 5

1. Locke contends that the self is an unalienable possession of the individual: "every man has a property in his own person ... the labour of his body and the work of his hands ... are properly his" ("Of Property" [1689] 203). Rousseau's notion of "The Social Contract" (1762) is that the natural state of every individual is freedom. In *Phenomenology of Spirit* (1807), Hegel, whose thinking influences subsequent theories of freedom, argues that slavery existed at an early stage of civilization and that in more developed stages the slave achieves self-consciousness through activity and is able to overthrow the master.

2. Hegel, for example, asserts: "It is only through the development of his own body and mind, essentially through his self-consciousness's apprehension of itself as free, that he takes possession of himself and becomes his own property and no one else's" ("Property" 57, p. 47).

3. As Heller observes, "the novel expresses a strong critique of Victorian women's disadvantaged economic and legal position, especially within marriage. The weapon that allows Percival Glyde and Fosco to launch their conspiracy against Laura Fairlie is a marriage settlement that deprives her of power over her inheritance, a plot that emphasizes the lack of legal control Victorian wives had over their money prior to the Married Women's Property Acts of 1870 and 1882" (112).

4. This relationship suggests another parallel to Radcliffe's novel. Both heroines encounter evil because they have foolish aunts who marry villainous Italians.

5. Recalling Montoni's similarly quasi-legal attempts in *Udolpho*.

6. Fosco's admiration seems sincere and is likely a marker of his villainy; in Collins's world only a foreign villain could prefer Marian, who opposes all that is cherished in the Victorian Englishwoman, over Laura.

7. One more character in the novel is remarkable for her self-possession, Mrs. Catherick, Anne's mother, who knows the "secret" of Sir Percival's identity. During her brief appearance in the novel Walter repeatedly describes her in these terms. "Her manner [is] aggressively self-possessed" (433); she is a "self-possessed" woman (438) even though she knows that her daughter "has been lost" (433). She continues her discussion with Walter, "with additional self-possession" (434) and ends the discussion with a "defiant self-possession of... manner" (438). Although proper Walter, who favors childish women, finds her "cruel," "wicked" and hard, there is something to be admired in a woman who takes such pride in her self-possession. Significantly, Mrs. Catherick requires no rescuing when her identity is threatened; she recovers herself after she had been "robbed of my character" (436) and buys back her identity by blackmailing the villainous Sir Percival regarding his.

8. Walter also reveals his belief in the power of the written word to convey narrative meaning; he is the ostensible compiler and sometime initiator of the various documents that compose the novel.

Chapter 6

1. Drawing on Newton's idea of empirical science, which posited an orderly world available to the apprehension of the rational mind, and reinforced by the empiricism of Locke,

Berkeley and Hume, the eighteenth-century Enlightenment philosophy espoused by Voltaire promoted the powers of the rational mind to apprehend and control the world and itself. Gothic madness subverts the Enlightenment project of "putting man in possession of himself" (Foucault *Madness and Civilization* 214) and of the world.

2. A predicament that Heller suggests emblematizes specific Victorian concerns. Laura undergoes "a specifically Victorian version of Gothic that encodes contemporary concerns about the treatment of the insane, particularly of mentally ill women who were subject to unjust incarceration" (114).

3. Elaine Showalter's early study on madness (*The Female Malady* 1985) identifies historical associations of women and madness as a symptom of the powerlessness of women. She quotes Shoshana Felman: "Men, on the other hand, 'appear not only as the possessors, but also as the dispensers, of reason, which they can mete out to—or take away from—others'" (4). Marta Caminero-Santangelo returns to this notion in 1998: "insanity is not subversive," or not entirely and successfully subversive. Although, Caminero-Santangelo acknowledges, madness "can be legitimately read as a 'rejection' of the social order" (180), she asserts that it is ultimately "the final surrender to ... dominant discourses, precisely because it is characterized by the (dis)ability to produce meaning" (13). But in 1985, Showalter was already moving from this position, recalling that Phyllis Chesler "maintains that the women confined to American mental institutions are failed heroic rebels against the constraints of a narrow femininity" (4). In discussing *Wrongs*, Showalter continues: "the madwoman has become as emblematic a figure for contemporary feminists as she was for Mary Wollstonecraft in 1797" (4), that is, a figure of female resistance to socially imposed norms. While Jane thus presents a model of insanity as powerful resistance, so too does Bertha Rochester, burning down her prison Thornfield, as does a precursor of Bertha, the Saxon heiress who asserts her national identity in burning down the Norman-occupied family castle in Walter Scott's *Ivanhoe* (1819).

4. Of course, Wollstonecraft's contention that her text, constructed as a critique of the legal horrors of marriage, revealing "matrimonial despotism of heart and conduct" ("Author's Preface" 74) is unlike what she (mis)represents as the escapist fantasies of the Gothic, is disputed by the myriad instances of Gothic attention to law and society.

5. That Eliot tends to masculinize power in this and her other work exemplifies the struggle that Gilbert and Gubar see in her writing "a woman's reaction against her own internalization of a tradition that she recognizes as especially dangerous for females" (462).

6. Eliot's reading of Brontë's Bertha is indicated in a letter to she wrote to Charles Bray, dated 11 June 1848; Bertha is "a putrefying carcase" to whom Rochester is enchained by "diabolical law."

7. Latimer's discovery of the banality that lies beyond the lifted veil re-enacts Emily's experience in *Udolpho*; after a novel-length agony regarding a supposedly decaying body that is hidden behind a black veil, Emily and the reader discover that it is only a wax image.

8. Certainly the preponderance of the walls indicates the extent of the anxiety. As Nina Auerbach colorfully declaims, virtually every Gothic text displays instances of physical containment: "in these extravagant novels ... all roads ... lead to some sort of prison" ("Jane Austen and Romantic Imprisonment" 9).

9. Reading *The Mysteries of Udolpho*, Natalka Freeland finds in Emily's self-imposed standards of virtue and self-seclusion "law or convention ... so completely internalized that it is indistinguishable from personal and private morality" (156).

10. Julia's decision to cast her lot with her confined mother, discussed below, is another instance of this pattern.

Chapter 7

1. This is the most significant but not the only doubled relationship in the novel. The feminine feeble-minded Laura is also doubled by her masculinely intelligent half-sister (through her mother), Marian Halcombe. Walter and Sir Percival are paired as Laura's dual suitors and Sir Percival and Fosco are paired as the dual villains of the novel.

2. The threat posed to the integrity and stability of the self by the double is famously documented by Gilbert and Gubar who read Bertha Rochester as Jane Eyre's double: both are named Mrs. Rochester; Bertha comes to Jane's room wearing Jane's wedding veil; both are orphans. Gilbert and Gubar argue that Bertha represents what Jane wants to do, what she fears doing were she to lose the self-possession that characterizes her actions. Bertha expresses the anger that Jane represses and is what Jane wishes to be: Rochester's equal in size and strength. As the reading of Gilbert and Gubar indicates, the double is also a means of escape from physical and social

confinement. While Jane remains enclosed within the social roles of proper woman and wife, Bertha escapes her confinement. Yet in addition to indicating possibilities of escape, Bertha suggests the loss of self-control. Typical of the Gothic form, *Jane Eyre* demonstrates many other sets of doubles: John Reed and Mr. Rochester; Miss Temple and Helen Burns; Rochester and St. John; Diana and Mary. Here, as in the other texts discussed, the overwhelming pattern of the double unsettles the notion that each individual is the sole proprietor of individual qualities.

3. *The Italian*, like *Udolpho*, contains doubled fathers—the evil Schedoni and his good brother, the Count di Bruno, Ellena's father—as well as twin (or even quadrupled) mothers: the good pair—Ellena's aunt, Signora Bianchi and her hidden mother, Olivia—and the evil pair –Vivaldi's mother, the Marchesa, and the Abbess. In *Udolpho*, almost every major character is doubled: Emily's dead mother is doubled by her two aunts: Madame Montoni and the dead Marchioness de Villeroi. Emily's good father is paired with Montoni, her evil uncle. Emily herself is mirrored by her friend, Blanche. Her lover, Valancourt, is paired with Montoni and also with DuPont, another suitor of Emily. Valancourt also provides a more explicit instance of self-division; there is within the novel a good Valancourt, the young suitor who courts Emily, and later the bad Valancourt, who renders himself unsuitable for Emily by becoming enmeshed in a life of decadence. In this doubled narrative, even places are paired: the Castle of Udolpho is mirrored by La Vallée, Emily's home of origin and also by Chateau-le-Blanc, the home of Blanche.

4. Certainly one effect of all these doublings is to foreground the controlling father as the source of familial unhappiness and horror. Yet, equally certain is the superfluity of this strategy. Radcliffe's characterization and plot are never guilty of subtlety; her characterization of Mazzini is typically overwrought. We learn on the first page of the novel that he is "voluptuous and imperious ... arrogant and impetuous ... haughty and overbearing," unkind and neglectful toward his wife, "his heart dead to paternal tenderness" (3). Moreover, Radcliffe's descriptions of the crimes he perpetrates against his family—forced marriage, imprisonment, attempted murder—are all sufficient to implicate patriarchal power.

5. Writers who deploy the explained supernatural align themselves deferentially toward the Enlightenment. Such writers, like Radcliffe and Reeves, initially interrogate rational claims to possession of reality while eventually ceding to Enlightenment claims. Writers of the unexplained supernatural like Walpole and Lewis (and these examples do support Clery's observation regarding the gendering of this strategy) persist in a sustained refusal of the Enlightenment claim of the powers of the rational mind to possess reality.

6. The husband's possession of the wife is made explicit in the narrative of the bandit's wife. Her marriage is effected when the members of the band "cast lots to decide to whose possession I should fall; I became the property of the infamous Baptiste" (123). The role of the Catholic Church as possessor and prison of young women is shown in Agnes's fate; she is "destined to the Convent from her cradle" (130).

7. Veeder explains: "the amount of blood allotted to the reproductive system during the catamial period meant that only a dangerously small amount of blood remained in the brain" (60–61).

8. That the ghastly ghost is a Nun also reinforces the sense of anxiety originating in the power of the Catholic Church to take possession of others.

9. By, for example, Patrick McGrath.

10. In *The Melodramatic Imagination*, Peter Brooks locates this interiorization, which he calls "melodrama of consciousness," as a Modern development, found in the work of Henry James. In discussing *The Turn of the Screw*, Brooks observes that the reader does not know whether it is the house that is haunted by ghosts or the individual, the governess, who is haunted by madness.

Chapter 8

1. Bondeson's *Buried Alive* is certainly the most exhaustive work on the subject. In addition to tracing the phenomenon of live burial through history, Bondeson provides a chapter on "Literary Premature Burials."

2. Julian Litten states that the "one abiding fear during the early nineteenth century ... that of being buried alive ... is documented" (166) and gives examples of provisions made to avert this fate, and Ariès notes that "indications of anxiety continued to appear through the first half of the nineteenth century, although the references became less common in the more discreet wills" (400). Another culturally and historically determined fear associated with the loss of the body was the fear of losing the body after death. The presence of grave-robbers of the late eighteenth century threatened even the seemingly permanent security of the body in the grave. Ariès cites

instances of grave robbing, for purposes of scientific dissection, in Paris and in London in the late eighteenth century. In a report from London, dated 1793, "'Every night the watchman's rattle announced that more cadavers had just been stolen'" (369). This fear surfaces in *Frankenstein*; Victor Frankenstein, realizing that he cannot create a body ("with all its intricacies of fibres, muscles and veins" [47]) to animate, resorts to "the unhallowed damps of the grave" (48), "charnel-houses" (48)," "the dissecting room" (48). Victor Frankenstein is, then, in addition to his various other crimes, a grave-robber, appropriating the body parts that constitute his creation from their rightful owners. Kilgour notes that the fear of this figure also surfaces in Burke's rhetorical association of the grave-robber and the revolutionary in France (Kilgour *Rise of the Novel* 29). As Kilgour notes, this association suggests that the revolutionary, like Victor Frankenstein, has set in motion a force that he cannot control. Sherry Holman's historical novel, *The Dress Lodger*, provides a wonderfully vivid picture of the grave-robbing milieu in nineteenth-century England.

3. Ariès asserts: "The crisis of death is possibly the most severe of all the problems resulting from an individualistic philosophy" (10). Ariès indicates that one result of this new set of fears is the associated recognition, or construction, of a breach dividing death and life. In this, Ariès's research recalls Foucault's insight that new social categories of the eighteenth century called for new institutions devoted to maintaining the separation between the categories. The newly distinct categories of the dead and the living called for the development of new institutions to perpetuate the newly discovered, or invented, separation. These new institutions included the development of burial sites distant from the centers of living. As the idea of death and the dead was constructed as a separate category, to be distanced physically and socially, the dead were placed farther from the living, the locus of burial moving from church yard and church building to more distant cemeteries.

4. The distinction is drawn by Radcliffe herself in "On the Supernatural in Poetry." Radcliffe aligns terror with the unseen, with suspense that "awakens the faculties to a high degree of life." Horror, on the other hand, "freezes and nearly annihilates" (168) the faculties through a brutal exposure to the irrefutable and visible.

5. This episode echoes an anecdote told by Lawrence Stone of a mother who refused to relinquish the body of her baby (249). Stone uses his story to illustrate the increasing divide between death and everyday life; like Ariès, he traces this development to the rise of individuation.

6. Walter indicates another instance of lost self-possession associated with death: the dead and the memory of the dead possess the living, a psychological reality emblematized by the hauntings of ghosts.

7. The release from premature burial echoes the larger pattern of release from enclosure: Walpole's Theodore escapes the giant helmet to become the heir of Udolpho; Isabella is freed to become Theodore's bride; Reeve's Edmund escapes the haunted room to become the heir of Castle Lovel; Emily escapes from the Castle of Udolpho; Radcliffe's Ellena, too, escapes from her various prisons as does her lover, Vivaldi; Bertha Rochester escapes her attic, albeit through death.

8. Markman Ellis indicates (in *The History of Gothic Fiction*) that the fear of vampires was so vivid that it leaked out of the pages of fiction into the more respectable press. Reports of vampire attacks appeared in the press beginning in the 1730s, including an account in the respectable *London Journal* in March 1732 that resulted in much controversial discussion of the topic (161–162).

Chapter 9

1. Dale Porter indicates that British merchant ships had been transporting Negro slaves from Africa to the West Indies since the end of the sixteenth century. By 1775, when the British West Indies had reached a peak of prosperity and non–British territories were rapidly expanding, merchants from British ports carried nearly 60,000 slaves a year across the Atlantic. F.O. Shyllon establishes the concurrence of British slavery and Gothic literature, disputing the notion that black slaves were emancipated in England as early as 1772. Shyllon notes that the decision of Lord Mansfield, Chief Justice of England on June 22 of that year determined only that black slaves could not be forcibly removed from England (3). Shyllon finds in the case of Grace Jones (in which in 1827 Lord Stowell of the High Court of Admiralty ruled that a slave brought into England did not become free by that fact alone) proof that slavery was not fully erased from Britain as a result of the 1772 Mansfield judgment. In fact, not until 1834 (or 1838 with the end of the apprenticeship system) were black slaves in Britain fully emancipated, as were slaves in British colonies in the West Indies. The period of the most intense anti-

slavery rhetoric was also congruent with the period of the high Gothic. Dale Porter notes that the abolition of the British slave trade was formally proposed in 1788, in the form of the Slave Trade Regulating Act of 1788, and that arguments for and against abolition filled the intervening years before slavery was finally abolished (37). Clare Midgely notes that with the passage of the Abolition Act of 1807 abolishing British slave trade, the campaign against slavery itself began (76). This lasted until slavery was abolished in 1834. David Turley notes that the "period of slave emancipation" (9) lasted from 1780s until the 1830s. Several historians note even earlier anti-slavery sentiment. Moira Ferguson writes of the "growing anti-slavery protest" (108) during the 1770s and David Dabydeen argues that "by 1750 there was already considerable public awareness of the brutality of the slave trade" (38). "From the 1770's onward, English was deluged by antislavery verse" (44).

2. Toussaint L'Oeverture's bloody slave rebellion in St. Domingue, lasting from 1791 to 1803, provided much raw material for horrifying fantasies of slave vengeance. And, as Dabydeen indicates, the rebellions presented an actual example of the political uses of horror: "The revolts had an impact on the dismantling of slavery" (14).

3. Ruth Cowhig writes of the long "tradition of the black villain-hero" (2) in Shakespeare, including Aaron in *Titus Andronicus* and Othello. This is of particular relevance when we remember that Shakespeare is an early and important influence on the Gothic, beginning with Walpole and Radcliffe.

4. In *Women Against Slavery*, Midgely traces the roots of the women's rights movement in the abolition movement in England (a progression that also occurred in the United States), noting that women were involved in the anti-slavery movement through local ladies' anti-slavery associations. In "Remember Those in Bonds," Midgeley writes, "The antislavery movement spanned the period between Mary Wollstonecraft's key feminist work, *A Vindication of the Rights of Women* (1792) and the formation of the first women's suffrage societies in 1867."

5. This rhetorical conflation endures well into the nineteenth century: in *The Subjection of Women* (1869) John Stuart Mill connects the legal position of woman in marriage with that of the slave and appeals to the English distaste for slavery (by then abolished in England) in arguing for women's rights (Section I).

6. Dickenson notes that "if a person is not a possessive individual, then he—or much more likely she—cannot enter into a social contract." Locke asserts: "Every Man has a Property in his own Person. This no body has any Right to but himself.... But women lack a property in their own person ... they do not own the labour of their bodies ... because they have no property in their bodies" (72).

7. The setting of Dacre's novel is of great interest. *Zofloya* was written shortly after the collapse of the Serene Republic of Venice in 1797. The structures of this Republic and the threat of its Inquisition loom at the margins of the novel; contemporary readers would have noticed that these structures had within recent memory collapsed. Dacre's allusion to political revolution is one of many instances in which she evokes Lewis's *The Monk*, a text that explicitly gestures to the horrors of the French Revolution. The setting of Venice indicates other important literary influences. Of course, the story of a Moor in Venice alludes to *Othello*; additionally, *Zofloya* gestures to *The Merchant of Venice* in an interesting way. There are strong indications that Dacre, like Shylock, was Jewish. Kim Ian Michasiw quotes from a letter of Bryon calling Dacre "this lovely little Jessica, [alluding of course to *Merchant*] the daughter of the noted Jew K" (xii). One possible explanation for Dacre's pseudonym is that it indicates an aristocratic connection to "Acre ... the last city held by the crusaders in Palestine" (*Zofloya* Appendix 269). Dacre's cultural identity imparts significance to a seemingly meaningless episode in which Leonardo, the brother of the heroine, takes refuge in the household of a rich benefactor. When the wife of the benefactor tries to seduce him, Leonardo refuses; the wife accuses him of seduction and Leonardo is cast out (86–93). This story evokes the Biblical story of Joseph in the house of Potiphar, a story that is particularly telling because it leads to the Biblical narrative of the enslavement of the Israelites in Egypt, a story that of course has great resonance within this novel of slavery and enslavement.

8. Indicated henceforth as Satan/Zofloya to differentiate from the unpossessed Zofloya

9. In a continuation of the motif of the appropriated body, Victoria later dreams that the body is discovered in a chest by a servant of Berenza: "Forth from the chest they drew the disclosed, half mouldered skeleton, that once had been Berenza" (228).

10. "Leonardo took possession of the homely bed" to go to sleep (97)—an instance of the complicated locution that results from Dacre's insistent use of the language of possession.

11. The form of the demonic contract is worth noting here: Victoria need only state that she is Zofloya's in order to consign herself to satanic possession. This contrasts with the insistence upon the written contract that Brantlinger (45) notes in *The Monk* when Satan appears, like an efficient bureaucrat, with the implements of possession—paper and parchment—in hand.

12. This demonic marriage appears to be a source for the marriage of Isidora to Melmoth the Wanderer in Maturin's novel; in each case marriage is equated with demonic possession.

13. Malchow overlooks the trope of the dark patriarch when he writes of darkly dangerous marginalized characters like Heathcliff and Frankenstein as encoded slaves, representing contemporary anxiety regarding slave rebellion.

14. A useful overview of the legal status of women regarding property possession in England before the enactment of the liberalizing laws of the late-nineteenth century is to be found in "A Brief Summary in Plain Language, of the Most Important Laws Concerning Women" (1854) compiled by Barbara Bodichon, "the first great campaigner for the reform of the property laws" (Dolin 2). A more exhaustive discussion of the topic is to be found in Susan Staves's *Married Women's Separate Property*.

15. In "Patriarchal Territories," Peter Stallybrass turns to Bakhtin to suggest a philosophical foundation for the containment of the female body through coverture, as it recollects the uncontrolled and transgressive grotesque body that Bakhtin delineates. Stallybrass traces the trajectory of thought: since the woman's body is "*naturally* grotesque" it must be subject to "constant surveillance" (126). "In the process, 'woman,' unlike man, is produces as a *property* category.... Economically, she is the fenced-in enclosure of the landlord, her father, or husband" (127).

16. The category of the "unperson" had a contemporary equivalent. As Clery notes, Locke's minimum condition for civil rights is the ownership of property; loss or lack of property denoted loss of civil rights (Clery *Supernatural Fiction* 125). Immanuel Kant too, links political viability with property (and with maleness—embedded in the parenthetical "of course" of the following sentence). In "On the Relationship of Theory to Practice in Political Right" he writes: "The only qualification required by a citizen (apart, of course, from being an adult male) is that he must be *his own master*... and must have some *property*" (78).

17. As Shanley points out, "aggravating a married woman's plight was the fact that it was extremely difficult for her to extricate herself from the bonds of matrimony" (9). Thus marriage as slavery.

18. Clery makes a similar observation in *The Rise of Supernatural Fiction*. Writing of Mme. Montoni's death in *Udolpho*, she notes "legal metaphor [is] represented as a lived experience. The 'civil death' required by common law is actualised in Mme Montoni's death. Elsewhere, married women are reduced to 'ghosts' or the 'living dead' by the law or exist as supposed ghosts" (126). To support the latter statement, Clery cites *A Sicilian Romance*. Clery also evokes Maria's statement in *Wrongs of Woman* that she is bastilled by marriage and argues that the "metaphor does not remain a figure of speech but is objectively realized in the plot" (127). What Clery overlooks is that these instances exemplify literalization, a strategy expressly associated with women's writing.

19. Both acts are, of course, evocations of incestuous rape.

20. The passage is curiously echoed in the slave narrative *Incidents in the Life of a Slave Girl* by Harriet Jacobs, an instance of Jacobs appropriating the strategies of popular literature to lend power to her autobiographical narrative.

21. Joan Perkin cites instances of fathers appropriating their children that are as horrifying to read as any Gothic novel.

22. Although a fragmentary note provided by William Godwin after her death suggests that Wollstonecraft planned a resolution in which Jemima finds and restores Maria's child (203). The pattern of struggle for possession of the child and the father's frequent appropriation of the child continues in the twentieth-century in E.M. Forster's curiously Gothic first novel, *Where Angels Fear to Tread* (1920). In this narrative, the English family of the mother, who has been abjected first by a brutish Italian husband and then by death, tries to wrest the child from the Italian father. The eventual death of the child, whose body is the site of the central struggle of the novel, is a revision of the conventional Gothic closure in which the contested castle is destroyed, rendering it useless to all disputants. E.M. Foster's complicated variation of this theme creates ambiguity in the conventional paradigm; in representing the imperialistic attempt by the English family to take the child from the Italian father, Forster interrogates the conventional categories of appropriating father and dispossessed mother.

23. Radcliffe's representation of the powers of the state as emblem of moral authority in

Udolpho and *The Italian* is atypical of the eighteenth-century Gothic and is, perhaps an example of her conservative tendencies. The presence of the police as an emblem of political order and control that D. A. Miller notes in *Novel and the Police* is a more common phenomenon in the Victorian novels that Miller discusses. However, Miller does evoke Foucault to indicate that the rise of the disciplining power of the state begins in the late eighteenth century, the period in which *Udolpho* was written.

24. Accounting, in part, for the continuing popularity of the mode among women, who have most to gain by this ludic subversion.

25. As Erickson points out, "The romantic ideal of companionate marriage ...was articulated in the eighteenth century.... However, feminist historians observe that these romantic ideals were simply a new means of maintaining male dominance at a time when overt demands of submission were no longer acceptable" (7).

26. In contextualizing *Clarissa*, written five years before the Hardwicke Marriage Act, Mary Vermillion, asserts that the act was an attempt on the part of parents "to legislate a reverence for dynasticism and parental authority that they themselves could not inspire" (411).

27. Foucault's discussion of incest in *The History of Sexuality* is also relevant to the Gothic. As Anne Williams observes, "Freud's theory of the repression of incestuous passions demanded by the Oedipus complex are staples of the Gothic tradition" (Williams 90); that is, the Gothic is riddled with instances of incest or near-incest. Foucault sheds light on this preoccupation in arguing that "since the eighteenth century the family has become an obligatory locus of affects, feelings, love ... a hotbed of constant sexual incitement" (108–109) and that the taboo of incest derives from the economic necessity of diverting sexual interest and marriage bonds away from the immediate family outward to other families with whom union would be economically beneficial.

Chapter 10

1. Within this framework, Mary Shelley's representation of parenthood in *Frankenstein* (1818) might be fruitfully read as a critique of primogeniture through the literalization of the absent mother. Many critics see Shelley's novel as a critique of the male appropriation of the mother's biological act of procreation, as in Victor's nine-month labor to produce a child without a mother. However, within the legal context of patriarchy and the textual context of other novels that are preoccupied with the issue of paternity, it is tempting to read Shelley's deployment of the motif of the absent mother (in addition to the nonexistent mother of the monster, many other mothers are absent from Shelley's text) as a critique of the legal structures—primogeniture and paternal possession—that are reflected in so many Gothic texts. Certainly one indication of the monster's subversiveness is his demand for a female partner to share equally in the production of an heir.

2. As Jane Gallup precisely indicates, the system of patriarchal law and the structure of primogeniture decree that the womb is a passive receptacle and (citing Luce Irigaray) "the womb is 'itself possessed as a means of (re)production'" (43). The Gothic responds to this dispossession with the trope of the missing mother, which literalizes the legal situation of the mother under the system of primogeniture.

3. As Carolyn Dever notes, "the mother is constructed as an emblem of the safety, unity, and order that existed before the very dangerous chaos of the child's Gothic plot" (24).

4. That which Miller defines as "instances of disequilibrium, suspense, and general insufficiency from which a given narrative appears to arise ... opposed to the 'nonnarratable' state of quiescence assumed by a novel before the beginning and supposedly recovered by it at the end" (ix).

5. In *The Madwoman in the Attic*, Gilbert and Gubar build upon Woolf's insight, and echo Chesler's observation that "women are motherless children in patriarchal society." They thus identify the absent mother as an emblem for the inability of women to create and to sustain a female tradition within the patriarchy, leading to an "anxiety of authorship."

6. The OED confirms the validity of the double definition of this word; as early as 1774, "confinement" means "the being in child-bed; childbirth, delivery, accouchement" in addition to meaning imprisonment.

7. The contemporary double meaning of this word is also validated by the OED.

8. A reality recognized by one OED definition of the word "deliver": "to disburden (a woman) of the foetus."

9. In "Revising Gothic Primogeniture," Michael Macovski surveys the scholarship on "the primogenitury plots that distinguish both the eighteenth- and nineteenth-century literary traditions" (33)—and notes that "critics ranging from David Punter to Emma Clery and from Maggie Kilgour to Anne Williams, all limn primogeniture and its various subversions—including female inheritance, bastard lines, and the broken law of the Father—as constitutive of the Gothic ... adversions of

Gothic primogeniture become even more pronounced during the Romantic era ... the authors begin to promulgate directly transgressive ideas of meritorious inheritance, redefined property, and truncated paternity" (32).

10. This instance recalls the moment in *The Old English Baron* in which possession of the castle is similarly destabilized by the opening of the containing doors.

11. Of significance to the following discussion of narrative possession, Gilbert's social power is accompanied by his narrative power. He is the narrator of the text; Helen's diary, the narrative of her dispossession, is framed by Gilbert's narrative and is shared by him with his reader.

12. A principle later articulated by Freud in "Family Romances": "'*pater semper incertus est*,' while the mother is 'certissima'" (299).

13. Donna Dickensen adds: "This deficiency in men—their crucial inability to assure their own fatherhood— ... motivates them to devise the sexual contract. The prior subordination of women to men and male sex-right over female bodies—the sexual contract—is required to ground the social contract" (75).

14. Edgeworth's propensity to satirize the Gothic is more explicit in a more obscure work that Railo compares to Austen's *Northanger Abbey* (1817): "Miss Edgeworth, too, mocked at the romanticism of her times in her story, 'Angelina or L'Amie Inconnue,' *Moral Tales* (1801)" (78).

15. This recurring trope indicates the women's dispossession of identity within the patriarchy.

16. Long's essay "Wavering, Witless, and Without Council: The Widow in Restoration and Eighteenth-Century England" confirms that, fictional representations notwithstanding, the situation of the widow in patriarchal pre-industrial England was powerful and prosperous.

17. Macovski writes of a related connection, commenting on "a striking parallel between the handing down of inheritance and the handing down of texts. That is, we can trace a remarkable correspondence between the way that landed property, family castles, and dowries are inherited across generations—and the way texts are read, copied, imitated, plagiarized and forged through time" (32).

Chapter 11

1. Another variation of the multiple narrative voice in the Victorian Gothic is to be found in one of Dickens's later Christmas books, *The Haunted House* (1862). In this ghost story, Dickens provides introductory material and two stories: "The Ghost in Master B.'s Room" and "The Ghost in the Corner Room." All the other chapters—each devoted to the story of the exorcism of a room in the eponymous house—are provided by other authors including Wilkie Collins and Elizabeth Gaskell. In this text the narrative literally and explicitly moves beyond the control of the aging author who, Ackroyd suggests in the introduction, was incapable of the task of completing yet another Christmas book on his own. Thus while the haunted house is exorcised of its ghosts, the text, *The Haunted House*, remains haunted by the voices of the contributors to Dickens's work.

2. A number of critics have noted the multiple narratives to be found in *Wuthering Heights* in which Brontë's decentralized voices tend to destabilize meaning as well as authorial power. In writing of the repetition that results from the multiple narratives in Brontë's novel and of the multiple interpretative responses made possible by this narrative frame, J. Hillis Miller comments that critics, readers and characters are forced to conclude that there is no "single, unified and logically coherent" (*Wuthering Heights* 384) meaning to be found in the text. Beth Newman reads the resistance of *Wuthering Heights* to readerly and critical possession as a feminist strategy; the multiple narratives resist containment by the male monolithic gaze that is characteristic of much nineteenth-century fiction.

3. James's *The Turn of the Screw* also exemplifies this atypical structure.

4. Noteworthy as the year of publication of *Otranto*.

5. Is this unnamed Italian the title character? After all, every character in the book is Italian. Even though Schedoni the quintessentially evil Italian is typically considered the eponymous character, the narrative authority of the unnamed Italian might indicate that Radcliffe accords him this dubious honor.

6. In the case of the document, the passage of time further invalidates the meaning. As Clarence indicates: "even if it [the will] can be made out, it will hardly invalidate our possession after a hundred and thirty years" (II.172).

7. Jan B. Gordon makes an interesting connection between the fragmented narrative and other Gothic tropes of disruption: "The very proliferation of fragments in Gothic fiction—abandoned houses, rusty locks, ill-fitting bolts, crumbling graves, incompleted manuscripts, half-formed sensibilities—share the ontology of the interrupted" that which left in an open-ended state avoids "any terminal judgement"

(213–214). To this evocative set, I would add the tropes of the interrupted wedding and the deferred closure.

Chapter 12

1. Susan Stewart observes that "within the eighteenth-century transformations of the literary marketplace the decline of patronage, the rise of booksellers, the advent of mass literary production and copyright, the development of the concept of 'intellectual property'—lies a central set of questions regarding the relationship among speech and writing authorship, authenticity, and audience" (4).

2. Mark Rose traces the culmination of the "question of literary property" in the consolidation of the "world's first copyright statute [the Statute of Anne] ...enacted [in Britain] in 1710" (4), "a legislative extension of the long-standing regulatory practice of the stationer's Company, the ancient London guild of printers and booksellers [with] two major innovations: the statute limited the term of protection (the guild copyrights were perpetual), and authors were legally recognized as possible proprietors of their words (previously only members of the guild could hold copyrights)" (4).

3. Kayman indicates the linguistic basis of this conceptual conflation; copyright law involves "not a plot of land, but a plot whose value waits on the time of unfolding" ("The Reader and the Jury" 378).

4. Significantly, Michael North draws on Gothic tropology to define earlier anxieties: "the need to distinguish the creative imitation from the servile and thus to distinguish memorable writers from ignorable ones haunted Renaissance notions of authorship" (1380).

5. This argument lies at the center of Françoise Meltzer's *Hot Property*. Meltzer asserts that "'originality' itself [is] a construct, or even ... a mythology" and that "within the literary establishment, any claim of originality seeks to protect its fruits as being (on) private property" (1). North articulates the paradox of the claim to originality: "at some basic level, at least that of language, the materials of language are common property" (1381).

6. In "The Death of Author," Barthes similarly argues that the concept of "author" is an ideological construct that allows us to imagine a text as univocal, emanating from a unified source when in fact a text resists the containment and hermeneutic apprehension implied by the concept of author: "To give a text an Author is to impose a limit on that text, to furnish it with a final signified, to close the writing" (146–147).

7. It is at this moment of the construction of text as property, Foucault argues, that "the transgressive properties always intrinsic to the act of writing became the forceful imperative of literature. It is as if the author, at the moment he was accepted into the social order of property, which governs our culture, was compensating for his new status by reviving the older bipolar field of discourse in a systematic practice of transgression and by restoring the danger of writing which, on another side, had been conferred the benefits of property" (125). This observation provides yet another explanation for the rise of the transgressive Gothic in the eighteenth century.

Chapter 13

1. Melmoth is the diabolical eponymous character of the novel, living from the seventeenth to the nineteenth century; he is to be distinguished from his relative John Melmoth who untangles the story through the course of the novel and who inhabits the nineteenth century.

2. The doubled name denotes the character's dual personae: she is known as Immalee when stranded on a remote island, Isadora after she is recovered by her aristocratic Spanish family.

3. This situation vividly echoes the plight of Agnes in *The Monk*. Another pointed evocation of *The Monk*, beyond the obvious echoes of Satanic temptation and the demonization of the Catholic Church, is the scene of the death of the parricide in Melmoth's narrative. The parricide is reduced by a mob to "a mangled lump of flesh" (255); his death evokes the gruesome death of the prioress in *The Monk*; each death at the hands of a ferocious mob re-enacts the horrors of the French Revolution.

4. Maturin also revisits more conventional anxieties of property possession. In his introduction to the novel, Baldick comments: "It is money, after all that sets this story in motion, from John Melmoth's first arrival at his rich uncle's deathbed to the fatal inheritance which ruins the Mortimers in "the Lovers Tale." More particularly, it is family wealth which repeatedly brings disaster to the novel's leading characters: Stanton, Monçada, Immalee, and Elinor are all in their "various ways imprisoned by their own mercenary relatives" (xviii).

5. Patrick Brantlinger notes Maturin's special place in the Gothic tradition, observing that recurrence of tropes of narrative dispossession throughout the canon, "editorial frames, stories-within-stories, documents and fragments of documents.... The record for this

sort of textual doubling and redoubling probably belongs to Charles Maturin's *Melmoth the Wanderer*" (39).

6. Drawing on the vocabulary of antique furniture, Stewart coins the term "distressed genres" to describe new narratives that are made to look old. Although Stewart does not specify Maturin, this term is usefully applied to some of the narratives in *Melmoth* that satisfy "the nostalgia for authenticity and subjectivity inherent in this Romantic relation to time" (23). Indeed, the term "distressed narrative" (revealing a double-meaning unintended by Stewart) may be applied to much of the Gothic mode in which contemporary narratives are frequently presented as antique.

Chapter 14

1. Chris Baldrick notes that "Maturin has overloaded the character with several functions working at cross-purposes.... Melmoth is not just a Faust, he is a Mephistopheles at the same time ... the Wanderer has to act the role of Milton's Satan in Eden while also doubling up as the archangel Raphael who justifies the ways of God to Eve and warns her against the archtempter ... like the Irish landlords of his day, Melmoth is an absentee villain" (xvi). Baldick is quite correct, but he misses some of the meanings of this overdetermined character; Melmoth is also the wandering outcast Cain and the Wandering Jew. As Rosenberg asserts, "the theme of the Eternal Wanderer who discovers the horror of his compact and devotes his life to the search for a proxy reaches its full climax only with the story of Melmoth" (230). Margaret Drabble also notes that "there are elements of the story" of the Wandering Jew in *Melmoth* (1053). The most comprehensive discussion of the connections between the figures of the Wandering Jew, Cain and Melmoth is to be found in Railo's *The Haunted Castle* in which Railo traces the figure of the Wandering Jew in the western canon.

2. Margaret Drabble expands upon this in *The Oxford Companion to English Literature*: The monk of 1228 was Roger of Wendover who tells the story in his *Flores Historiarum*: "An Armenian archbishop visited England in 1228" and told of dining with "Joseph, who was present at the Crucifixion, and was said to be still alive, as a testimony of the Christian faith.... He had been Pontius Pilate's porter, by name Cartaphilus, who when they were dragging Jesus from the Judgement Hall, had struck him on the back, saying, "Go faster, Jesus, why dost thou linger?,' to which Jesus replied, 'I indeed am going, but thou shalt tarry till I come.' This man had been converted soon after and named Joseph. He lived for ever, and was now a very grave and holy person" (1052).

3. From a theological perspective, the figure of the uncanny Wandering Jew represents the return of the repressed theological past of Christianity. Bonnie Friedman observes that the figure of the Wandering Jew provides a Christian account for the survival of the Jews in the face of their rejection of Jesus; the myth "interprets Jewish triumph as punishment, Jewish endurance as victimization" (11). The location of the Jew underneath the lintel prefigures his wandering—he is a liminal figure, belonging to no time or place.

4. This mysterious and dangerous figure appears in a number of Gothic texts including William Godwin's *St Leon* (1779) and Lewis's *The Monk* (1795). The mysterious "Great Mogul" (167) who exorcizes the ghost of the Blooding Nun in *The Monk* is revealed to be "the celebrated Character known universally by the name of '*the wandering Jew*'" (177). Lewis's representation of the Wandering Jew anticipates Maturin's: until his identity is revealed, the Great Mogol, like Melmoth, is described as "a Foreigner," (167); he too is associated with "Doctor Faustus, whom the Devil had sent back to Germany" (167) and with Cain: "God has set his seal upon me, and all his Creatures respect this fatal mark!" (169). Lewis's Wandering Jew tells Raymond that he is doomed to wander eternally: "Fate obliges me to be constantly in movement," words that are derived from "a poem by Christian Friedrich Daniel Schubart entitled 'Der Ewige Jude' (1787)." Schiller also revisits this myth in his poem "Der Geisterseher" (McEvoy Note 169 *Monk* 450). The persistence of the figure of the Wandering Jew in the Gothic is one example of the tendency of the Gothic text to reconfigure the supernatural Other, horrifying because unknown, as the racial and cultural Other, equally horrifying because equally unknown.

5. An intermediary stage on this journey is represented by Lytton's *Zanoni*, which is discussed by Railo in his lengthy section on "The Wandering Jew"—a section that curiously omits discussion of *Trilby*. In Railo's description of Lytton's text we see foreshadowings of Du Maurier's. The "second chief character of the book, the singer Viola, a character whose whole soul is filled with music" (Railo 210), anticipates Trilby who is fated to become a musical instrument. The Wandering Jew figure, Zanoni, is of unknown origins and "dusky sheen.... Many old persons profess to have seen him ... in the days of their youth, yet his appearance has not changed." Zanoni is even

more closely evocative of Svengali in his "glance. He is able to impart to it such power that he can govern the minds of others" (Railo 212).

6. This was not the case when Du Maurier first published his sensational novel; *Trilby* was a great success, becoming "the first modern best seller in American publishing" (Showalter ix). Indeed, in a trend that prefigured the excesses of twentieth-century popular culture, "Trilby [the eponymous heroine of the novel] generated a craze—'Trilby-mania'—that went beyond the novel itself. Socialites performed *tableaux vivants* from the book, and sang Trilby's songs to raise money for charity; art galleries exhibited the manuscript, illustrations ... manufacturers vied to produce Trilby products from ice-cream to shoes; and a town in Florida named its streets after characters in the book" (Showalter ix-x).

7. Figured by Rosenberg as "the Wandering Jew driving about London in a gilded landau, with a nice Gibson girl in tow" (235).

8. Du Maurier's evocation of this anti–Semitic trope connects to his representation of Svengali's sexual lasciviousness. Sander Gilman elaborates on this association: "in turn-of-the-century Europe there was an association between the genitalia and the nose" (188). The exaggerated focus upon the nose of the Jew reflected an anxious interest in "the hidden sign of his sexual difference, his circumcised penis" (189). Gilman argues that the emphasis on the difference of the nose (or phallus) of the Jew was another way to distinguish an Other whose otherness was rapidly becoming invisible.

9. In *Zofloya*, for example, the dark powerless slave slips into the role of the dark powerful master, anticipating the movement of Heathcliff, the dark outcast in *Wuthering Heights*.

10. The common association of Jewish blood with uncontainable danger in European anti–Semitic rhetoric invites Halberstam and other critics to see the germ of anti–Semitism within the image of the vampire and his insidiously invasive blood.

11. We see in Du Maurier's anxious description of little Billee and in the project of his text a demonstration of the anxieties generated by the "*peculiar nature* of the threatening otherness of the Jew.... Whereas in general the Other's most threatening aspect seems to reside in an identifiable difference, the most ominous aspect of the Jewish threat appeared as related to sameness. The Jews' adaptability seemed to efface all boundaries and to subvert the possibilities of natural confrontation. The Jew was the *inner* enemy *par excellence*"

(Friedländer 213). This fear surfaces in another fact that we learn about Billee: "Little Greek that he was, he worshipped the athlete" (170). Since we already know that little Billee is also a little Jewish, the association in this phrase jolts us once again. For in this tiny character, Du Maurier appears to capture a synthesis between Hebrew and Hellene –the two cultures that Arnold works so hard to disentangle in his influential work *Culture and Anarchy* (1869).

12. Rosenberg notes that in this description, Du Maurier "recovers ... the often potent medieval metaphor [of anti–Semitism], that of the dog" (256).

13. Wistrich's description of the iconography of the Devil in Christian art confirms the source of Svengali's description: the Devil is typically figured as "an undeniably repulsive figure with an oversized head, bulging eyes, horns, a tail, and long, flamelike hair" (Wistrich 4).

14. This passage evokes "a favourite image of late nineteenth-century medical art ... the image of the aged pathologist contemplating the exquisite body of the dead prostitute before he opens it" (Gilman 108). Gilman illustrates this image with an example: "the striking image by Enrique Simonet (1890)." In this photograph we see a beautiful dead woman lying on a slab in a morgue while a bearded physician gazes at her half-draped body: the fate that Svengali envisions for Trilby is before us.

15. Richard Kelly argues for another association of Svengali with the devil. He notes that when Little Billee first hears about La Svengali from another famous singer, "her voice is described in terms of an instrument: 'Everything that Paganini could do with his violin she does with her voice—only better'" (258, Kelly's citation). Legend had it that the only way Paganini could have achieved his virtuosity on the violin was by selling his soul to the devil. Du Maurier's association of Svengali with the devil is subtly reinforced through this allusion. Kelly also cites the conversation between Trilby and the conductor when Svengali dies. "The references to God, the devilish musicians and the Satanic music further strengthen the relationship between Svengali's demonic character and the music" (99).

16. An interesting and relevant discussion of the figure of the artist's model in nineteenth-century French literature may be found in Marie Lathers's *Bodies of Art*. Lathers considers "how the female model is narrated and read by readers and spectators" (1) and the relation of the figure of the artist's model to realism. "Through the figure of the model ... realist authors were able to produce and dispute claims concerning representation, mime-

sis, and the real, as well as sexual and other forms of difference" (2). Lathers shows the significance of the ethnicity of the model, tracing an evolution "in the preference for different racial and ethnic model types, from the Jewish model, most popular in the 1830's and 1840's, to the Italian immigrant model favored by painters in the 1850's, 1860's, and 1870's, to the Parisian poser ... of the 1880's and 1890's" (15–16). This discussion becomes relevant when we remember that Trilby is an Anglo/Irish artist's model and that Du Maurier sets the opening scenes of his story in the 1850s. Of further interest: Lathers identifies "the novel of the artist's life as a "popular subgenre of French literature" (4) and also identifies an English strain, exemplified by the American Nathaniel Hawthorne's *The Marble Faun* and Oscar Wilde's *The Picture of Dorian Gray*. Of great significance to the discussion of this essay is that both Hawthorne's and Wilde's texts, like Du Maurier's, veer toward the supernatural Gothic in their stories of artist life. Reading from a different perspective, Lukacs notes that the relationship of the artist to his model is "only a special and immediately palpable case of the changed relationship between art and life in general" and indicates that Flaubert, Baudelaire, Ibsen and Anatole France wrote of this relationship" ("Tribune" 221).

17. That George Eliot associates realism with moral imperatives is evident from her essay "Realism" in which she equates realistic writing with honest writing, providing "a faithful account of men and things" (113), finding the truth of "the secret of deep human sympathy" (115).

18. Kelly adds, "for Svengali, music, like mesmerism is power and control" (98). For a fuller discussion of mesmerism and its representations in literature see Maria Tatar's *Spellbound*.

19. This discrepancy was likely due to the mores of Jewish culture that promotes music in liturgical forms while disparaging the visual arts as a violation of the second commandment prohibition of graven images.

20. An association echoed in Eliot's *Daniel Deronda*: Daniel's Jewish mother is an actress and singer.

21. These intensely gazing eyes connect this photograph to the portrait in *Melmoth*.

22. Benjamin connects the capacity of the photograph to disrupt the relationship of artist and art to the disruptive effects of printing: "The enormous changes which printing, the mechanical reproduction of writing, has brought about in literature are a familiar story" (218–219). This comparison indicates the concerns that result in the anxieties of ownership of textual art and visual art that inform *Trilby*.

23. This is, of course, part of Roland Barthes's argument in "The Death of the Author." In his formulation the death of the author is particularly visible in the medium of photography.

24. Benjamin asserts "the nineteenth-century dispute as to the artistic value of painting versus photography ... was in fact the symptom of a historical transformation" (226). In fact, Du Maurier's photographic portrait of Svengali recalls Maturin's vividly realistic painting of Melmoth in *Melmoth the Wanderer*. Maturin's unexpected attraction to realism accounts for the significance of the portrait in his text. *Melmoth* begins with an episode that valorizes the death-defying power of the realistic portrait. John Melmoth returns to Ireland (in 1816) to see his uncle who is dying of fright from seeing alive a man whose portrait is dated 1646. We see the portrait from John's perspective: "There was nothing remarkable in the costume, or in the countenance, but *the eyes*" (17). John is reminded of a poem by Southey that describes "eyes ... [that] gleamed with demon light" (18). This portrait is a representation that (like the Wandering Jew) cannot be destroyed; although John burns the portrait, it uncannily reappears in "a miniature likeness of that extraordinary being ... so faithfully [rendered] that the pencil appeared rather held by the mind than by the fingers" (72). Maturin's image of the realistically drawn portrait uncannily prefigures Du Maurier's later representation of Svengali, whose supernatural power rests in his eyes.

25. The movement toward realism in the late nineteenth century was—as George Levine suggests in his influential analysis—"a self-conscious rejection of certain conventions of literary representation and of their implications" (*The Realistic Imagination* 5), "in pursuit of the unattainable unmediated reality" (8).

26. Brantlinger observes that "at the same time that George Eliot was investing the novel with a new philosophical gravity, the sensationalists were breaking down the conventions of realist fiction" (164).

27. It is this problem that Tom Lloyd locates as the "radical uncertainty at the heart of realism as it continually questions itself in the process of creating relative order out of a world in social and cultural flux" (11–12). Katherine Kearns also defines the unsettling paradox at the center of the realist project: "one must guard against reproducing exactly the effects of reality, with its welter of detail, its bewildering subversions of expectation, and its capricious tendency toward a coincidentally

perfect order that would embarrass any artist worth her salt" (51).

28. As narrated by Joel Carmichael: "At the end of the nineteenth century the 'Dreyfus Affair' highlighted and focused the tension surrounding the Jews.... Captain Alfred Dreyfus, son of a rich textile manufacturer, had a position in the French War Ministry; in 1894 he was charged with treason (selling military secrets to the Germans); on 22 December he was convicted and sentenced to life imprisonment on Devil's Island.... The tone of the press, however, was unusually vindictive; its theme was that Dreyfus symbolized the inherent disloyalty of French Jews to France. Anti-Semitic elements led the chorus of outrage.... This coupled with severe doubt raised by extraordinary irregularities in the trial, created a violent counter-movement.... For twelve years all France ... was polarized.... Dreyfus's innocence [was] demonstrated a few years later" (140–141).

29. In the diabolic construction of Svengali, *Trilby* recalls another late–Victorian text that unleashes the Gothic in the form of Satan: Marie Corelli's *The Sorrows of Satan* (1895—the year after the publication of *Trilby*) in which Satan is figured as the sorrowful (and thus atypically ambiguous) Prince Rimânez. Like *Trilby*, *The Sorrows of Satan* was an enormous popular success and like *Trilby*, *Sorrows* quickly vanished from the canon. In his introduction to *The Sorrows of Satan* Peter Keating suggests that the recontextualization into the Gothic tradition accounts for the disappearance of this popular work (and hence *Trilby* as well) from the canon. "She [Corelli] was willing to draw on older popular traditions of sensation and horror fiction.... She was everything that the most admired [realist] late–Victorian novelists were not" (xx). Thus *Sorrows of Satan* and *Trilby* do not enter the canon because, as Jane Tompkins suggests in *Sensational Designs*, texts that do not fit the dominant notions of literary form—frequently sensation texts—are excluded from the canon.

30. Nor does *Trilby* establish a position in the sensation canon. *Trilby* does gesture to the strategies of the sensation novel as noted by Patrick Brantlinger who observes that sensation writers destabilize the conventions of realism, "importing Gothic elements back into contemporary settings, reinvesting the ordinary with mystery (albeit only of the secular, criminal variety), and undoing narrative omniscience to let in kinds of knowledge—suspicions, at least—that realistic fiction had banished" (164). Yet by taking his text closer to the realm of the Gothic, in identifying evil with the religious and supernatural rather than with the secular and criminal, Du Maurier dislodges his text from the sensation canon as well.

31. The tendency of generic and textual instability also works to dispossess critical apprehension of the text resulting in a refusal of the confinements of interpretation and a refusal of the possession of hermeneutics, as the following chapter will assert.

32. To appropriate Wilt's title phrase.

33. Garber whose *Shakespeare's Ghost Writers* also considers the haunting nature of writing and reading locates a similar moment in Keats's poem "This Living Hand," that ends with the writer extending his living hand—now dead because in the distant future—to the reader. Thus "the act of writing is a sleight of hand through which the dead hand of the past reaches over to *our* side of the border" (xv). Keats's image is revisited in Katherine Rowe's *The Dead Hand*, which locates the centrality of that image in the Gothic canon. Rowe's association of the image with a disrupted sense of "self-possession," disrupting the "modern notion of the body as proper to the self" (xi), suggests a link between the disrupted notions of self-possession and of possession of one's art, the product of one's self.

34. Conversely, we readers, too, are ghosts, casting our ephemeral presence over the texts we read; as David Punter remarks, "all readers ... hover, like ghosts, over the terrain of the text" (*Gothic Pathologies* 2). Indeed, neither reader nor writer can securely possess the haunted Gothic narrative that resists authorial, readerly and hermeneutic possession.

Chapter 15

1. Or to use a more complicated label, "historiographic metafiction" (Hutcheon xi).

2. In *Neo-Victorian Gothic: Horror, Violence and Degeneration in the Re-Imagined Nineteenth Century*, editors Marie-Louise Kohlke and Christian Gutleben work to contextualize the neo–Victorian in the Gothic tradition, arguing persuasively that the neo–Victorian is, like the Gothic a self-reflexive and subversive genre.

3. Rosario Arias and Patricia Pulham—in their introduction to *Haunting and Spectrality in Neo-Victorian Fiction*—note the Victorian tendency to engage with the past: "The return to classical, medieval and renaissance pasts is evident in the works of nineteenth-century writers and poets ranging from Sir Walter Scott to Oscar Wilde" (xiii). Yet they fail to recognize that these writers tend to return to

the pasts when they turn to the Gothic tradition in their work.

4. Waters's texts that operate out of the neo–Victorian tradition also show an affinity for the Gothic. For example, *The Little Stranger* (2009), which takes place in the English countryside after World War II, reconsiders the old Gothic concerns with class and ownership (including ghostly) of the hereditary grand house.

5. These are crimes at least for the poor. Although Margaret's suicide attempt is not a complete secret, her socio-economic class protects her from prison.

6. At the novel's end we realize that Ruth has also been carefully watching Margaret

7. Thus creating a strong connection to A.S. Byatt's neo–Victorian novel *Possession* (1990).

8. This is one of many moments when Waters conflates the nineteenth and twentieth century meanings of "queer" in her novel.

9. Yet another doubling, that of names: Mrs. Brink's name is Margery (174).

10. She is also able to identify the limits imposed upon her by her culture. When a foolish woman asks, Margaret is able to supply Tennyson's restrictive and misogynistic couplet: *"For men at most differ as Heaven and Earth, / But women, worst and best, as Heaven and Hell"* (33).

11. Heilmann also observes that the Governess's monitoring of the children, including watching for signs of potential homosexuality of Miles is recast as Mrs. Prior's monitoring of Margaret. Margaret's perspective thus provides insight into the frustration of Miles in the face of the Governess's control.

12. In a particularly nasty aside, de Groot writes about Waters, "She is stridently articulate about the way that the genre itself allows space for experimentation and complexity of expression" (59), including exploration of submerged sexuality. De Groot somewhat narrowly complains that Waters's novels work to fulfill her scholarly project rather than accurately presenting the "standard view of Victorian Britain" (68), at least in the case of *Tipping the Velvet*, criticizing the "utopic conclusion" (68) of that novel which seeks "to disrupt (to 'queer') the smooth running of history" (69). De Groot, seemingly, (mis)reads *Velvet* as a historical novel rather than as an example of neo–Victorian Gothic, holding it to a standard of historical accuracy without recognizing the interpretative imperatives of the metanarrative, an instance, perhaps, of a Gothic text destabilizing a scholarly reader.

13. Waters does point to the ghostly nature of all women and spinsters in particular. Margaret considers that "it is the same with spinsters as with ghosts; and one has to be of their ranks in order to see them at all" (58). In the jail, Margaret has to squint to read the "ghostly titles" (63) of the books given to the prisoners—is it women's literature and writers that are spectralized?

14. Recalling the namelessness of the governess in James's *Turn of the Screw*.

15. A similarly invisible literary allusion that points to the invisible Ruth as the driving force of the novel is missed by Sarah Parker who considers Robin Vole, "the femme fatale" (4) of Djuna Barnes's *Nightwood* (1936), which she discusses in the context of *Affinity*, without noting that she shares Ruth's initials.

16. Shor's statement that Gaskell "as a reader of Ruskin and a fellow inheritor of the Romantic tradition" (166) considers the shift from woman as object of gaze to subject, might be an interesting prism through which to examine Margaret's fixation on the relationship between Selina's appearance and the Crivelli picture of *Veritas*.

17. Although Selina seems fully implicated by the conclusion of the novel, betraying Selina and running off with Ruth, there is a strong likelihood that the tragic dispossession of the ending is doubled, and that Selina, like Margaret is robbed of her love and her happiness. There is evidence that Selina ultimately falls into her own trap, coming to love Margaret, while still continuing to be possessed by Ruth, who is, as Stefania Cicia proposes "the real villain of the piece" (11). As Selina appears to reel Margaret in, in the last stages of the escape plot, she weeps as she bids Margaret goodbye in prison. Selina "placed her face against my throat. '*My affinity,*' she whispered" (309). The emotion truly seems real, and closer to love than to remorse. On the night of her betrayal as she waits for Selina to appear in her bedroom, Margaret thinks she hears Selina's voice, although Selina never comes to her. "It was Selina's voice I think I heard, and it was my name she called" (318). We later learn that Selina did spend that night in Ruth's room, directly above Margaret's. Does Selina actually cry out in longing or dream for Margaret from Ruth's bed?

18. Rachel Carroll notes "a devastating culmination to the narrative both for Margaret and the reader who has become affectively identified with her" (2).

Chapter 16

1. The strange mixture—the mixture of the actual/legal and the supernatural that pervades

the Gothic meditation on possession—is exemplified in James's ghost story: the haunting ghost pays the legal owner of the property a rental, "in good American gold and silver" (69).

2. This discussion, of course, takes place against the larger background of the debate concerning the ideology of the novel: is the novel a conservative force for social control as argued, for example, by D.A. Miller in *Novel and Police* and Armstrong in *Desire and Domestic Fiction* or is it a subversive force for rebellion as argued, for example, by Mikhail Bakhtin and by Terry Castle in *Masquerade and Civilization*? Significantly D.A. Miller evokes the panopticon, Foucault's iconic image, to argue that the novel is a method of disseminating social control. In doing so, Miller highlights Foucault's implicit stance toward art and his denial of the possibilities of art to resist the power of social control.

3. In her study of the politics of *Jane Eyre* and "the progress of Jane Eyre from dispossession to ownership" (715), Parama Roy poses a similar question couched in similar terms. Recalling Armstrong's reading of *Wuthering Heights*, Roy argues that *Jane Eyre* is "profoundly divided between revolutionary and conservative impulses since the rejection of country-house norms and values" (719) "is diluted considerably by Jane's latter-day assumption of wealth and gentility" (725). To Roy, the closure of the novel indicates Brontë's "clandestine submission to the dicates of the institutions she had sought to reevaluate and dislocate" (726).

4. The Gothic dangers illustrated by the Affair were recognized by both Émile Zola and George Lukacs in their writing. Zola suggests that the Affair was certain to destabilize modern history and wrench it back to the dark past. In a letter dated 1896 (pre-dating by two years the famous "J'accuse") Zola evokes Gothic tropology in writing of the Affair: "It seems to me a *monstrosity* [italics mine]; by that I mean something that is altogether beyond the bounds of common sense, truth and justice, a blind and stupid thing that would drag us back centuries in time" (2): the time, that is, of the pre-rational demonization of Jews. Lukacs also observes the dangerous tendency of demonizing the Other and of naturalizing this process, of allowing Gothic rhetoric into political discourse. Writing of the Dreyfus trial Lukacs argues that only when the tendency to naturalize demonization was resisted and reversed, was justice restored and the course of history restabilized (at least for the moment): "When first of all an intellectual vanguard, but later followed by broad masses, no longer came to accept the fate of an individual man, the unjustly condemned Captain Dreyfus, as normal and natural, refusing to 'accustom' themselves to it, then a state crisis developed in France," leading to Dreyfus's exoneration ("Tribune" 213).

5. In arguing for the humanism of realism that reads beyond the stereotypes, Kearns warns against the opposing Gothic tendency to respond to difference with fear instead of curiosity: "that thing which refutes all attempts at being bespoken, that thing for which the trope of visibility is always insufficient— becomes phatasmic, made of monsters, women, beasts, and Others" (Kearns 142).

6. My three essay collections consider the process whereby the application of Gothic rhetoric translates the human Other into the inhuman Gothic monster. *The Gothic Other, Horrifying Sex* and *Demons of the Body and Mind*, all published by McFarland, consider instances in which human difference is reframed as quasi-supernatural danger.

7. With the understanding that, as Rosemary Jackson points out, Todorov's *The Fantastic* "fails to consider the social and political implications of literary forms" (Jackson 6). Yet although Jackson's project of locating the fantastic in the political spectrum is laudable, her argument that the fantastic is in alignment with the subversive in literature fails to account for the full range of tension in the fantastic.

Conclusion

1. Marshall's monograph, *The Transatlantic Gothic Novel and the Law* (2011), is of particular relevance to this discussion as she also writes of the relationship between the Gothic novel and legal codes, recognizing the Gothic as an accessible "vehicle through which authors and readers alike could explore … justice" (161), recognizing that the system "is not rational, measured and reasoned" (161). Marshall's discussion tends to focus on the systems of criminal law—including confessions, the jury system—and punishment.

2. One consequence being that much interplay between American and English literature occurs within the space of the Gothic. For example, a consideration of the trope of confinement in the Gothic benefits from the insight of Nancy Armstrong and Leonard Tennenhouse in *The Imaginary Puritan* (1992) that the American captivity narrative brought to England in the late seventeenth and early eighteenth centuries influenced the development of the English novel in the form of Richardson's tales of captivity *Pamela* and *Clarissa*.

Bibliography

Adorno, Theodor. "Theses Against Occultism." *Minima Moralia: Reflections from a Damaged Life.* Trans. E. F. N. Jephcott. London: NLB, 1974. 238–244.

Altmann, Alexander. *Moses Mendelssohn: A Biographical Study.* Tuscaloosa: University of Alabama Press, 1973.

Arias, Rosario, and Patricia Pulham, eds. *Haunting and Spectrality in Neo-Victorian Fiction.* New York: Palgrave Macmillan, 2010.

Ariès, Philippe. *The Hour of Our Death.* Trans. Helen Weaver. New York: Knopf, 1981.

Armitt, Lucie, and Sarah Gamble. "The Haunted Geometries of Sarah Waters's *Affinity.*" *Textual Practice* 20.1 (2006): 141–159.

Armstrong, Nancy. *Desire and Domestic Fiction: A Political History of the Novel.* New York: Oxford University Press, 1987.

———. "Emily Brontë In and Out of Her Time." *Wuthering Heights.* By Emily Brontë. Norton Critical Edition. Ed. William M. Sale and Richard J. Dunn. New York: Norton, 1990. 365–377.

———. *Fiction in the Age of Photography: The Legacy of British Realism.* Cambridge: Harvard University Press, 1999.

Armstrong, Nancy, and Leonard Tennenhouse. *The Imaginary Puritan.* Berkeley: University of California Press, 1992.

Auerbach, Nina. "Jane Austen and Romantic Imprisonment." *Romantic Imprisonment.* New York: Columbia University Press, 1986. 3–21.

Austen, Jane. *Northanger Abbey.* London: Penguin, 1995.

Backus, Margot Gayle. *The Gothic Family Romance: Heterosexuality, Child Sacrifice, and the Anglo-Irish Colonial Order.* Durham: Duke University Press, 1999.

Baldick, Chris. Introduction. *Melmoth the Wanderer.* By Charles Maturin. New York Oxford University Press, 1989. vii-xix.

Barthes, Roland. "The Death of the Author." *Image, Music, Text.* Trans. Stephen Heath. New York: Hill and Wang, 1977. 142–148.

Battiscombe, Georgina. *Charlotte Mary Yonge: The Story of an Uneventful Life.* London: Constable, 1943.

Baum, Joan. *Mind-Forge'd Manacles: Slavery and the English Romantic Poets.* North Haven, CT: Archon, 1994.

Beales, H.L. *The Industrial Revolution, 1750–1850.* London: Cass, 1967.

Benjamin, Walter. "The Work of Art in the Age of Mechanical Reproduction." *Illuminations.* Ed. Hannah Arendt. Trans. Harry Zohn. New York: Schocken, 1968. 217–251.

Bernstein, Stephen. "Form and Ideology in the Gothic Novel." *Essays in Literature* 18 (Fall 1991): 151–65.

Blackstone, William. *Commentaries on the Laws of England.* 5 vols. Philadelphia: Rees Welsh, 1897.

Bloom, Harold. *The Anxiety of Influence.* New York: Oxford University Press, 1975.

———. *A Map of Misreading.* New York: Oxford University Press, 1975.

Bodichon, Barbara Leigh Smith. "A Brief Summary, in Plain Language, of the Most Important Laws Concerning Women: Together with a Few Observations Thereon." 1854. *Mistress of the House: Women of Property in the Victorian Novel.* By Tim Dolin. Aldershot: Ashgate, 1997.

Bondeson, Jan. *Buried Alive: The Terrifying History of Our Most Primal Fear.* New York: Norton, 2001.

Boswell, James. *The Journal of a Tour to the Hebrides. The Journey to the Western Islands Scotland* and *The Journal of a Tour to the Hebrides.* By Samuel Johnson and James Boswell. New York: Penguin,1984.

Braid, Barbara. "Victorian Panopticon: Confined Spaces and Imprisonment in Chosen Neo-Victorian Novels." *Space in Cultural and Literary Studies.* Newcastle upon Tyne: Cambridge Scholars, 2010.

Brantlinger, Patrick. *The Reading Lesson: The Threat of Mass Literacy in Nineteenth-Century British Fiction.* Bloomington: Indiana University Press, 1998.

Brindle, Kym. "Diary as Queer Malady: Deflecting the Gaze in Sarah Waters's *Affinity.*" *Neo-Victorian Studies* 2.2 (2009): 2009–2010.

Brogan, Kathleen. *Cultural Haunting: Ghosts and Ethnicity in Recent American Literature.* Charlottesville: University Press of Virginia, 1998.

Brontë, Anne. *The Tenant of Wildfell Hall.* New York: Penguin, 1979.

Brontë, Charlotte. *Jane Eyre.* Ed. Q.D. Leavis. New York: Penguin, 1985.

Brontë, Emily. *Wuthering Heights.* Norton Critical Edition. Ed. William M. Sale and Richard J. Dunn. New York: Norton, 1990.

Brooks, Peter. *The Melodramatic Imagination: Balzac, Henry James, Melodrama and the Mode of Excess.* New Haven: Yale University Press, 1976.

Brown, Charles Brockden. *Edgar Huntly.* New York: Penguin, 1988.

Buckle, Stephen. *Natural Law and the Theory of Property.* Oxford: Clarendon Press, 1991.

Burke, Edmund. *A Philosophical Enquiry into the Origin of Our Ideas of the Sublime and the Beautiful.* New York: Oxford University Press, 1990.

Burke, Kenneth. *Permanence and Change: An Anatomy of Purpose.* Los Altos, CA: Hermes, 1954.

Burt, Richard, and John Michael Archer. *Enclosure Acts: Sexuality, Property, and Culture in Early Modern England.* Ithaca: Cornell University Press, 1994.

Buse, Peter, and Andrew Stott, eds. *Ghosts: Deconstruction, Psychoanalysis, History.* New York: St. Martin's Press, 1999.

Butler, Marilyn. "The Woman at the Window: Ann Radcliffe in the Novels of Mary Wollstonecraft and Jane Austen." *Gender and Literary Voice.* Ed. Janet Todd. New York: Holmes and Meier, 1980. 128–148.

Byerly, Alison. *Realism, Representations, and the Arts in Nineteenth-Century Literature.* Cambridge: Cambridge University Press, 1997.

Caminero-Santangelo, Marta. *The Madwoman Can't Speak: Or Why Insanity Is Not Subversive.* Ithaca: Cornell University Press, 1998.

Carmichael, Joel. *The Satanizing of the Jews: Origin and Development of Mystical Anti-Semitism.* New York: Fromm, 1992.

Carroll, Rachel. "Becoming My Own Ghost: Spinsterhood, Heterosexuality and Sarah Waters's *Affinity.*" *Genders* 45 (2007). *Opposing Viewpoints in Context.* Web. 10 Feb. 2015.

Castle, Terry. *The Apparitional Lesbian: Female Homosexuality and Modern Culture.* New York: Columbia University Press, 1993.

_____. Introduction. *The Female Thermometer: Eighteenth Century Culture and the Invention of the Uncanny.* By Castle. New York: Oxford University Press, 1995.

_____. *Masquerade and Civilization: The Carnivalesque in Eighteenth Century English Culture and Fiction.* Stanford: Stanford University Press, 1986.

_____. "The Spectralization of the Other in *The Mysteries of Udolpho.*" *The Female Thermometer.* New York: Oxford, 1995. 120–139.

Chesler, Phyllis. *Women and Madness.* Garden City, N.Y.: Doubleday, 1972.

Chodorow, Nancy "The "The Psychodynamics of the Family." *Psychoanalysis and Woman.* Ed. Shelley Saguaro. New York: New York University Press, 2000. 108-127.

Clery, E.J. "The Politics of the Gothic Heroine in the 1790's." *Reviewing Romanticism.* Ed. Philip Martin and Robin Jarvis. New York: St. Martin's, 1992. 69–85.

_____. *The Rise of Supernatural Fiction.* Cambridge: Cambridge University Press, 1995.

Collins, Wilkie. *The Woman in White.* New York: Bantam, 1985.

Corelli, Marie. *The Sorrows of Satan.* New York: Oxford University Press, 1996.

Cowhig, Ruth. "Blacks in English Renaissance Drama and the Role of Shakespeare's Othello." *The Black Presence in English Literature.* Ed. David Dabydeen. Manchester: Manchester University Press, 1985. 1–25.

Dabydeen, David. "Eighteenth-century English Literature on Commerce and Slavery." *The Black Presence in English Literature.* Manchester: Manchester University Press, 1985. 26–49.

Dacre, Charlotte. *Zofloya; or, the Moor.* New York: Oxford University Press, 1997.

Derrida, Jacques. *Specters of Marx.* Trans. Peggy Kamuf. New York: Routledge, 1994.

Dever, Carolyn. *Death and the Mother from*

Dickens to Freud: Victorian Fiction and the Anxiety of Origins. Cambridge: Cambridge University Press, 1998.

Dickens, Charles. "The Chimes." *The Christmas Books*. Ed. Sally Ledger. London: Dent, 1999. 87–177.

———. *A Christmas Carol. The Christmas Books*. Ed. Sally Ledger. London: Dent, 1999. 1–85.

———. *The Haunted House*. Foreword by Peter Ackroyd. London: Hesperus Press, 2002.

Dickenson, Donna. *Property, Women and Politics: Subjects or Objects?* New Brunswick: Rutgers University Press, 1997.

Dolin, Tim. *Mistress of the House: Women of Property in the Victorian Novel*. Aldershot: Ashgate, 1997.

Drabble, Margaret. "The Wandering Jew." *The Oxford Companion to English Literature*. Rev. ed. Ed. New York: Oxford University Press, 1995. 1052–1053.

Du Maurier, George. *Trilby*. Intro. Elaine Showalter. New York: Oxford University Press, 1995.

Eco, Umberto. "Travels in Hyperreality." *Travels in Hyperreality: Essays*. San Diego: Harcourt Brace Jovanovich. 1986. 3–58.

Edgeworth, Maria. *Castle Rackrent*. New York: Oxford University Press, 1964.

Edmundson, Mark. *Nightmare on Main Street: Angels, Sadomasochism, and the Culture of the Gothic*. Cambridge: Harvard University Press, 1997.

Elbert Monika, and Bridget M. Marshall. *Transnational Gothic: Literary and Social Exchanges in the Long Nineteenth Century*. Burlington, VT: Ashgate, 2013.

Eliot, George. *The Lifted Veil*. New York: Penguin, 1985.

———. "On Realism." *Documents of Modern Literary Realism*. Ed. George J. Becker. Princeton: Princeton University Press, 1963. 112–116.

Ellis, Kate Ferguson. *The Contested Castle: Gothic Novels and the Subversion of Domestic Ideology*. Urbana: University of Illinois Press, 1989.

Ellis, Markman. *The History of Gothic Fiction*. Edinburgh: Edinburgh University Press, 2000.

———. *The Politics of Sensibility: Race, Gender and Commerce in the Sentimental Novel*. Cambridge: Cambridge University Press, 1996.

Erickson, Amy Louise. *Women and Property in Early Modern England*. New York: Routledge, 1993.

Felman, Shoshana. "Turning the Screw of Interpretation." *Literature and Psychoanalysis: The Question of Reading Otherwise* 55–56 (1977): 94–207.

Ferguson, Moira. *Subject to Others: British Women Writers and Colonial Slavery, 1670–1834*. New York: Routledge, 1992.

Fiedler, Leslie Fiedler, Leslie A. *Love and Death in the American Novel*. New York: Criterion, 1960.

Forster, E. M. *Where Angels Fear to Tread*. New York: Vintage, 1992.

Foucault, Michel. *The Archaeology of Knowledge*. Trans. A.M. Sheridan Smith. New York: Pantheon, 1972.

———. *Discipline and Punish: The Birth of the Prison*. Trans. Alan Sheridan. New York: Vintage, 1979.

———. *The History of Sexuality. Vol 1. An Introduction*. Trans. Robert Hurley. New York: Vintage, 1990.

———. *Madness and Civilization: A History of Insanity in the Age of Reason*. Trans. Richard Howard. New York: Vintage, 1988.

———. *The Order of Things: An Archaeology of the Human Sciences*. New York: Vintage, 1973.

———. "Truth and Power." *Power/Knowledge: Selected Interviews and Other Writings, 1972–1977*. Ed. Colin Gordon. New York: Pantheon, 1980. 109–133.

———. "What is an Author?" *Language, Counter-Memory, Practice: Selected Essays and Interviews*. Trans Donald F. Bouchard and Sherry Simon. Ithaca: Cornell University Press, 1977.

Freeland, Natalka. "Theft, Terror, and Family Values: The Mysteries and Domesticities of Udolpho." *Ghosts: Deconstruction, Psychoanalysis, History*. Ed. Peter Buse and Andrew Stott. New York: St. Martin's, 1999. 144–162.

Freud, Sigmund. "The 'Uncanny.'" *Writings on Art and Literature*. Stanford: Stanford University Press, 1997. 193–233.

Friedländer, Saul. "'Europe's Inner Demons: The 'Other' as Threat in Early Twentieth-Century European Culture." *Demonizing the Other: Antisemitism, Racism, and Xenophobia*. Ed. Robert S. Wistrich. Amsterdam: Harwood, 1999.

Friedman, Bonnie. "A Wondering Jew with a Post-Holocaust Sensibility." *Forward* 5 (July 2002): 11.

Gallup, Jane. "The Father's Seduction." *The (M)other Tongue: Essays in Feminist Psychoanalytic Interpretation*. Ed. Shirley Nelson Garner, Claire Kahane and Madelon Sprengnether. Ithaca: Cornell University Press, 1985. 334–351.

Gamble, Sarah. "'I Know Everything. I Know

Nothing': (Re)reading *Fingersmith*'s Deceptive Doubles." In *Sarah Waters: Contemporary Critical Perspectives*. Ed. Kaye Mitchell. London: Bloomsbury, 2013.

Garber, Frederick. "Meaning and Mode in Gothic Fiction." *Studies in Eighteenth Century Culture*. Vol. 3: *Racism in the Eighteenth Century*. Ed. Harold E. Pagliaro. Cleveland: Case Western Reserve University Press, 1973. 155–169.

Garber, Marjorie. *Shakespeare's Ghost Writers: Literature as Uncanny Causality*. New York: Routledge, 1987.

Gilbert, Sandra M., and Susan Gubar. *The Madwoman in the Attic: The Woman Writer and the Nineteenth-Century Literary Imagination*. New Haven: Yale University Press, 1979.

Gilman, Sander. "The Jewish Foot: A Footnote to the Jewish Body." *Feminism and the Body*. Ed. Londa Schiebinger. Oxford: Oxford University Press, 2000. 355–374.

_____. *The Jew's Body*. New York: Routledge, 1991.

Gittings, Clare. *Death, Burial and the Individual in Early Modern England*. London: Croom Helm, 1984.

Gordon, Jan B. "Narrative Enclosure as Textual Ruin: An Archaeology of Gothic Consciousness." *Dickens Studes Annual*. Vol. 2. Ed. Michael Timko, Fred Kaplan and Edward Guiliano. New York: AMS Press, 1983. 209–238.

Gray, K. "Property in Thin Air." *Cambridge Law Journal*. (1991): 252–307.

Groot, Jerome de. "'Something New and a Bit Startling': Sarah Waters and the Historical Novel." In *Sarah Waters: Contemporary Critical Perspectives*. Ed. Kaye Mitchell. London: Bloomsbury, 2013.

Haggerty, George E. *Gothic Fiction/Gothic Form*. University Park: Pennsylvania State University Press, 1989.

Halberstam, Judith. *Skin Shows: Gothic Horror and the Technology of Monsters*. Durham: Duke University Press, 1995.

Hall, Demelza. "Apprehending the Apparitional: Spatial/Sexual Transgressions in Sarah Waters's Affinity." *Quest* 2: 1–13.

Hawthorne, Nathaniel. *The House of the Seven Gables*. New York: Penguin, 1986.

_____. *The Marble Faun*. New York: New American Library, 1987.

Hay, Douglas. "Property, Authority, and the Criminal Law." *Albion's Fatal Tree: Crime and Society in Eighteenth-Century England*. Ed. Douglas Hay et al. New York: Pantheon, 1975. 17–63.

Hegel, Georg. "Property." *Philosophy of Right*. Oxford: Clarendon Press, 1945. 40–57.

Heilbroner, Robert. *The Worldly Philosphers*, 6th ed. New York: Simon & Schuster, 1992.

Heilman, Ann. "The Haunting of Henry James: Jealous Ghosts, Affinities and *The Others*." *Haunting and Spectrality in Neo-Victorian Fiction*. Ed. Rosario Arias and Patricia Pulham. New York: Palgrave Macmillan, 2010.

Heller, Tamar. *Dead Secrets: Wilkie Collins and the Female Gothic*. New Haven: Yale University Press, 1992.

Holcombe, Lee. *Wives and Property: Reform of the Married Women's Property Law in Nineteenth-Century England*. Toronto: University of Toronto Press, 1983.

Homans, Margaret. *Bearing the Word: Language and Female Experience in Nineteenth Century Women's Writing*. Chicago: University of Chicago Press, 1986.

_____. "Dreaming of Children: Literalization in *Jane Eyre* and *Wuthering Heights*." *The Female Gothic*. Ed. Juliann E. Fleenor. Montreal: Eden Press, 1983. 257–279.

Horkheimer, Max, and Theodor W. Adorno. "Elements of Anti-Semitism: Limits of Enlightenment." *Dialectic of Enlightenment*. Trans. Edmund Jephcott. Stanford: Stanford University Press, 2002. 137–172.

_____. "The Theory of Ghosts." *Dialectic of Enlightenment*. Trans. Edmund Jephcott. Stanford: Stanford University Press, 2002. 178–179.

Howells, Cora Ann. *Love, Mystery and Misery*. London: Athlone Press, 1978.

Hughes, William, and Andrew Smith, eds. *Queering the Gothic*. Manchester: Manchester University Press, 2009.

Hunt, Lynn. *The Family Romance of the French Revolution*. Berkley: University of California Press, 1992.

Hutcheon, Linda. *A Poetics of Postmodern: History, Theory, Fiction*. New York: Routledge, 1988.

Jackson, Rosemary. *Fantasy: The Literature of Subversion*. New York: Methuen, 1981.

Jaffe, Audrey. "Under Cover of Sympathy: Ressentiment in Gaskell's *Ruth*." *Victorian Literature and Culture* 21 (1993): 51–65.

James, Henry. "The Ghostly Rental." *Twelve Victorian Ghost Stories*. Ed. Michael Cox. Oxford: Oxford University Press, 1997. 54–85.

_____. "The Turn of the Screw." *American Gothic Literature*. Ed. Charles L. Crowe. Malden, MA: Blackwell, 1999. 276–338.

Johnson, Nancy E. "Rights, Property and the Law in the English Jacobin Novel." *Mosaic*. 27 (Dec. 1994): 99–120.

Kahane, Claire. "The Gothic Mirror." *The*

(M)other Tongue: Essays in Feminist Psychoanlytic Interpretation. Ed. Shirley Nelson Garner, Claire Kahane and Madelon Sprengnether. Ithaca: Cornell University Press, 1985. 334- 351.

Kant, Immanuel. "On the Relationship of Theory to Practice in Political Right." *Kant's Political Writings.* Ed. Hans Reiss. Trans. H.B. Nisbet. Cambridge: Cambridge University Press, 1970. 73–86.

Kayman, Martin. "The Reader and the Jury: Legal Fictions and the Making of Commercial Law in Eighteenth Century England." *Eighteenth Century Fiction* 9 (1997): 373–394.

Kearns, Katherine. *Nineteenth-Century Literary Realism: Through the Looking Glass.* Cambridge: Cambridge University Press, 1996.

Kelly, Richard. *George Du Maurier.* Boston: Twayne, 1983.

Kilgour, Maggie. *The Rise of the Gothic Novel.* London: Routledge, 1995.

Kliger, Samuel. *The Goths in England: A Study in Seventeenth and Eighteenth Century Thought.* Cambridge: Harvard University Press, 1952.

Kohlke, Marie-Louise, and Christian Gutleben, eds. *Neo-Victorian Gothic: Horror, Violence and Degeneration in the Re-Imagined Nineteenth Century.* New York: Rodopi, 2012.

Kristeva, Julia. *Powers of Horror: An Essay on Abjection.* Trans. Leon S. Roudiez. New York: Columbia University Press, 1982.

Lathers, Marie. *Bodies of Art: French Literary Realism and the Artist's Model.* Lincoln: University of Nebraska Press, 2001.

Lawrence, D.H. *Studies in Classic American Literature.* New York: Viking Press, 1961.

McKendrick, Neil, John Brewer, and J. H. Plumb. *The Birth of a Consumer Society: The Commercialization of Eighteenth Century England.* Bloomington: Indiana University Press, 1982.

Lefebvre, Henri. *The Production of Space.* Trans. by Donald Nicholson-Smith. Oxford: Blackwell, 1974.

Levine, George. *The Realistic Imagination: English Fiction from Frankenstein to Lady Chatterley.* Chicago: University of Chicago Press, 1981.

Lewis, Matthew. *Journal of a West India Proprietor, 1815–17.* Boston: Houghton Mifflin, 1929.

_____. *The Monk.* Oxford: Oxford University Press, 1995.

Lewis, W. S. Introduction. *The Castle of Otranto.* By Horace Walpole. New York: Oxford University Press, 1982. vii–xvi.

Litten, Julian. *The English Way of Death: The Common Funeral Since 1450.* London: Robert Hale, 1991.

Llewellyn, Mark. "'Queer? I Should Say It Is Criminal': Sarah Waters's *Affinity* (1999)." *Journal of Gender Studies* 13.3 (2004): 203–214.

Lloyd, Tom. *Crises of Realism: Representing Experience in the British Novel, 1816–1910.* Lewisburg, PA: Bucknell University Press, 1997.

Locke, John. "Of Property." *Second Treatise: An Essay Concerning the True End of Civil Government.* 1689. *On Moral Business: Classical and Contemporary Resources for Ethics in Economic Life.* Ed. Max L. Stackhouse et al. Grand Rapids: Eerdmans, 1995. 203–207.

Long, Mikhail Ann. "Wavering, Witless, and without Council: The Widow in Restoration and Eighteenth-Century England." *Misogyny in Literature.* Ed. Katherine Anne Ackley. New York: Garland, 1992. 67–88.

Lonsdale, Roger. *The Poems of Thomas Gray, William Collins, Oliver Goldsmith.* New York: Norton, 1972.

Lukacs, George. *The Theory of the Novel: A Historico-Philosophical Essay on the Forms of Great Epic Literature.* 1920. London: Merlin, 1971.

_____. "Tribune of Bureaucrat?" *Essays on Realism.* Ed. Rodney Livingstone. Trans. David Fernbach. Cambridge: MIT Press, 1980. 198–237.

Marshall, Bridget M. *The Transatlantic Gothic Novel and the Law, 1790–1860.* Burlington, VT: Ashgate, 2011.

McCuskey, Brian. "Not at Home: Servants, Scholars, and the Uncanny." *PMLA* (2006): 421–436.

McGrath, Patrick. Introduction. *The New Gothic.* Ed. Patrick McGrath and Bradford Morrow. New York: Vintage, 1992. xi–xiv.

Macovski, Michael. "Revisiting Gothic Primogeniture: The Kinship Metaphor in the Age of Byron." *Gothic Studies* 3 (April 2001): 32–44.

Malchow, H.L. *Gothic Images of Race in Nineteenth-Century Britain.* Stanford: Stanford University Press, 1996.

Maturin, Charles. *Melmoth the Wanderer.* New York: Oxford University Press, 1968.

Meltzer, Françoise. *Hot Property: The Stakes and Claims of Literary Originality.* Chicago: University of Chicago Press, 1994.

Michasiw, Kim Ian. Introduction. *Zofloya.* By Charlotte Dacre. New York: Oxford University Press, 1997.

Midgley, Clare. "'Remember Those in Bonds, As Bound with Them': Women's Approach to Anti-slavery Campaigning in Britain 1780–1870." *Women, Migration and Empire.* Ed. Joan Grant. London: Trentham, 1996. 73–102.

____. *Women Against Slavery: The British Campaigns: 1780–1870.* London: Routledge, 1992.

Milbank, Alison. Introduction. *A Sicilian Romance.* By Ann Radcliffe. Oxford: Oxford University Press, 1993. ix–xxix.

Miles, Robert. *Ann Radcliffe: The Great Enchantress.* Manchester: Manchester University Press, 1995.

Miller, D. A. *Narrative and its Discontents: Problems of Closure in the Traditional Novel.* Princeton: Princeton University Press, 1981.

____. *The Novel and the Police.* Berkeley: University of California Press, 1988.

Miller, J. Hillis. *The Disappearance of God: Five Nineteenth-Century Writers.* Cambridge: Harvard University Press, 1963.

____. *Fiction and Repetition: Seven English Novels.* Cambridge: Harvard University Press, 1982.

____. "*Wuthering Heights*: Repetition and the 'Uncanny.'" *Wuthering Heights* by Emily Brontë. Norton Critical Edition. Ed. William M. Sale and Richard J. Dunn. New York: Norton, 1990. 378–393.

Mitchell, Kaye. "'I'd Love to Write an Anti-*Downton*!': An Interview with Sarah Waters." In *Sarah Waters: Contemporary Critical Perspectives.* Ed. Kaye Mitchell. London: Bloomsbury, 2013.

Mogen, David, Scott P. Sanders and JoAnne Karpinski, eds. Introduction. *Frontier Gothic: Terror and Wonder at the Frontier in American Literature.* Rutherford, N.J.: Fairleigh Dickinson University Press, 1993.

Morrison, Toni. "Romancing the Shadow." *Playing in the Dark: Whiteness and the Literary Imagination.* New York: Vintage, 1993. 31–59.

Mowl, Tim. *Horace Walpole: The Great Outsider.* London: Murray, 1996.

Neeson, J.M. *Commoners: Common Right, Enclosure and Social Change in England, 1700–1820.* Cambridge: Cambridge University Press, 1993.

Newman, Beth. "The Situation of the Looker-On: Gender, Narrator and Gaze in *Wuthering Heights.*" *PMLA* 105 (1990): 1029–1041.

North, Michael. "Authorship and Authography." *PMLA* 116 (2001): 1377–1385.

Offer, Avner. *Property and Politics, 1870–1914: Landownership, Law, Ideology, and Urban Development in England.* Cambridge: Cambridge University Press, 1981.

Palmer, Paulina. *Lesbian Gothic: Transgressive Fictions.* London: Cassell, 1999.

Parker, Patricia. *Literary Fat Ladies: Rhetoric, Gender, Property.* New York: Methuen, 1987.

Parker, Sarah. "'The Darkness is the Closet in Which Your Lover Roosts Her Heart': Lesbians, Desire and the Gothic Genre." *Journal of International Women's Studies* 9 (Mar. 2008):4–19.

Paulsen, Ronald. *Representations of Revolution (1789–1820).* New Haven: Yale University Press, 1983.

Perkin, Joan. *Women and Marriage in Nineteenth-Century England.* Chicago: Lyceum, 1989.

Perkin, Harold. *The Origins of Modern Society, 1780–1880.* London: Routledge, 1969.

Pocock, J.G.A., ed. *Three British Revolutions: 1641, 1688, 1776.* Princeton: Princeton University Press, 1980.

Pohl, Rebecca. "Sexing the Labyrinth. Space and Sexuality in Sarah Waters' *Affinity.*" In *Sarah Waters: Contemporary Critical Perspectives.* Ed. Kaye Mitchell. London: Bloomsbury, 2013.

Poole, Keith B. *Britain's Haunted Heritage.* Leicester: Magna, 1995.

Poovey, Mary. "Ideology in the *Mysteries of Udolpho.*" *Criticism* 21 (1979): 307–330.

____. *Making a Social Body: British Cultural Formation, 1830–1864.* Chicago: University of Chicago Press, 1995.

Porter, Dale H. *The Abolition of the Slave Trade in England, 1784–1807.* Hamden, CT: Archon, 1970.

Punter, David. *Gothic Pathologies: The Text, the Body and the Law.* New York: St. Martin's Press, 1998.

Radcliffe, Ann. *The Castles of Athlin and Dunbayne.* New York: Oxford University Press, 1995.

____. *The Italian.* New York: Oxford University Press, 1968.

____. "On the Supernatural in Poetry." *Gothic Documents: A Sourcebook, 1700–1820.* Ed. E.J. Clery and Robert Miles. Manchester: Manchester University Press, 2000.

____. *The Mysteries of Udolpho.* New York: Dutton, 1973.

____. *A Sicilian Romance.* New York: Oxford University Press, 1993.

Ragussis, Michael. *Figures of Conversion: "The Jewish Question" and English National Identity.* Durham: Duke University Press, 1995.

Railo, Eino. *The Haunted Castle: A Study of the Elements of English Romanticism.* New York: Dutton, 1927.

Rajan, Tilottama. *The Supplement of Reading.* Ithaca: Cornell University Press. 1990.

Reeve, Clara. *The Old English Baron*. Ed. James Trainer. London: Oxford University Press, 1967.

Rich, Adrienne. "The Temptations of a Motherless Woman." 1973. *On Lies, Secrets, and Silence: Selected Prose 1966–1978*. New York: Norton, 1979. 89–106.

Roberts, Siân Silyn. "A Transnational Perspective on American Gothic Criticism." In *Transnational Gothic: Literary and Social Exchanges in the Long Nineteenth Century*, ed. by Monika Elbert and Bridget M. Marshall. Burlington, VT: Ashgate, 2013.

Robinson, Joan. *Economic Philosophy*. Chicago: Aldine, 1962.

Rose, Mark. *Authors and Owners: The Invention of Copyright*. Cambridge: Harvard University Press, 1993.

Rosenberg, Edgar. *From Shylock to Svengali*. Stanford: Stanford University Press, 1960.

Rousseau, Jean-Jacques. "A Discourse upon the Origins and Foundation of Inequality Among Mankind." *The Social Contract and Discourses*. Ed. G.D.H Cole. New York: Dutton, 1913. 143–229.

Rowe, Katherine. *Dead Hands: Fictions of Agency, Renaissance to Modern*. Stanford: Stanford University Press, 1999.

Roy, Parama. "Unaccomodated Woman and the Poetics of Property in *Jane Eyre*." *Studies in English Literature 1500–1900* 29 (1989): 713–727.

Ruskin, John. "The Nature of Gothic." *The Stones of Venice*. Ed. J.G. Links. New York: Da Capo Press, 1985. 157–190.

Ryan, Alan. *Property and Political Theory*. New York: Blackwell, 1984.

Sade, Marquis de. "Reflections on the Novel." 1800. *The 120 Days of Sodom and Other Writings*. Ed. and trans. Austryn Wainhouse and Richard Seaver. New York: Grove Weidenfeld, 1996. 97–116.

Sanger, Charles Percy. "The Structure of *Wuthering Heights*." *Wuthering Heights*. By Emily Brontë. Norton Critical Edition. Ed. by William M. Sale and Richard J. Dunn. New York: Norton, 1990. 331–336.

Schifrin, Daniel R. "A Play for all Seasons." *Hadassah Magazine* 78 (May 1997): 32–35.

Schroeder, Jeanne Lorraine. *The Vestal and the Fasces: Hegel, Lacan, Property, and the Feminine*. Berkeley: University of California Press, 1998.

Shanley, Mary Lyndon. *Feminism, Marriage, and the Law in Victorian England, 1850–1895*. Princeton: Princeton University Press, 1989.

Shelley, Mary W. *Frankenstein*. New York: Dutton, 1973.

Shor, Hilary. "The Plot of the Beautiful Ignoramus: *Ruth* and the Tradition of the Fallen Woman." In *Sex and Death in Victorian Literature*. Ed. Regina Barreca. Bloomington: Indiana University Press, 1990.

Showalter, Elaine. *The Female Malady: Women, Madness, and English Culture, 1830–1980*. New York: Pantheon, 1985.

———. Introduction. *Trilby*. By George Du Maurier. New York: Oxford University Press, 1995. ix-xxiii.

Shyllon, F. O. *Black Slaves in Britain*. London: Oxford University Press, 1974.

Smith, Richard M. "Some Issues Concerning Families and Their Property in Rural England 1250–1800." *Land, Kinship and Life-Cycle*. Ed. Richard M. Smith. New York: Cambridge University Press, 1984. 1–86.

Smith, Robert A. "Walpole's Reflections on the Revolution in France." *Horace Walpole: Writer, Politician, and Connoisseur*. Ed. Warren Hunting Smith. New Haven: Yale University Press, 1967. 91–114.

Spivak, Gayatri Chakravorty. "Can the Subaltern Speak." In *Marxism and the Interpretation of Culture*. Ed. C. Nelson and L. Grossberg. Chicago: University of Illinois Press, 1988.

Stallybrass, Peter. "Patriarchal Territories: The Body Enclosed." *Rewriting the Renaissance: The Discourses of Sexual Difference in Early Modern Europe*. Ed. Margaret Ferguson, Maureen Quilligan, and Nancy J. Vickers. Chicago: University of Chicago Press, 1986.

Staves, Susan. *Married Women's Separate Property in England, 1660–1833*. Cambridge: Harvard University Press, 1990.

Stewart, Susan. *Crimes of Writing: Problems in the Containment of Representation*. New York: Oxford University Press, 1991.

Stone, Lawrence. *The Family, Sex and Marriage in England, 1500–1800*. New York: Harper & Row, 1977.

Sturrock, June. *"Heaven and Home": Charlotte M. Yonge's Domestic Fiction and the Victorian Debate over Women*. Victoria, BC: University of Victoria, 1995.

Tatar, Maria M. *Spellbound: Studies on Mesmerism and Literature*. Princeton: Princeton University Press, 1978.

Thirsk, Joan. "The European Debate on Customs of Inheritance, 1500–1700." *Family and Inheritance: Rural Society in Western Europe, 1200–1800*. Ed. Jack Goody, Joan Thirsk, E.P. Thompson. Cambridge: Cambridge University Press, 1976. 177–191.

Thompson, Allan. *The Dynamics of the Industrial Revolution*. New York: St. Martin's, 1973.

Thompson, E.P. "The Grid of Inheritance: A Comment." *Family and Inheritance: Rural Society in Western Europe, 1200–1800*. Ed. Jack Goody, Joan Thirsk, E.P. Thompson. Cambridge: Cambridge University Press, 1979. 328–60.

Thompson, James. *Models of Value: Eighteenth-Century Political Economy and the Novel*. Durham: Duke University Press, 1996.

Todorov, Tzvetan. *The Fantastic: A Structural Approach to a Literary Genre*. Trans. Richard Howard. Cleveland: Case Western University Press, 1973.

Tompkins, Jane. *Sensational Designs: The Cultural Work of American Fiction, 1790–1860*. New York: Oxford University Press, 1986.

Tucker, Irene. *A Probable State: The Novel, the Contract, and the Jews*. Chicago: University of Chicago Press, 2000.

Turley, David. *The Culture of English Antislavery, 1780–1860*. London: Routledge, 1991.

Turner, Michael. *English Parliamentary Enclosure: Its Historical Geographic and Economic History*. Hamden, CT: Archon, 1980.

Veeder, William. "The Nurture of the Gothic; or, How Can a Text Be Both Popular and Subversive?" *Spectral Readings: Towards a Gothic Geography*. Ed. Glennis Byron, and David Puntner. New York: St. Martin's, 1999. 54–70.

Vermillion, Mary. "*Clarissa* and the Marriage Act." *Eighteenth-Century Fiction* 9 (1997): 395–412.

Walpole, Horace. "An Account of the Giants Lately Discovered." *The Works of Horace Walpole*. Ed. Mary Berry. Vol. 2. London: Robinson, 1798. 91–102.

_____. *The Castle of Otranto*. New York: Oxford University Press, 1964.

_____. *The Yale Edition of Horace Walpole's Correspondence*. Ed. W.S. Lewis. New Haven: Yale University Press, 1937–1983.

Watt, Ian. *The Rise of the Novel: Studies in Defoe, Richardson and Fielding*. Berkeley: University of California Press, 1957.

_____. "Time and Family in the Gothic Novel: *The Castle of Otranto*." *Eighteenth Century Life* 10 (Oct. 1986): 159–170.

Webb, Igor. *From Custom to Capital: The English Novel and the Industrial Revolution*. Ithaca: Cornell University Press, 1981.

Weisbuch, Robert. *Atlantic Double-Cross: American Literature and British Influence in the Age of Emerson*. Chicago: University of Chicago Press, 1989.

Wheen, Francis. *Karl Marx: A Life*. New York: Norton, 2000.

Wiesner, Merry E. *Women and Gender in Early Modern Europe*, 2d ed. Cambridge: Cambridge University Press, 2000.

Williams, Anne. *Art of Darkness: A Poetics of Gothic*. Chicago: University of Chicago Press, 1995.

Williams, Raymond. *The Country and the City*. New York: Oxford University Press, 1973.

Wilt, Judith. *The Ghosts of the Gothic*. Princeton: Princeton University Press, 1980.

Wistrich, Robert S. "Introduction: The Devil, The Jews, and Hatred of the 'Other.'" *Demonizing the Other: Antisemitism, Racism, and Xenophobia*. Amsterdam: Harwood, 1999.

_____, ed. *Demonizing the Other: Antisemitism, Racism, and Xenophobia*. Amsterdam: Harwood, 1999.

Wollstonecraft, Mary. *A Vindication of the Rights of Woman and Vindication of the Rights of Men*. Oxford: Oxford University Press, 2008.

_____. *The Wrongs of Woman: or, Maria. Mary and The Wrongs of Woman*. New York: Oxford University Press, 1980.

Wolstenholme, Susan. *Gothic (Re)Visions: Writing Women as Readers*. Albany: State University of New York Press, 1993.

Woolf, Virginia. "Professions for Women." *The Death of the Moth and Other Essays*. London: Hogarth Press, 1942. 235–242.

_____. *To the Lighthouse*. New York: Harcourt Brace Jovanovich, 1955.

Yonge, Charlotte. *Chantry House*. London: Macmillan, 1886.

_____. *The Heir of Redclyffe*. New York: Oxford University Press, 1997.

Zola, Émile. *The Dreyfus Affair: 'J'Accuse' and Other Writings*. Ed. Alain Pagès. Trans. Eleanor Levieux. New Haven: Yale University Press, 1996.

Index

Agricultural Revolution 5, 24; *see also* enclosure
American Gothic 197–202
American Revolution 22, 23, 199
aristocrats and aristocracy 5, 17, 18, 20, 21, 25, 28, 49, 50–51, 64–65, 119, 126, 201; *see also* castle; inheritance; patriarchy; primogeniture
asylum 50, 63, 65, 138; *see also* confinement; prison
author *see* writers and writing

Barrett Browning, Elizabeth 175
barriers 7, 8, 20, 21, 63; *see also* asylum; Bastille; confinement; enclosure; internalized boundaries; prison
Barthes, Roland: "The Death of the Author" 216n6
Bastille 8, 22, 138; *see also* French Revolution; prison
Bible 1, 2, 43–44, 49, 74, 105, 143–147, 149, 185, 212n7
Blackstone, William *see* English common law
Brockden Brown 201; *Edgar Huntly* 197, 199
Brontë, Anne: *The Tenant of Wildfell Hall* 115–116, 125
Brontë, Charlotte: *Jane Eyre* 58–60, 83, 96, 99, 104, 108
Brontë, Emily: *Wuthering Heights* 35–37, 83
brothers *see* sons
burial, reburial and premature burial 40, 65, 75, 76–80, 181, 207n5
Burke, Edmund: sublime 190, 194

castle 3, 8; destruction of 24, 28, 30–31, 43, 192; haunted 13

Castle, Terry: "apparitional lesbian" 178–181; "The Spectralization of the Other in *The Mysteries of Udolpho*" 70
Catholic church and Catholics 15, 24, 41, 66, 73–77, 107, 128, 138, 144–147; *see also* Italy and Italians; Lewis, Matthew: *The Monk*
childbirth *see* mothers
closure 24, 29, 31, 100, 111, 115, 119–120, 123, 124, 148, 189, 192–193, 195; *see also* deferred ending; explained supernatural
Collins, Wilkie: *The Woman in White* 49–55, 65, 67–71, 79, 81, 96, 99, 104, 123–124, 170, 176
confinement 3, 62–65, 127, 173; *see also* asylum; burial; Catholic church and Catholics; coverture; prison
conservative tendencies in the Gothic 26, 30–31, 33, 42–44, 191–196, 213n23; *see also* realism; restoration of property; subversive tendencies in the Gothic
copyright 132–135
Corelli, Marie: *The Sorrows of Satan* 220n29
coverture 54, 92–97, 118; *see also* marriage laws

Dacre, Charlotte: *Zofloya; or, The Moor* 85–92, 99, 106–107, 117
daughters 103–106, 142; *see also* fathers; mothers; sons
death and resurrection 65, 76–80; *see also* burial
deferred ending 32; *see also* closure
denouement *see* closure
devil *see* Satan
Dickens, Charles: *Bleak House* 176; "The Chimes" 204n9; "A Christmas Carol" 166

231

double 3, 4, 50, 59, 67–71, 73, 75, 107, 155, 174–177, 184–185, 201
Dreyfus Affair 164
Du Maurier, George: *Trilby* 150–166
dynasty *see* patriarchy

Edgeworth, Maria: *Castle Rackrent* 117–120, 127
Eliot, George 8, 157; *The Lifted Veil* 61–62, 80
enclosure 5, 6, 19–21, 203n5, 205n1, 205n3; *see also* aristocrats and aristocracy
English common law 14, 95–96; William Blackstone *Commentaries on the Laws of England* 13, 84, 93, 134
Enlightenment 4, 5, 15, 47, 48, 56–57, 59, 60, 72–73, 187–188
explained supernatural 33, 70, 186–187

fathers 22, 97, 101, 210n3, 210n4: *see also* husbands; mothers; patriarchy
female Gothic 38–39, 42, 198; *see also* Radcliffe, Ann; Reeve, Clara; Yonge, Charlotte
female inheritance 32–34, 42–43, 112–114; *see also* primogeniture
Forster, E.M.: *Where Angels Fear to Tread* 213n22
Foucault, Michel 4, 5, 6, 7, 66, 80; *Discipline and Punish* 6, 21, 24–25; *The History of Sexuality* 6, 101–102; *Madness and Civilization* 5, 56–59, 62–63; *The Order of Things* 5, 7, 69–70; panopticon 178–179; "What Is an Author?" 6, 135
French Revolution 22, 33; *see also* Bastille
Freud, Sigmund 95, 109–110, 180, 200; "The Uncanny" 70, 182

Gaskell, Elizabeth: *Ruth* 185–186
ghosts 4, 16, 17, 29, 36–37, 40, 70, 71–75, 95, 105, 142, 162, 176, 182–184, 188, 199, 201; *see also* Castle, Terry: "apparitional lesbian"; supernatural
Gothic tropes: in political discourse 164, 194–195; repetition of 42, 175

haunting 4, 13, 15, 73, 75, 165–166; *see also* ghosts; supernatural
Hawthorne, Nathaniel: *The House of the Seven Gables* 201; *The Marble Faun* 200
homosexuality and queerness 180, 189
husbands 49, 57–62, 89, 96, 115–116; *see also* fathers; marriage; patriarchy; wives

identity 3, 7, 17, 48–54; *see also* double
Industrial Revolution 5, 24–25, 27, 82
inheritance 3, 25–27, 33–34, 42, 43; *see also* female inheritance; identity; primogeniture; restoration of property

insanity 3–6, 50, 56–62, 188; *see also* asylum
internalized boundaries 66, 209n5, 209n9, 209n10
interrupted wedding 98
Ireland and Irish 138, 205n2, 217n1; *see also* Edgeworth, Maria
Irving, Washington: "Legend of Sleepy Hollow" 201; "Rip van Winkle" 200–201
Italy and Italians 49, 51, 126–127, 129, 181; *see also* Hawthorne, Nathaniel: *The Marble Faun*; Radcliffe, Ann; Walpole, Horace: *The Castle of Otranto*

James, Henry: "The Ghostly Rental" 191; *The Turn of the Screw* 176
Jews 150–166, 212n7; *see also* Satan

Keats, John: "Eve of Saint Agnes" 175–176

Lacan, Jacques 95, 105, 109–110, 184
law 1, 33, 35, 37, 43, 52–53, 72–73, 134, 170–171, 173, 196; *see also* copyright; English common law; marriage law; realism; state
Lawrence, D.H.: *Studies in Classic American Literature* 200
Le Fanu, Sheridan 175
lesbians 173–176, 183, 187; *see also* Castle, Terry: "apparitional lesbian"; homosexuality and queerness
Lewis, Matthew 22, 83; *Journal of a West India Proprietor* 82; *The Monk* 73–78, 98, 105, 117, 125
literalization 94–97, 110, 111–112, 130
Locke, John 2, 47, 82

madhouse *see* asylum
madness *see* insanity
manuscript, lost, recovered or fragmented 3, 129–130, 139–142, 147; *see also* narrators, multiple; writers and writing
marriage 26–27, 30–31, 41–42, 83–85, 92–92, 100–102; *see also* coverture; husbands; interrupted wedding; marriage law; patriarchy; wives
marriage law 100, 200; Divorce Act 93; Infant Custody Acts 94, 116; (Married Women) Act 94; Married Women's Property Acts 54, 94, 171; Matrimonial Causes Act 94; *see also* coverture
Marx, Karl, and Marxism 28–29
Maturin, Charles: *Melmoth the Wanderer* 76–77, 125, 130, 137–149, 219n24
mesmerism 155, 157, 161, 169–170, 173–175, 177, 180–187
Morrison, Toni: *Beloved* 201; "Romancing the Shadow" 81, 91–92, 200

Index

mothers 115–117, 173, 208n7; missing 97, 104–114, 117–120, 144; *see also* coverture

narrative, embedded *see* narrators, multiple
narrator, unreliable 127
narrators, multiple 3, 4, 125, 139–141; *see also* writers and writing
neo-Victorian novel 169–170
nostalgia 28, 39

patriarchy 23, 25, 27, 36, 112–113: failure of 97–98; *see also* aristocrats and aristocracy; fathers
peasants 18, 22, 119–120, 126, 127; *see also* aristocracy
penitentiary *see* prison
photograph 160–163
Poe, Edgar Allan 201
premature burial *see* burial
primogeniture 25–27, 40–41, 43, 54, 103–104, 111–115, 117, 119; *see also* female inheritance; inheritance
prison 6, 47, 172–173; *see also* Foucault: panopticon

race 36, 81, 83, 85, 90, 92; *see also* slaves and slavery
Radcliffe, Ann 22, 49, 63, 67, 76, 97, 193: *The Italian* 126; *Mysteries of Udolpho* 32–34, 79, 96, 98, 99; *Sicilian Romance* 33–34, 63–66, 68–71, 76, 79, 96–98, 103–104, 109–114, 117; "On the Supernatural in Poetry" 211n4
rape 3, 61, 101; *see also* sexual possession
reader 3: destabilized 126–127, 135–136, 141, 145–146, 148–149, 188–190
realism 33–34, 36–37, 42, 99, 116, 120, 156–158, 161–165, 193; *see also* explained supernatural; law
reason and rationality *see* Enlightenment
reburial *see* burial
Reeve, Clara: *The Old English Baron* 13, 15, 16, 17, 21, 25–26, 29–32, 48, 63, 125, 128, 129
restoration of property 16, 17, 18, 28–33, 35–43, 119–120
resurrection *see* death and resurrection
revolution 8, 22, 25; *see also* Agricultural Revolution; American Revolution; French Revolution; Industrial Revolution
Rossetti, Christina: "Goblin Market" 176
Rousseau, Jean-Jacques 2; "A Discourse on the Origin of Inequality" 13, 14
Ruskin, John: "The Nature of the Gothic" 8, 9

Satan 85, 87–92, 138, 139, 143, 150, 153–156, 163–164, 165
Scott, Walter: *Ivanhoe* 209n3

sensation novel 220n30; *see also* Collins, Wilkie
sexual possession 153–156, 173–174; *see also* coverture, rape
servants and service 64, 171–172, 181–186; *see also* peasants; slaves and slavery
Shakespeare, William 126, 212n3
Shelley, Mary: *Frankenstein* 9, 80, 83, 214n1
sisters *see* daughters
slave narratives 201
slaves and slavery 5, 81–92, 199, 211n1, 212n2; *see also* Dacre, Charlotte: *Zofloya*; race; servants
sons 113–114; *see also* fathers
space, Gothic 15, 39, 108, 172–173, 199, 201; *see also* castle; Catholic church and Catholics; haunting; prison
spiritualism *see* mesmerism
Spivak, Gayatri Chakravorty: subaltern 182
state 15, 128, 173; *see also* law
subaltern *see* servant; Spivak, Gayatri Chakravorty: subaltern
subversive tendencies in the Gothic 20–23, 26, 30, 33–34, 191–196
supernatural 196; *see also* ghosts
Svengali 150–166

Todorov, Tzvetan: fantastic 195–196
Transatlantic Gothic *see* American Gothic

vampire 80
villain 8, 170; *see also* fathers; husbands; Italy and Italians; Jews

walls *see* barriers
Walpole, Horace: "An Account of the Giants Lately Discovered" 23, 82; *The Castle of Otranto* 9, 13, 15, 16, 17, 21, 23–27, 29–31, 48, 56, 63, 96, 98, 103–104, 112, 126, 128–131, 204n; on enclosure 19–20; homosexuality 180; on revolution 23
Wandering Jew *see* Jews
Waters, Sarah: *Affinity* 169–202; *Fingersmith* 170, 176, 189
wives *see* husbands; marriage; marriage law; mothers
Wollstonecraft, Mary: *A Vindication of the Rights of Men* 2, 34, 60, 65; *The Wrongs of Woman* 60–61, 79, 84, 93, 96–97, 104
Woolf, Virginia: "Professions for Women" 108; *To the Lighthouse* 44
writers and writing 3, 6, 7, 53–54, 108, 123–124, 131, 135–136, 142–145, 148–149, 165, 176–178, 181

Yonge, Charlotte: *Chantry House* 38–44, 125, 130; *The Heir of Redclyffe* 207n3

www.ingramcontent.com/pod-product-compliance
Lightning Source LLC
Chambersburg PA
CBHW051220300426
44116CB00006B/658